Tcl/Tk Programming for the Absolute Beginner

P9-BJH-651

KURT WALL

CENGAGE
Learning

Professional • Technical • Reference

Australia, Brazil, Japan, Korea, Mexico, Singapore, Spain, United Kingdom, United States

CENGAGE Learning

Professional • Technical • Reference

Tcl/Tk Programming for the Absolute Beginner
Kurt Wall

Publisher and General Manager, Cengage Learning PTR:
Stacy L. Hiquet

Associate Director of Marketing:
Sarah O'Donnell

Manager of Editorial Services:
Heather Talbot

Marketing Manager:
Mark Hughes

Acquisitions Editor:
Mitzi Koontz

Project Editor and Copy Editor:
Marta Justak

Technical Reviewer:
Rick Reynolds

PTR Editorial Services Coordinator:
Erin Johnson

Interior Layout Tech:
Value Chain

Cover Designer:
Mike Tanamachi

Indexer:
Sharon Shock

Proofreader:
Melba Hopper

For product information and technology assistance, contact us at
Cengage Learning Customer & Sales Support, 1-800-354-9706

For permission to use material from this text or product, submit all requests online at **cengage.com/permissions**
Further permissions questions can be emailed to
permissionrequest@cengage.com

Library of Congress Control Number: 2007903971

ISBN-13: 978-1-59863-438-9

ISBN-10: 1-59863-438-0

Cengage Learning PTR
20 Channel Center Street
Boston, MA 02210
USA

Cengage Learning is a leading provider of customized learning solutions with office locations around the globe, including Singapore, the United Kingdom, Australia, Mexico, Brazil, and Japan. Locate your local office at: **international.cengage.com/region**

Cengage Learning products are represented in Canada by Nelson Education, Ltd.

For your lifelong learning solutions, visit **cengageptr.com**

Visit our corporate website at **cengage.com**

Printed in the United States of America
2 3 4 5 11 10 9 8

To my wife, Kelly, who truly is flesh of my flesh and bone of my bone.

ACKNOWLEDGMENTS

The image of writing as a solitary person laboring in the dark of night to produce a literary masterpiece is a grand fiction, usually perpetuated by writers who know better. I might have worked in the dark of night, but that's the only part of the image that holds up to serious scrutiny. Writing a book is a team effort. My agent, Marta Justak, helped me get the book and took some lumps intended for me when I fell behind on the schedule. As usual, Marta, you're the best. Let's do this again, but leave out the parts that weren't fun.

The editorial team was first rate. Special thanks to Mitzi Koontz for graciously accommodating my request to extend the schedule; Marta Justak, the copy editor, eliminated a distressing number of typos and grammatical mistakes; Melba Hopper, proofreader extraordinaire, gets extra credit for understanding the conventions I adopted and perversely managed not to follow; and Rick Reynolds, my technical editor, noted some algorithmic subtleties and downright blunders that would have embarrassed me and misled you. Sharon Shock, the indexer, had the thankless but vital task of creating the index. A good index makes the difference between a book that sits on the shelf and a book that gets dog-eared and marked-up. Thanks to you all—it's a much better book as a result of your ministrations.

I appreciate the help and support of my colleagues at Panasas, the inhabitants of the #tcl channel on Freenode, and my friends. Panasas tolerated my bleary-eyed appearances at the office. The Tcl and Tk pros on #tcl answered oddball questions about Tcl and Tk features. My friends provided support and encouragement and said: "Ooh! Aaah!" at just the right times.

I would be remiss if I failed to thank my wife. Kelly gave me the space and time to work on the book that I would otherwise have spent with her. She also told me not to stay up too late working on the book, advice I would have done well to heed. Poots the cat provided needed comic relief and company at 2:00 a.m.

All the support and assistance notwithstanding, I take full responsibility for any errors and mistakes that remain.

About the Author

When he isn't writing a book (including numerous Linux books), Kurt Wall might be found cooking, drinking coffee, working at his day job, playing in his garden, trying not to hurt himself while learning to build furniture, or sitting in front of his computers. Kurt dislikes writing about himself in the third person.

TABLE OF CONTENTS

Chapter 6   CREATING AND USING ARRAYS 115

Chapter 7   WRITING TCL PROCEDURES 133

INTRODUCTION

Tcl and Tk are enjoying a resurgence of popularity and interest in the computing community. There are some fine books dedicated to Tcl and Tk programming, but the book you hold in your hands addresses what I see as an underserved market, Tcl and Tk neophytes with little or no programming experience. Like other books in the *Absolute Beginner* series, I use simple games as a vehicle to demonstrate language-specific features and more general programming concepts.

Tcl is an uncomplicated language. With surprisingly few syntax rules and a limited yet comprehensive set of commands, technically competent readers can become competent Tcl programmers with a few weeks of practice. While Tcl, and its graphical extension, Tk, are simple to learn and use, they are remarkably powerful and can be used to create sophisticated, powerful, and full-featured applications in a short amount of time. In addition, the Tcl and Tk development community, by which I mean the people who develop the language and the (growing) number of people who use it on a day-to-day basis, is friendly, knowledgeable, and helpful. This is all to say that you can be productive without needing to be a Tcl or Tk guru, but when you need guru-level help, it is readily available.

WHO THIS BOOK IS FOR

What I wanted to create was a book that reflects the way *I* learn new programming languages. I learn best when introduced to a command, get to see simple examples that illustrate its use, and then am provided with enough information to facilitate and encourage experimentation. Toward that end, almost all of the examples in this book are complete and stand on their own. They don't rely on code from other chapters to work. I also reuse and rework earlier examples so you can see how functionality evolves. Finally, I provided a lot of examples. I firmly believe that the only way to learn a new programming language is to look at a lot of examples of other people's code.

I wrote this book with my own experience learning Tcl and Tk in mind. I'd found that the available books were either dated and based on ancient versions of Tcl and Tk or advanced texts that assumed either prior experience with Tcl and Tk *or* significant experience with other programming languages. There was plenty of tutorial material available on the Web, and the demonstration programs that came with the Tcl and Tk distributions were also excellent resources, but I couldn't find a single source that introduced the fundamental concepts that inform all Tcl programming, introduced Tcl commands with simple examples, or that covered most Tcl and Tk commands in a comprehensive way.

HOW THIS BOOK IS ORGANIZED

I organized this book into two parts. The first part, consisting of Chapters 1–8, introduces Tcl programming. The second part, Chapters 9–15, covers Tk programming. My approach is cumulative; you need to read and understand the material in one chapter before you proceed to the next. In some cases, I use commands in one chapter that I don't discuss until later in the book. I apologize in advance for this, but there are certain commands you need to know how to use in order to have a complete, functioning Tcl script. I clearly note these situations, and there aren't many of them.

I have not attempted to write a Tcl and Tk reference manual. In fact, I have deliberately avoided writing an exhaustive tome. I have not described every Tcl and Tk command that exists, have not covered every option and attribute of the commands I do discuss, and have avoided covering corner cases and elements of the language that I consider obscure or that would just serve to complicate the text or confuse newcomers to the language. In general, I wanted to cover the common case—the tasks that most people just beginning with Tcl and Tk want to perform. You could say I have tried to write a book that shows you how to use the 80 percent of Tcl and Tk's functionality; the other 20 percent is useful, but you won't need it for most of your programming with Tcl.

So you'll know what you're getting into, the chapter-by- chapter description follows.

- Chapter 1, "Introducing Tcl and Tk," consists of a short history of Tcl and Tk, a section highlighting their salient features, and a description of their distinguishing characteristics. If your computer doesn't already have Tcl and Tk installed, then don't skip "Getting Tcl and Tk," or you won't be able to work through the example programs, which would certainly defeat the purpose of buying this book.

- Chapter 2, "Running TCL Programs, describes how to use the Tcl interpreter interactively and in batch mode. Tcl is an interpreted language, so Tcl commands must be executed by an interpreter, tclsh, instead of being compiled and then executed directly. You can use tclsh interactively, allowing you to enter commands and see their results immediately. You can also save your Tcl commands to a file, called a *command file* (imaginative name, yes?) or *script*, and have the Tcl interpreter execute the script. After you become familiar with Tcl's simple syntax, I think you will find it much more efficient to save your scripts in a file and execute them by passing the command file to the interpreter.

- **Chapter 3, "Doing Mathematics,"** introduces the fundamental elements of the Tcl language, such as comments, variables, expressions, and commands. You also get your first exposure to the two most difficult elements of Tcl: command substitution and grouping. *Command substitution* describes the manner in which programming statements are built from Tcl's built-in commands and the results of those commands. *Grouping* refers to the way in which the operators "" and {} affect how command substitution works. This chapter also teaches you how to perform mathematical operations using Tcl's expr command.

- After learning how to perform basic math using Tcl, **Chapter 4, "Strings, Strings, Everywhere Strings!,"** shows you how to perform string operations. Tcl has a rich set of commands and functionality for manipulating strings, an unsurprising fact when you consider that Tcl is a string-based programming language. The final section continues the discussion of Tcl control structures I started in the previous chapter by introducing two looping commands: while and for.

- Lists are one of Tcl's two native or built-in data structures. In **Chapter 5, "Working with Lists,"** you spend some quality time with lists. Tcl has a broad set of commands for dealing with lists, and this chapter will get you up to speed with them. I also finish up the discussion of control structures by introducing the switch command, another command used for conditional execution, and the foreach command, a looping control structure that specializes in iterating over list items. The chapter ends with the two commands you can use to interrupt loop execution: break and continue.

- **Chapter 6, "Creating and Using Arrays,"** is devoted mostly to arrays. Tcl arrays, like Perl's hashes, are *associative,* meaning that they are indexed by strings, rather than integers or other numeric types. In addition to learning how to create and use arrays, this chapter also shows you commands and techniques for handling errors. Error handling combines well with material on arrays because common mistakes that occur when using arrays (such as accessing out-of-bounds or non-existent array indices) raise errors that need to be handled gracefully.

- Procedures are covered in depth in **Chapter 7, "Writing Tcl Procedures."** Procedures enable you to replace a commonly used sequence of commands with a single new command. Known as *subroutines* or *functions* in other programming languages, Tcl procedures can be called with or without arguments. You will also learn about variable and procedure scope, which determines when and where variables and procedures are visible. Together, procedures and an understanding of variable and procedure scope give you the tools you need to start implementing your Tcl scripts in a more modular and easy-to-maintain manner.

- Most non-trivial programs involve interacting with the host filesystem. In **Chapter 8, "Accessing Files and Directories,"** you'll learn how to open, close, delete, and rename files. The chapter also shows you how to perform file I/O using the `puts` (output) and `gets` (input) commands and how to use the `format` command to "pretty print" output. Finally, you'll learn how to navigate the filesystem programmatically and work with file and directory names in a platform-neutral manner.

- **Chapter 9, "Understanding Tk Programming,"** starts the discussion of graphical programming, introducing programming in Tk. As an introductory chapter, this chapter is light on code and long on text, as it discusses topics including event-driven programming and widget attributes and operations. Covering this information here simplifies my job in the rest of the chapters because most Tk programming assumes familiarity with material presented in this chapter. The chapter closes with a description of each of the widgets available to Tk programming.

- Unless you've been living in an unelectrified cave for the last decade, you are accustomed to clicking buttons. **Chapter 10, "Button Widgets,"** describes how to program Tk buttons. After providing more information about the first of Tk's three geometry managers, `pack`, this chapter looks at Tk's button widgets. In addition to learning how to use buttons, I'll show you how to use color in a Tk application and how to bind buttons to commands and events

- **Chapter 11, "Windows, Frames, and Messages,"** shows you how to use the `grid` geometry manager; I think you'll like `grid` better than `pack`. I'll also introduce you to three more Tk widgets: `frames`, `toplevels` (that is, top-level windows), and `messages`.

- **Chapter 12, "Entry and Spinbox Widgets,"** introduces the `entry` and `spinbox` widgets. Tk's `entry` widget is a specialized type of text-entry field best suited to high-speed, head-down data entry, but applicable for many types of data entry in which you want to control or validate the data that is input. The `spinbox` widget, often referred to as a *spinner* in other GUI toolkits, is based on the entry widget.

- In **Chapter 13, "Listbox Widgets,"** you learn how to use Tk's `listbox` widget. A `listbox` displays a series of read-only text lines. The list is vertically scrollable and can be scrolled horizontally as necessary. You can select zero, one, or more items in a list, so the listbox widget has methods for determining which items are selected (and for selecting items programmatically). You can add and delete items from a `listbox`, but items themselves cannot be edited. As usual, you can also control the colors, relief, and other visual attributes of `listbox` widgets.

- Chapter 14, "Scrollbar, Scale, and Text Widgets," discusses three Tk widgets: scrollbars, scales, and text boxes. Scrollbars allow you or your users to scroll the viewable area of a window. A *scale widget* is a slider whose value changes as the slider is moved. Text widgets provide areas for displaying and editing text. As you will see later in the chapter, Tk's `text` widget is a full-featured text display and manipulation tool. The price of this feature set is that the `text` widget is complex.

- Chapter 15, "The Canvas Widget," concludes the book with a tour of the `canvas` widget. The `canvas` is a general purpose widget you can use to display drawing primitives, such as arcs, lines, polygons, and other shapes; images in a variety of formats; text; and even other embedded widgets. I will show you how to use many of the canvas widget's other features in this chapter.

Conventions Used in This Book

A note on textual conventions used in the text is in order. Code listings are shown in a `monospaced font`. Similarly, code that appears in text is also shown in a `monospaced font`. Commands or text that you type will appear in **`bold, monospaced font`**. Placeholders, such as variable names in syntax diagrams, are shown in *`italicized monospaced font`*. Finally, new terms and phrases are shown in *regular-faced italicized text*.

Where's the Code?

The source code for the example code can be downloaded from the book's companion Web site at http://www.courseptr.com/downloads (search by author, ISBN, or title) or from my personal Web site at http://www.kurtwerks.org/bookwerks/tcl/. In addition, suggested solutions for the end-of-chapter exercises can also be downloaded from the companion Web site or from my personal Web site.

INTRODUCING TCL AND TK

This is the one chapter in every book about programming languages that readers usually skip. It consists of a short history of Tcl and Tk, a section highlighting their salient features, and a recitation of their distinguishing characteristics (which bears a disturbing resemblance to marketing). While I hope you read, or at least skim, the entire chapter, if your computer doesn't already have Tcl and Tk installed, then don't skip "Getting Tcl and Tk," or you won't be able to work through the example programs, which would certainly defeat the purpose of buying this book.

WHAT IS TCL?

Tcl, pronounced like "tickle," stands for *tool command language*. As the odd name suggests, Tcl was designed to be a glue language enabling users to control other programs and utilities. Tcl, and its graphical complement, Tk (discussed in the next section), were created by Dr. John Ousterhout at the University of California-Berkeley in the 1980s. As originally conceived, Dr. Ousterhout intended Tcl to be used both as a scripting language, allowing programs to communicate with each other by invoking Tcl commands, and as an embeddable interpreter in those programs, allowing users to configure and customize the programs using the Tcl scripting language they already knew. In this way, Tcl is roughly analogous to Visual Basic for Applications (*VBA*) from Microsoft. Just as you can use VBA to pull functionality from Microsoft Word, Excel, and PowerPoint into a single application, you can use Tcl (and Tk) to pull functionality from a variety of programs together into a single application.

Like any successful programming language or application, though, Tcl long ago met and exceeded its creator's original intent. Originally built as a high-level tool to allow other programs to interact with each other, it is now much more common to encounter complete Tcl/Tk applications that consist of hundreds or thousands of lines of code. The capabilities of Tcl's core language have grown as well so that Tcl programmers can create fully network-aware and -capable applications, interact with databases, browse the Web or serve Web pages, and control MIDI devices. Indeed, there are enough extensions to the language, written in Tcl itself or using its extensions *API* (application programming interface), that what you can do with Tcl is truly limited only by your imagination and your facility with the language.

Cross-platform. Did I mention that Tcl is cross-platform? *Cross-platform* means that the Tcl code you write on, for example, Linux should execute unmodified on any system to which the Tcl interpreter has been ported. Which is to say that Java is not the first language to claim: "Write once, run anywhere." Tcl's cross-platform capabilities free developers from having to learn the specifics of, say, interacting with the Linux file system or the Windows TCP/IP stack. Instead, the Tcl interpreter handles the low level, platform-specific details of writing to files or opening network sockets, freeing you to focus on your application, such as what you are going to write to a file or what you are going to do with the data you just read from that socket. It is certainly true that you need to have some platform-specific knowledge, such as the difference between how filenames are constructed on Windows and UNIX systems, but the point is that Tcl shields you from these low-level details.

What Is Tk?

At the simplest level, Tk (pronounced "tee kay") is an extension to Tcl (strictly speaking, a library) that provides a toolkit for creating and using graphical user interfaces. Tk includes commands for creating buttons, text boxes, and other user interface widgets. You can also control the colors of Tk applications and the fonts that they use. Tk provides an interface to the graphical windowing system of the host operating system on which it is being executed. As a Tcl extension, Tk gives you access to all of Tcl's core commands and other extensions.

Tk does for creating graphical applications what Tcl does for creating nongraphical applications. Usually, when you create a graphical application, you have to spend as much time developing the buttons, text boxes, and scroll bars and wiring them into your application as you do developing the application itself, that is, the logic and functionality for which the graphical components are merely an interface. Tk handles the difficulty and tedium of creating the graphical components, freeing your time and effort for the application itself.

Tk has a reputation for looking old and resulting in an awkward user interface. To some degree, this is deserved; Tk's development lagged behind other toolkits. However, things have begun to change. A popular extension, Tile, is available that gives most Tk widgets the look and feel of their native operating system's applications. Work is underway to integrate the Tile extension into the Tk core. In addition to providing a native look and feel to Tk applications, Tile supports the most recent trend in GUI customization, which are themes (also known as *skins*). So, while Tk might have been slow in the past to adapt to changes in windowing toolkits, it is quickly closing the gap.

WHAT MAKES TCL AND TK DIFFERENT?

What makes Tcl and Tk different from other programming languages and graphical toolkits? Tcl compares favorably to scripting languages like Perl, Python, and Ruby and shells such as Bourne, Korn, and Bash because it has the same features and capabilities, albeit with a different syntax and language structure. What distinguishes Tcl from other scripting languages is its ability to be embedded into other applications. It is relatively straightforward to add a Tcl interpreter to your existing application and so provide a full-featured configuration and macro language.

Tk, likewise, gives you access to the same basic user interface widgets as most other graphical toolkits. However, once you are familiar with Tk, you can write graphical applications faster with it than you can with other toolkits. Not many scripting languages offer graphical functionality as an integral part of the language. As a result, you can often, even routinely, develop an application in weeks using Tk, something that would have taken months with another language and graphical framework.

Finally, a graphical application developed with Tk can be remarkably short. The following three-line Tcl script displays a clock whose display updates every second:

```
proc every {ms body} {eval $body; after $ms [info level 0]}
pack [label .clock -textvar time]
every 1000 {set ::time [clock format [clock sec] -format %H:%M:%S]}
```

Don't worry about the syntax and commands in this program, just appreciate the brevity of the code. You'll understand what these commands do soon enough. Figures 1.1, 1.2, and 1.3 show what this clock looks like on Linux, Windows, and OS X, respectively.

clock.tcl running on a Linux system

FIGURE 1.1

A three-line Tk clock program running on Linux.

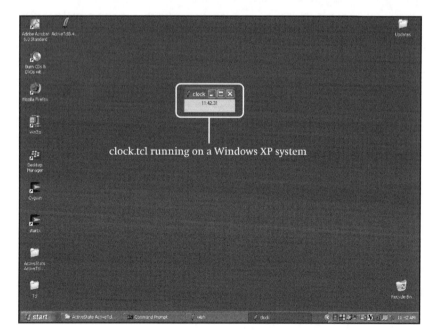

clock.tcl running on a Windows XP system

FIGURE 1.2

A three-line Tk clock program running on Windows XP.

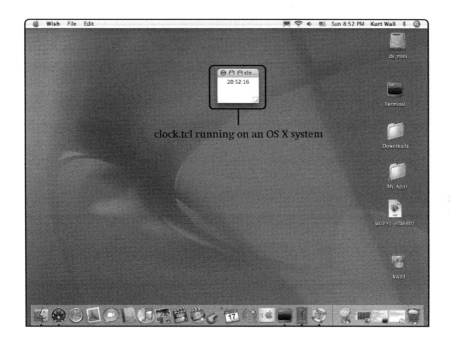

clock.tcl running on an OS X system

WHY USE TCL AND TK?

I use Tcl and Tk for a number of reasons. First, it is fast, easy to use, and capable. Although Tcl will never win a foot race with a compiled language like C if you need to do heavy number crunching or 3D animation, for the majority of your needs, Tcl will be fast enough. It is also easy to use because the language itself consists of relatively few commands and a very small number of syntax rules. Tcl is also capable because a good deal of functionality is built into the core command set or is available as extensions. If you can't find what you want, though, you can create a new command that *does* do what you want.

Tcl has remained true to its roots as a glue language, a way to glue external programs and utilities together into a single, coherent application. For example, one friend of mine used Tcl and a smidgen of Tk to create a spam tagging and reporting application. He wrote just enough Tcl and Tk code to provide a user interface that he can use to tag a message as spam and track the spam back to its source, using network monitoring and diagnostic utilities (ping and whois) and some DNS lookup tools.

You can work fast with Tcl and Tk. Tk-based development is much faster than traditional library- or framework-based development because Tk handles the mechanics of creating and manipulating graphical widgets. Moreover, as an interpreted language, Tcl spares you long compile times. Granted, the programs you will write and use in this book will be short, but as your own programs grow in length and complexity, you will appreciate being able to take the compile step out of the usual edit-compile-debug development process.

One of the most compelling reasons I can think of for using Tcl and Tk is that they are easy to learn and yet amply powerful. As I remarked earlier, Tcl has relatively few commands and an extremely simple syntax, so with a reasonable amount of practice, you will be able to write small but useful (and, in the case of this book, fun and entertaining) applications. At the same time, Tcl has all the elements you would expect in a programming language, such as variables, procedures, loops, conditionals, data structures, and interfaces to operating system services such as file I/O (input/output), process control, threads, and network sockets.

Finally, Tcl and Tk are satisfying and rewarding to use. If you are reading this book, you are probably already interested in programming and have experienced the sense of accomplishment that comes from writing a program that automates a tedious task or simplifies a complicated one. Tcl and Tk can satisfy that part of you that likes to build things. In my opinion, once you become proficient, Tcl and Tk shorten the time it takes you to get your reward: a completed program.

GETTING TCL AND TK

Obviously, in order to take advantage of Tcls and Tk's benefits, you need to get them. Fortunately, this is not difficult. Tcl and Tk are freely available for a variety of operating systems. In most cases, you can get ready-to-run binaries. In other cases, you might have to download the source code and build it yourself. The instructions in this section describe how to obtain and install Tcl and Tk for the three most popular operating systems available: Linux, OS X, and Windows. I'll also explain how to install Tcl and Tk from source, if binaries for your system are not available.

Installing Tcl and Tk on Linux

If you are running a Linux system, chances are better than average that you already have Tcl and Tk installed. Chances are better still that if you do not have it installed, it is readily available for installation from your vendor's package repository or CD-ROM. For example, if you are using Fedora or Fedora Core, the following command should install the latest versions of Tcl and Tk:

```
# yum install tcl tk
```

On Debian-based systems, such as Debian itself or Ubuntu and its derivatives, the following command should suffice:

```
# sudo apt-get install tcl tk
```

I can't provide instructions for every Linux distribution out there, but you get the idea. If a binary version of Tcl and Tk isn't available for your favorite flavor of Linux, skip ahead to the section titled "Installing Tcl and Tk from Source."

If you want to ensure that everything is working properly after the installation is complete, start the Tcl interpreter, tclsh, by typing tclsh at a command prompt and typing the following Tcl command at the % prompt:

```
% puts "Hello, Tcl/Tk World!"
Hello, Tcl/Tk World!
%
```

Installing Tcl and Tk on Windows

Installing Tcl and Tk on a Windows system is easy. First, point your Web browser at the ActiveState Web site (www.activestate.com), click Downloads, and click the ActiveTcl link under Language Downloads on the right-hand side of the page (see Figure 1.4).

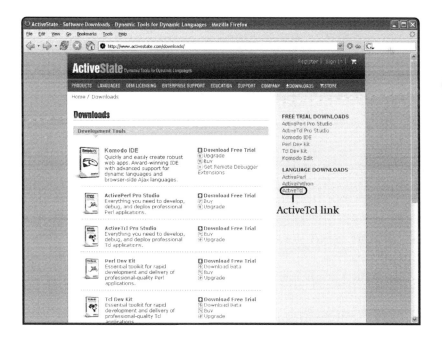

FIGURE 1.4

Downloading ActiveTcl on Windows.

You can either drop $40 to get a DVD shipped to you or click the Download link to start the download process. If you want to get promotional information from ActiveState, fill out the form. Otherwise, just click the Continue button. For Windows, you want the "AS Windows" package. "AS" stands for "ActiveState," and the AS Windows package includes the

Tcl download and ActiveState's installer. The download weighs in at slightly less than 22MB (see Figure 1.5).

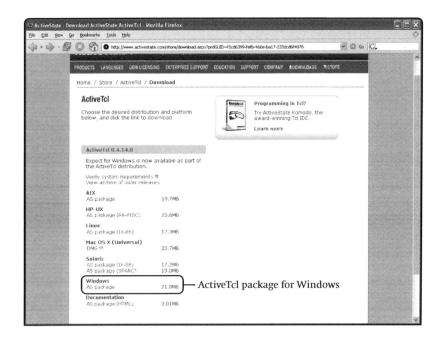

ActiveTcl package for Windows

While the download proceeds, read the next paragraph to find out a little bit more about ActiveState and ActiveTcl.

ActiveState provides high quality software development products, such as Tcl, JavaScript, Perl, PHP, Python, and Ruby, and complementary tools such as integrated development environments and debuggers. In addition, ActiveState provides services for developers and for companies using ActiveState products. In most cases, their core products, like ActiveTcl, are free and licensed by their creators in such a way that the core languages, like Tcl and Tk, must be made available by companies like ActiveState for free. ActiveTcl is ActiveState's binary distribution of Tcl, Tk, and a number of the most popular Tcl extensions. All of the extensions are tested, integrated, and ready to use. ActiveTcl closely tracks Tcl's development, so it is as current and close to mainline Tcl as possible.

After you download the ActiveTcl installer, installation is quick and uncomplicated.

1. Double-click the installer icon, which looks like a feather (a feather for tickling, get it?), as shown in Figure 1.6.

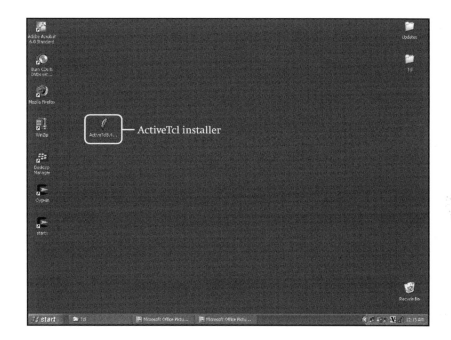

FIGURE 1.6

ActiveState's
ActiveTcl installer
icon.

2. After reviewing all the packages and extensions that will be installed, click Next (see Figure 1.7).

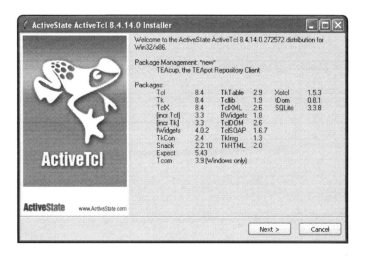

FIGURE 1.7

ActiveTcl includes
a rich set of
extensions.

3. Read the license (or not) and click Next to continue the installation (see Figure 1.8).

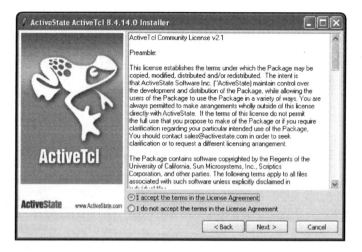

4. If you have administrator rights on your Windows system, you can choose whether all
   users can use ActiveTcl or just the current user. Similarly, you can choose which file
   associations to allow the installer to make and modify the installation directory, which
   defaults to C:/Tcl, as shown in Figure 1.9. Make your selections and then click Next to
   proceed.

No, the "/" is not a typo, and you don't need glasses. Unlike Windows, UNIX and UNIX-
like systems use "/" to separate directory names, not "\". Although "C:/Tcl" looks a bit
odd, you're just seeing an artifact of Tcl's UNIX heritage peeking through. Not to worry,
though, the installer does the right thing under the covers.

5. On the next screen, you can choose where to install the demonstration applications. I recommend keeping it simple and accepting the default directory, `C:/Tcl/demos` (shown in Figure 1.10). Click Next to continue the installation.

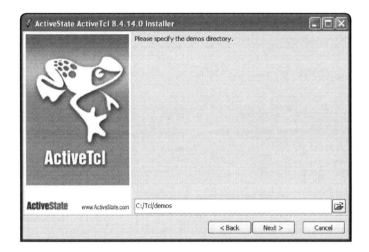

FIGURE 1.10

Decide where to install the demos.

6. Confirm your selections on the Summary screen, illustrated in Figure 1.11, and then click Next to start (finally!) the installation.

FIGURE 1.11

Ready to start the installation.

Again, the mixture of "/" and "\" in directory names is unfortunate, but the installer really *does* work properly.

7. The installation finishes quickly, and you're left with the dialog box shown in Figure 1.12, which shows you some settings and a short ActiveState marketing blurb. Click the Finish button to close the installer.

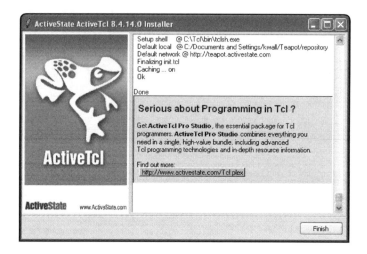

If you want to ensure that everything is working properly after the installation is complete, start the Tcl interpreter, tclsh, by selecting Start → All Programs → ActiveState ActiveTcl 8.4.14.0 → Tclsh84 and typing the following Tcl commands at the % prompt:

```
% puts "Hello, Tcl/Tk World!"
```

If everything has gone as planned, the resulting output should look like Figure 1.13.

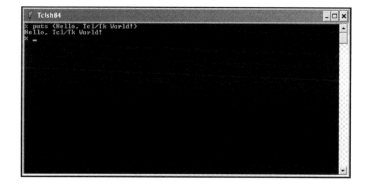

At this point, you're ready to start learning Tcl.

Installing Tcl and Tk on OS X

Installing Tcl and Tk on an OS X system is as simple and uncomplicated as installing it on Windows. Browse to the ActiveState Web site (www.activestate.com), click Downloads, and then click the ActiveTcl link under Language Downloads on the right-hand side of the page (see Figure 1.14).

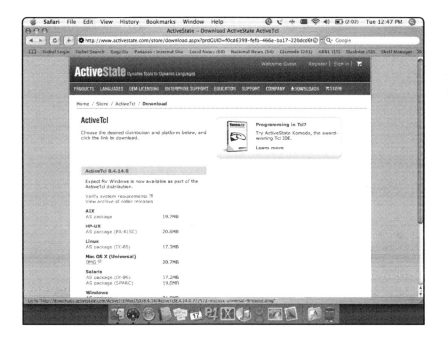

FIGURE 1.14

Finding the ActiveTcl package for OS X.

You can either drop $40 to get a DVD shipped to you or click the Download link to start the download process. If you want to get promotional information from ActiveState, fill out the resulting form. Otherwise, just click the Continue button. For OS X, you want the Mac OS X (Universal) package, which is an ActiveTcl package for both PPC and x86 versions of OS X. The download checks in at just less than 21MB (see Figure 1.15). After the download completes, use the following procedure to install ActiveTcl.

Double-click the package icon on the desktop (see Figure 1.16) to extract the archive.

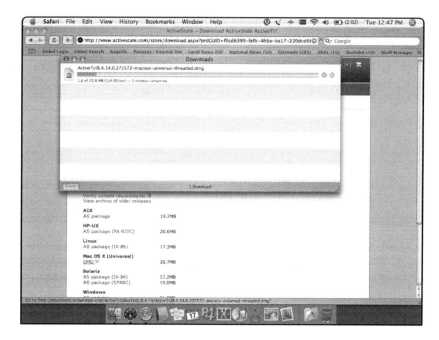

FIGURE 1.15

Downloading the
ActiveTcl package
for OS X.

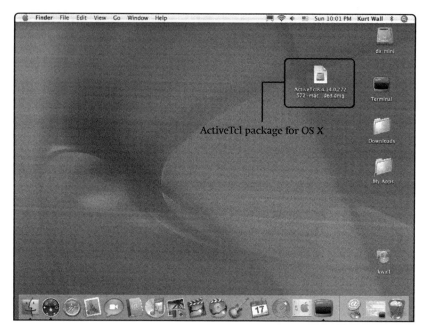

ActiveTcl package for OS X

FIGURE 1.16

Unpack the
archive.

Double-click the package icon, shown in Figure 1.17, to start the installation.

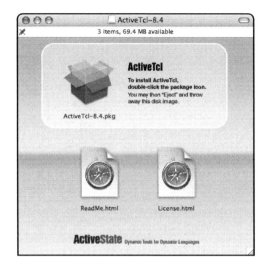

FIGURE 1.17

Start the installer.

Figure 1.18 shows the items that the installer will install on your system. Click the Continue button to proceed.

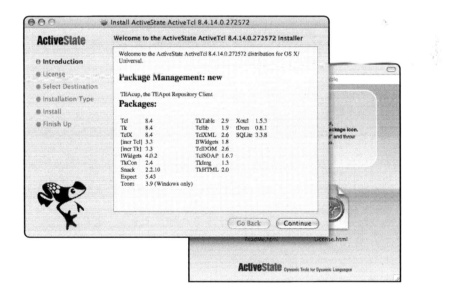

FIGURE 1.18

View the components you are about to install.

You must agree to the ActiveState license if you are going to proceed with the installation (see Figure 1.19).

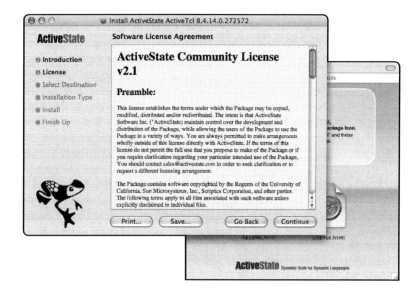

FIGURE 1.19

Accept the license
to proceed.

Select the destination into which to install the ActiveTcl package, as Figure 1.20 shows.

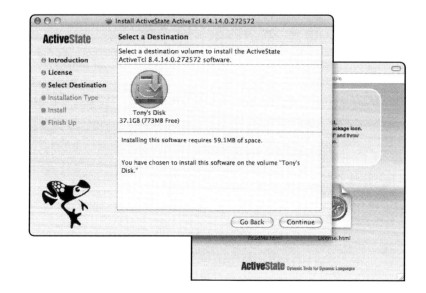

FIGURE 1.20

Choose the
installation
volume.

Figure 1.21 illustrates the installation progress bar. Watching the installation progress is about as exciting as watching paint dry.

FIGURE 1.21

Finally, the installation starts.

At length, the installation completes successfully (see Figure 1.22).

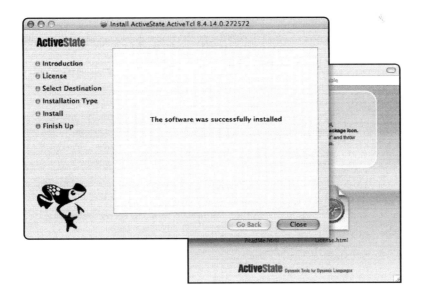

FIGURE 1.22

A completed, successful installation.

If you want to ensure that everything is working properly after the installation is complete, start the Tcl interpreter, tclsh, by picking Applications → Utilities in Finder and double-clicking Wish 8.4 and typing the following Tcl command at the % prompt:

```
% puts "Hello, Tcl/Tk World!"
```

If everything has gone as planned, the resulting output should look like Figure 1.23.

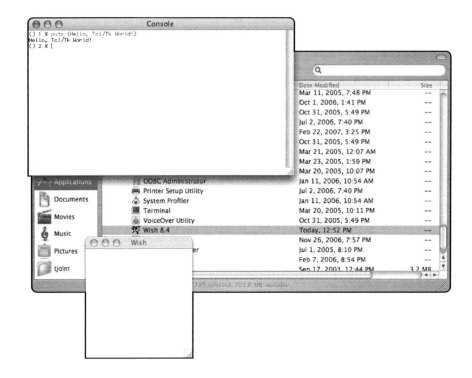

FIGURE 1.23

Verify that Tcl is
properly installed.

At this point, you're ready to start learning Tcl.

Installing Tcl and Tk from Source

Installing Tcl and Tk from source, as opposed to using a binary distribution, is the option of last resort. Not because it is difficult—it isn't—and not because it is time consuming—it isn't. Rather, it is a last resort simply because it's a darned rare platform (that is, combination of operating system and CPU) for which stable releases of Tcl and Tk are unavailable in binary format. I'm showing you how to build your own Tcl and Tk binaries for two reasons. In the first place, telling you how to build them from source is simply a matter of completeness. Secondly, and this is the really important reason, if you want to play with the latest and greatest Tcl and Tk releases, you have to use the development versions (8.5.mumble as I write this sentence), which are *rarely* available in binary form.

For Linux Users Only

The procedure I describe in this section is only for Linux users. OS X and Windows users should *really* use the binary distributions because building software on either of these platforms is complicated and usually requires expensive tools that you probably don't have. Even for Linux users, you'll need to have development packages installed, including g++ (the C++ compiler from the GNU project).

"Why would I want to use an unstable development version?" I'm glad you asked. You might want to play with its nifty new features. You might have encountered a bug in the stable release (yes, it's true, there *are* bugs in the code, even after 20 years), the solution for which is available in a development release. You might want to see if programs that work flawlessly in Tcl and Tk 8.4 work just as flawlessly in Tcl and Tk 8.5. Or you might like living on the bleeding edge and using development code that could crash your system, eat your lunch, burn your coffee, stain your shirt, and steal your girlfriend. Whatever your reason for wanting to do so, this section shows you how to install Tck and Tk from source code.

Without going into the gory details, you can download source tarballs of Tcl and Tk from the Tcl/Tk Web site at www.tcl.tk/software/. For this example, I downloaded the source release of Tcl/Tk 8.5a5, a development version, which consisted of two compressed tar files, tcl8.5a5-src.tar.gz and tk8.5a5-src.tar.gz. You need to build Tcl first, because Tk depends on it, that is, Tk needs files provided by Tcl in order to build successfully and execute properly.

1. Uncompress and extract the archive file:

    ```
    $ tar zxf tcl8.5a5-src.tar.gz
    ```

2. cd into the tcl8.5a5 directory:

    ```
    $ cd tcl8.5a5
    ```

3. cd into the unix directory:

    ```
    $ cd unix
    ```

4. Configure the build system:

    ```
    $ ./configure —prefix=/opt —enable-gcc
    ...
    config.status: creating Makefile
    config.status: creating dltest/Makefile
    config.status: creating tclConfig.sh
    ```

The argument —prefix=/opt tells the configure script where you want to install the compiled Tcl binaries. Traditionally, programs installed by system administrators which are not part of the system installation have usually been installed in /usr/local. On my system, I prefer to use the /opt filesystem. Wherever you install Tcl, I recommend installing it in a location that won't be overwritten if/when you upgrade your system. The —enable-gcc argument tells the configure script to configure the build to use gcc, the GNU Compiler Collection, rather than another C compiler that might be installed on your system. In most cases, it isn't necessary to use this argument, but it doesn't hurt anything to do so.

5. Build it:

```
$ make
...
gcc -pipe -O2    -Wl,--export-dynamic  tclAppInit.o -L/home/kurt/tclbook/tcl8.5a5/unix -
ltcl8.5 -ldl   -lieee -lm \
                -Wl,-rpath,/opt/lib -o tclsh
```

While the build proceeds, get a cup of coffee.

6. Run the test suite:

```
$ make test
...
3       unknownFailure
521     win
5       xdev
```

While the test suite runs, get another cup of coffee. It isn't uncommon to see tests skipped, so you can probably disregard messages about skipped tests. However, if you see more than a few failed tests, and you are motivated, you might consider reporting them to the Tcl developers using the Tcl bug tracker at sourceforge.net/tracker/? group_id=10894&atid=110894&func=add.

7. Install the Tcl binaries and libraries. This step requires root access. On my system, I use sudo. Use the method that suits you for becoming root on your system:

```
$ sudo make install
...
Installing and cross-linking top-level (.1) docs
Installing and cross-linking C API (.3) docs
Installing and cross-linking command (.n) docs
```

After successfully installing Tcl, you build and install Tk much the same way:

1. Uncompress and extract the Tk archive file:

   ```
   $ tar zxf tk8.5a5-src.tar.gz
   ```

2. cd into the tk8.5a5 directory:

   ```
   $ cd tk8.5a5
   ```

3. cd into the unix directory:

   ```
   $ cd unix
   ```

4. Configure the build system:

   ```
   $ ./configure —with-tcl=../../tcl8.5a5/unix —prefix=/opt —enable-gcc
   ...
   config.status: creating Makefile
   config.status: creating dltest/Makefile
   config.status: creating tkConfig.sh
   ```

5. The argument —with-tcl=../../tcl8.5a5/unix tells the Tk configure script where to find tclConfig.sh, which Tk needs in order to build and run properly. This is the reason that you built Tcl first. The other two arguments have the same meaning as they did for the Tcl installation.

6. Build it:

   ```
   $ make
   ...
   gcc -pipe -O2     -Wl,—export-dynamic  tkAppInit.o -L/home/kurt/tclbook/tk8.5a5/
   unix -ltk8.5
   \
                   -L/home/kurt/tclbook/tcl8.5a5/unix -ltcl8.5  -lX11  -ldl  -lieee
    -lm  -Wl,-rpath,/opt/lib -o wish
   ```

7. While the build proceeds, fetch your third cup of coffee.

8. Run the test suite:

   ```
   $ make test
   ...
    1       userInteraction
   ```

```
288     win
51      winSend
```

While the test suite runs (it takes longer for Tk than for Tcl), your screen will seem to have been taken over by an invisible user. If it's too disturbing to watch, get another cup of coffee. Or perhaps you should have a beer to counteract all the coffee you've been drinking. It isn't uncommon to see tests skipped, so you can probably disregard messages about skipped tests. However, if you see more than a few failed tests, and you are motivated, you might consider reporting them to the Tcl developers using the Tk bug tracker at sourceforge.net/tracker/?group_id=12997&atid=112997&func=add.

9. Assuming the test passed, install the Tk binaries and libraries. This step requires root access. On my system, I use sudo. Use the method that suits you for becoming root on your system:

```
$ sudo make install
Installing and cross-linking top-level (.1) docs
Installing and cross-linking C API (.3) docs
Installing and cross-linking command (.n) docs
```

That's it. Tcl and Tk are installed.

This chapter answered the five most burning questions of the day: "What is Tcl?" "What is Tk?" "What makes Tcl and Tk different?" "Why should I use Tcl and Tk?" and "How do I get Tcl and Tk?" The next chapter starts answering the question, "How do I use Tcl and Tk?"

RUNNING TCL PROGRAMS

This chapter describes how to use the Tcl interpreter interactively and in batch mode. Tcl is an interpreted language, so Tcl commands must be executed by an interpreter, tclsh, instead of being compiled and then executed directly. You can use tclsh interactively, allowing you to enter commands and see their results immediately. You can also save your Tcl commands to a file, called a *command file* (imaginative name, yes?) or script, and have the Tcl interpreter execute the script. After you become familiar with Tcl's simple syntax, I think you will find it much more efficient to save your scripts in a file and execute them by passing the command file to the interpreter.

INVOKING THE INTERPRETER

To start the Tcl interpreter, tclsh, just type `tclsh` at a command prompt and press Enter (on Windows, select Start → All Programs → ActiveState ActiveTcl 8.4.14.0 → Tclsh84). If you invoke it with no arguments, tclsh runs interactively. In interactive mode, tclsh reads commands from *stdin* (a common abbreviation for *standard input*, which is ordinarily the keyboard) and displays the output of those commands to *stdout* (*standard output*, usually your display). Figures 2.1, 2.2, and 2.3 show tclsh running interactively on Linux, OS X, and Windows, respectively.

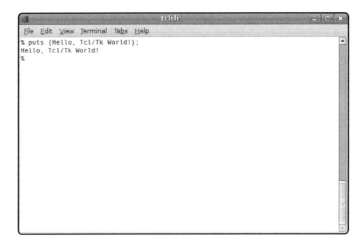

FIGURE 2.1

Running tclsh on a
Linux system.

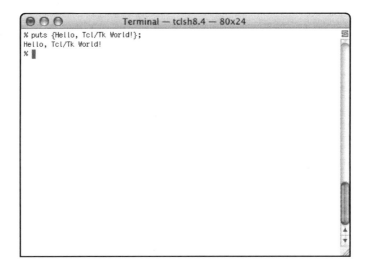

FIGURE 2.2

Running tclsh on
an OS X system.

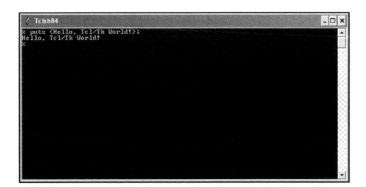

FIGURE 2.3

Running tclsh on a
Windows system.

The `puts` command writes its argument, `Hello, Tcl/Tk World!` in this case, followed by a newline to stdout (actually, `puts` is more powerful than this, as you'll learn in Chapter 8, "Accessing Files and Directories").

The default tclsh command prompt is %. This prompt means that the interpreter is waiting for a command to execute. A second prompt exists, referred to as the *secondary* or *input prompt*. The interpreter displays the input prompt when it is waiting for additional input to complete a command. You'll learn more about the input prompt in the next section.

When you are finished with your Tcl session, type `exit` and press Enter. As it happens, `exit` is a Tcl command, so it should work regardless of the operating system on which you are using Tcl. The interpreter also exits if it encounters an end-of-file (*EOF*) condition. EOF is operating system-specific: Linux and OS X users can send the EOF signal by pressing Ctrl-D. Windows users can press Ctrl-Z (Alt-F4 will close the window, but it isn't really an EOF signal *per se*). However, because EOF is operating system-specific, I encourage you to use the `exit` command so you and your Tcl usage is not tied to or dependent upon platform-specific idioms.

EXECUTING TCL COMMANDS INTERACTIVELY

Now that you know how to start and stop the Tcl interpreter (referred to hereafter as tclsh), you probably want to know how to execute commands, right? Well, due to poor planning on my part, you already know because I told you in the previous section: start tclsh with no arguments to enter interactive mode and then start typing commands.

By default, the input prompt is unset. If you want to set it, execute the following command while running the interpreter:

```
set tcl_prompt2 {puts -nonewline "> "}
```

This command sets the value of the special Tcl variable `tcl_prompt2`, which controls the appearance of tclsh's secondary prompt, to > (that's a right angle bracket followed by a single space). The primary or command prompt can be modified by setting the value of `tcl_prompt1`. The input prompt is useful because it is a visual cue that your command is incomplete. If you start typing a Tcl command but don't complete it, the interpreter will display "> " and then wait for you to enter the text required to complete the command (shown in the following example). You'll learn more about variables in the next chapter, so just take this at face value for the time being.

```
% set tcl_prompt2 {puts -nonewline "> "}
puts -nonewline "> "
% puts\
> "Hello, Tcl/Tk World!"
Hello, Tcl/Tk World!
```

In the example, I typed a `puts` command followed by \, which tells the interpreter that the `puts` command is continued on the next line. On the next line, tclsh displayed the input prompt and then waited for input to complete the command. I completed the command by typing `puts'` argument, `"Hello, Tcl/Tk World!"`, and pressing Enter. The interpreter then executed the command and displayed the requested output.

Setting tcl_prompt2 Automatically

Even though I don't use tclsh interactively very often, I prefer to have an input prompt. Rather than typing `set tcl_prompt2 {puts "> "}` each time I start tclsh, I put this command in the .tclshrc configuration file in my home directory. If you are familiar with Linux or UNIX, the file would be $HOME/.tclshrc (see example-tclshrc in this chapter's code directory on the Web site). If this file exists, tclsh reads it and executes the contents as a Tcl script. The behavior is the same for OS X and Windows. On OS X the file must also be named .tclshrc and located in your home directory; on Windows, the file must be named tclshrc.tcl and stored in your %HOME% directory. The typical use of tclshrc is to customize tclsh's run-time behavior, such as customizing the prompts, but you can use tclshrc to execute any arbitrary set of commands you want executed each time you start tclsh in interactive mode.

You can execute any valid Tcl command in interactive mode. The next example shows a few of the commands you can use. Feel free to try them yourself to become familiar with tclsh's admittedly Spartan interface. Don't worry about the details of the commands right now. I'll cover every command you see here in greater detail in later chapters.

```
% puts [clock format [clock seconds] -format {%A, %B %e, %Y}]
Saturday, April  7, 2007
% puts "You are using Tcl version $tcl_patchLevel"
You are using Tcl version 8.4.12
% puts "2 * 10 = [expr 2 * 10]"
2 * 10 = 20
% for {set i 0} {$i <= 5} {incr i} {puts "sine of $i is [expr sin($i)]"}
sine of 0: 0.0
sine of 1 is 0.841470984808
sine of 2 is 0.909297426826
sine of 3 is 0.14112000806
sine of 4 is -0.756802495308
sine of 5 is -0.958924274663
% puts My name is Kurt
wrong # args: should be "puts ?-nonewline? ?channelId? string"
```

The first command uses Tcl's clock command (twice) to retrieve, format, and display the current date. The second command prints the value of another special Tcl variable, tcl_patchLevel, which stores the version of Tcl that you are running. The third command illustrates how to perform mathematical calculations using the expr command. The fourth command uses an iterative loop command, for, to calculate the sine of each integer between 0 and 5. So far, so good.

The last command, puts My name is Kurt, has a deliberate syntax error so you can see how tclsh behaves when you make a mistake. I executed the puts command with the wrong number of arguments; puts accepts one argument, the string to display, but I passed four arguments, My, name, is, and Kurt. To help me correct my mistake, puts displays the correct syntax. In this case, I could correct my error by enclosing the sentence in double quotes or braces (more about string-handling syntax in Chapter 4, "Strings, Strings, Everywhere Strings!"). The error message also shows you one of Tcl's idiosyncrasies, the convention used to illustrate optional arguments in syntax diagrams: optional arguments are embedded between ? characters, rather than between a pair of brackets ([]). Tcl uses this convention because the language uses brackets for grouping arguments, as you'll learn in the next chapter.

Using tclsh in interactive mode is ideal when you are first learning to use Tcl because you can type commands and see their results immediately. If you make a syntax error, you'll see the error in context, which makes correcting it easy. Interactive mode is also handy for experimenting with new commands or features that you haven't used before. Another advantage of tclsh's interactive mode is that it lets you test small snippets of code before using them in a larger script. When I'm working on a program, I usually keep an interactive tclsh running in a separate window for just this purpose. Nevertheless, beginning with Chapter 3, I will use scripts almost exclusively because interactive mode is inefficient and inconvenient for writing and testing all but the shortest programs.

CREATING TCL COMMAND FILES

As you might have begun to see, interactive usage of tclsh, while convenient, quickly becomes tedious if you need to execute more than a few commands. If you need to execute the same set of commands frequently or repetitively, interactive use of tclsh will work, but is inefficient at best and infeasible at worst. Tcl command files, or *scripts*, are the solution. If you invoke tclsh with one or more arguments, it interprets the first argument as a Tcl command file or script and stores the second and following arguments as variables accessible in the script.

For example, suppose that you created a file named interactive.tcl and stored the five commands from the previous example in it. It might resemble the following script (see interactive.tcl in this chapter's code directory):

```
puts "[clock format [clock seconds] -format {%A, %B %e, %Y}]"
puts "You are using Tcl version $tcl_patchLevel"
puts "2 * 10 = [expr 2 * 10]"
for {set i 0} {$i <= 5} {incr i} {puts "sine of $i is [expr sin($i)]"}
puts My name is Kurt
```

To execute this script, invoke tclsh and pass the name of the script file, interactive.tcl, as the first argument to tclsh, as shown in the following example:

```
$ tclsh interactive.tcl
You are using Tcl version 8.4.12
2 * 10 = 20
sine of 0 is 0.0
sine of 1 is 0.841470984808
sine of 2 is 0.909297426826
sine of 3 is 0.14112000806
sine of 4 is -0.756802495308
sine of 5 is -0.958924274663
wrong # args: should be "puts ?-nonewline? ?channelId? string"
    while executing
"puts My name is Kurt"
    (file "interactive.tcl" line 5)
```

The output is the almost the same as the interactive session shown in the previous section. The exception is the nature of the error message shown while executing the fifth command, puts My name is Kurt. In addition to the error message from puts, tclsh shows you the command it was executing, the file in which the command was located, and the line number in the file. This information is invaluable when you are debugging a large program that consists of multiple files of tens, hundreds, or thousands of lines—imagine having to track down the offending command without these hints.

As you can see, using a script file is much more convenient than interactive tclsh usage. If you are using Tcl on a Linux, UNIX, or OS X system, it gets even easier because you can make the script itself executable by using special notation at the top of the script. Insert the text #!/usr/bin/tclsh as the first line of the script, then set the file's executable bit. Thus, interactive.tcl would look like the following script (see interactive2.tcl in this chapter's code samples):

```
#!/usr/bin/tclsh
puts "[clock format [clock seconds] -format {%A, %B %e, %Y}]"
puts "You are using Tcl version $tcl_patchLevel"
puts "2 * 10 = [expr 2 * 10]"
for {set i 0} {$i <= 5} {incr i} {puts "sine of $i is [expr sin($i)]"}
puts My name is Kurt
```

Finding the Path to tclsh **on Your System**

If you are using ActiveState ActiveTcl on OS X, the path to tclsh should be /usr/local/bin/tclsh. You can use the shell command which tclsh to find the path to tclsh on your system. On my Ubuntu system, the output looks like the following:

```
$ which tclsh
/usr/bin/tclsh
```

However, on my OS X system, the result was:

```
$ which tclsh
/usr/local/bin/tclsh
```

On Linux and OS X, set the execute bit as shown in the following command:

```
$ chmod 755 interactive2.tcl
```

Now you can execute the script without having to invoke tclsh specifically:

```
$ ./interactive2.tcl
Saturday, April  7, 2007
You are using Tcl version 8.4.12
2 * 10 = 20
sine of 0 is 0.0
sine of 1 is 0.841470984808
sine of 2 is 0.909297426826
sine of 3 is 0.14112000806
sine of 4 is -0.756802495308
sine of 5 is -0.958924274663
wrong # args: should be "puts ?-nonewline? ?channelId? string"
    while executing
"puts My name is Kurt"
    (file "./interactive2.tcl" line 7)
```

Unfortunately, executing Tcl scripts directly on Windows is not as easy as it is for Linux and OS X. The simplest (and least elegant) approach is to start a tclsh session and use the `source` command to invoke the script. You'll learn more about the `source` command in Chapter 7, "Writing Tcl Procedures," so what I'll say in this chapter is that the `source` command reads its argument, a filename, and executes the contents of the specified file as a script (see Figure 2.4).

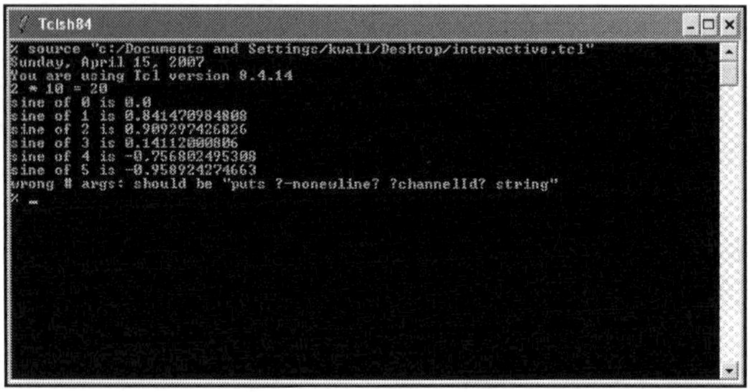

FIGURE 2.4

Use the `source` command to execute Tcl scripts on Windows.

As you can see in Figure 2.4, I executed the command `source interactive.tcl`, which read the contents of the script and executed it in the current tclsh session. This approach is easy, but it isn't terribly elegant for an application you want to deploy because few users will want to start a `tclsh` just to play your game.

Fortunately, you have two other options: creating a shortcut or a file association for files that have a .tcl extension. To create a shortcut, the target should resemble `C:\Tcl\bin\tclsh84.exe "C:\Documents and Settings\kwall\Desktop\interactive.tcl"` (see Figure 2.5).

Of course, you need to replace `C:\Documents and Settings\kwall\Desktop\interactive.tcl` with the path to your script. Using a shortcut is the appropriate way to make a deployed Tcl script self-executable, but it is less than ideal during development because you have to create a shortcut for each new script you write.

For development and learning purposes, the approach I recommend for making your Tcl script directly executable is to create a file association for the extension .tcl. Using My Computer or the Windows Explorer interface, create a new file type for .tcl, and add an "open" action. The command for the action should be something like `"C:\Tcl\bin\tclsh84.exe" "%1" "%*"` (see Figure 2.6).

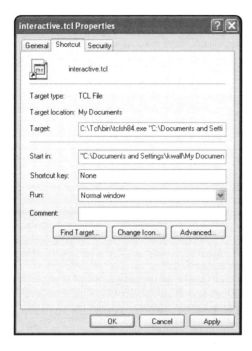

FIGURE 2.5

Create a shortcut
to execute Tcl
scripts on
Windows.

FIGURE 2.6

Create a file
association to
execute Tcl scripts
on Windows.

The "%1" parameter is a placeholder for the name of the script you want to execute. The "%*" parameter represents all of the arguments passed to the script, if any. Once you have set up the association, you can double-click Tcl script files in Explorer to execute them.

Dealing with Spaces in Filenames

If the path to the tclsh executable or to your Tcl script contains spaces, enclose the name in quotes.

The good news is that if you installed ActiveState's ActiveTcl distribution as described in the previous chapter, the ActiveState installer created a file association for Tcl scripts (that is, for files with the .tcl extension) for you. The bad news is that the association is to the wish (more about wish in Chapter 9, "Understanding Tk Programming") executable (C:\Tcl\bin\ wish84.exe, by default). To fix the association, change wish84.exe to tclsh84.exe.

There is one final *gotcha* with self-executing Tcl scripts on Windows to address. If you create a shortcut or use a file association, when the script ends, the tclsh window closes, making it difficult to see what the script has done. An easy workaround to prevent this is to add the command gets stdin as the very last line in your script, as shown in the following example. This command waits for you to type input and press Enter.

```
puts "[clock format [clock seconds] -format {%A, %B %e, %Y}]"
puts "You are using Tcl version $tcl_patchLevel"
puts "2 * 10 = [expr 2 * 10]"
for {set i 0} {$i <= 5} {incr i} {puts "sine of $i is [expr sin($i)]"}
gets stdin
```

For the purposes of this book, the idea is to pause the script until you press Enter. After you press Enter, tclsh exits and the window closes. There are better ways to pause Tcl scripts, which you will learn later, but gets stdin will suffice for the time being.

This chapter showed you *how* to use Tcl, or rather, how to use the Tcl interpreter, tclsh. Interactive tclsh sessions enable you to experiment with new or unfamiliar Tcl commands and play with small snippets of code. For any non-trivial program, though, it is much easier to create Tcl scripts that invoke tclsh directly, what I referred to as *self-executing Tcl scripts*. Making Tcl scripts self-executable in the Windows environment is a bit challenging and somewhat kludgy, an awkward side effect of the text-oriented nature of straight Tcl scripts. When you learn how to create graphical Tcl programs with Tk, you'll see that Tcl, in its Tk skin, integrates smoothly into GUI environments.

DOING MATHEMATICS

This chapter introduces the most fundamental elements of the Tcl language such as comments, variables, expressions, and commands. You also get your first exposure to the two most difficult elements of Tcl: command substitution and grouping. *Command substitution* describes the manner in which programming statements are built from Tcl's built-in commands and the results of those commands. *Grouping* refers to the way in which the operators "" and {} affect how command substitution works. This chapter also teaches you how to perform mathematical operations using Tcl's expr command.

GUESSING NUMBERS

This chapter's game is a simple pick-a-number exercise. The game chooses a random number between 1 and 20, asks you to guess what it is, and then displays a message indicating whether you guessed correctly or not. To start the game, execute the script guess_rand.tcl in this chapter's code directory on the Web site. Here are a few runs of the script:

```
$ ./guess_rand.tcl
Enter a number between 1 and 20: 5
Sorry! The number was 15.
$ ./guess_rand.tcl
```

```
Enter a number between 1 and 20: 5
Sorry! The number was 1.
$ ./guess_rand.tcl
Enter a number between 1 and 20: 5
Correct! The number was 5.
```

Although simple to play, guess_rand.tcl shows you how to do the following tasks:

- Use Tcl's `expr` command to perform mathematical calculations.
- Use the `puts` command to display strings and variables.
- Use the `gets` command to get input from the user.
- Use the `flush` command to clear I/O channels.
- Use the `if` command to evaluate a Boolean expression and execute different blocks of Tcl code, depending on the value of the Boolean expression.
- Use mathematical and logical operators to perform numeric comparisons.

To understand the code, which you will be able to do by the time you get to the end of the chapter, you'll need some background information. This introduction to key Tcl language features will give you the context you need to understand the code. Not to worry, though, as there are plenty of code snippets to digest and try out before you get to the guess_rand.tcl itself at the end of the chapter.

LANGUAGE FUNDAMENTALS

Tcl possesses all the standard elements necessary to a programming language, such as comments, expressions, variables, loops, conditionals, and procedures. However, at least one feature you might expect to encounter, keywords, does not exist in Tcl. In place of keywords, Tcl uses commands. As you will see later in the chapter, this difference is more than one of terminology. Similarly, Tcl has at least two syntax elements, command substitution and grouping, which you rarely encounter in compiled programming languages. *Command substitution* refers to the process by which the results of one command can be obtained and used as the argument to a second command. The results of the first command replace, or substitute for, the arguments of the second command. *Grouping* combines multiple arguments into a single argument, which in turn affects how command substitution works. Together, you can use command substitution and grouping to build more complex commands. These two features pervade the Tcl language and exert a powerful influence on how you write a Tcl program. Command substitution and grouping are so important to understand and use properly that the next two chapters revisit them, pointing out potential pitfalls and illustrating how they are used. Before you get into the minutiae of Tcl, though, I should cover the basic language features.

Comments

Comments are explanatory text that the Tcl interpreter ignores at runtime. To put it more prosaically, comments exist for the programmer, not for the program. The Tcl interpreter does not execute comments. Rather, comments serve to provide information to someone reading the code. A Tcl comment is prefixed with the # character, colloquially referred to as the *hash;* must appear at the beginning of a command; and ends with the first unescaped newline (that is, a carriage return or end-of-line character). So, of the following two Tcl commands, only the first is a comment (see comments.tcl in the source code directory for this chapter):

```
# puts {Hello, Tcl/Tk World!}
set msg {Hello, Tcl/Tk World!} # set the msg variable
```

If you try to execute the second command, it results in a syntax error. If you really want to make the text following # in the second line a comment, use a semicolon at the end of the command, thus:

```
set msg {Hello, Tcl/Tk World!}; # set the msg variable
```

Tcl uses both newline characters and semicolons to terminate commands, so the trick here is that the Tcl interpreter parses the ;, interprets it as the end of the set command, then encounters the #, which it interprets as the beginning of a comment.

If you need to create multi-line comments, you have two options. The way I do it is to begin each comment line with #. For example:

```
# This is the first line of a two-line comment. It is not
# especially enlightening but it is two lines long
```

The alternative method is to escape the newlines at the end of all but the last line of a multi-line comment. The reason this works is that, as explained earlier, comments are terminated by the first unescaped newline. *Escaping a character* means to cause the interpreter to ignore the character or to treat it specially. In this case, you want to tell the Tcl interpreter to ignore the newline. How, then, do you escape the newline? Prefix it with a backslash. The following two lines are functionally equivalent to the example I just gave you:

```
# This is the first line of a two-line comment. It is not \
especially enlightening, but it is two lines long
```

I prefer the first form to the second for simple aesthetics and because I can immediately distinguish between comments and commands when scanning a source code file. My mental source code parser has a more difficult time initially recognizing the second form (with escaped newlines) as comments. Suit yourself, but I recommend prefixing each line of a multi-line comment with #.

For what are comments used? As I quipped earlier, comments are for programmers, not programs. You might use them to explain how an especially subtle section of your program works. Another good reason to add a comment is to explain *why* a certain block of code works the way it does. Still another use of comments is to tell later readers of the code who wrote it (or, more likely, to tell later readers whom to blame). Perhaps the most common reason to use comments in your programs is to remind *yourself* what the code is doing and why. Six months from now, when you look at that throwaway piece of code you wrote, it will be very handy to have comments that refresh your memory. I don't know about you, but I have trouble remembering what I was thinking last week, so all the hints I can get help.

Commands

Commands are the meat of Tcl. Like keywords in other languages, Tcl commands are *reserved words*, meaning that they have a predefined meaning and usage in the language. However, unlike the keywords in most programming languages, you can redefine Tcl commands and replace a built-in Tcl command with an implementation of your own. What makes Tcl commands and Tcl itself different from other programming languages is that commands are the core of the language. Tcl commands do the heavy lifting in the language, not the interpreter. Each command defines its own arguments and is responsible for processing them. All that the interpreter does is parse the program, perform Tcl-specific syntax checking, group arguments, process substitutions, and then invoke the specified command, passing the arguments to the command for processing.

For example, the `puts` command accepts up to two arguments, an optional channel ID and a string to display. The interpreter performs any grouping on the arguments that might be required and then executes the `puts` command, passing all of the arguments available to `puts`. `puts`, not `tclsh`, validates the number and type of arguments and, if they validate, writes the specified string to the specified I/O channel, or to stdout if no I/O channel is requested. If the arguments don't validate, it is again `puts`, not `tclsh`, that displays the error message and syntax diagnostic.

So what precisely is a Tcl command? A Tcl command is a list of one or more words, the first of which is the command you want to execute. The second and following words are arguments. For the time being, consider a *word* as any group of consecutive characters surrounded by white space. In Tcl, a *character* is either a letter, digit, or one of a limited set of special symbols. *White space* consists of one or more tabs, one or more space characters, or a combination of the two. Each word is considered a separate argument, so if you want to pass multiple words as a single argument (say, to the `puts` command), then you have to enclose them in quotes (`""`) or braces (`{}`). The double quotes or braces are *not* treated as part of the argument, however. They merely combine, or *group,* the words into a single logical unit.

Arguments to Tcl Commands

Most Tcl commands take multiple arguments, but some accept only one, and some don't accept any arguments. Moreover, many Tcl commands have both optional and required arguments.

Consider the following three commands:

```
puts "Hello, Tcl/Tk World!"
puts stdout {Hello, Tcl/Tk World!}
puts stdout Hello, "Tcl/Tk World!"
```

The first command has one argument, `Hello, Tcl/Tk World!`, because the string is enclosed in double quotes. The second command has two arguments, `stdout` and `Hello, Tcl/Tk World!`, because the string `Hello, Tcl/Tk World!` is enclosed in braces and is considered a single argument. The third command (which is invalid, by the way) has three arguments, `stdout`, `Hello`, and `Tcl/Tk World!`.

Command arguments fall into one of two categories: parameters and options. In general, *parameters* (the fancy computer science term is *formal parameters*) are arguments on which a command operates, such as data to print or numbers to add. For example, in the three `puts` commands just shown, all of the arguments are parameters; `stdout` is the (optional) channel ID and the various renderings of "Hello, Tcl/Tk World!" are the string `puts` should display.

Options, on the other hand, are arguments that modify how commands operate. Not all commands have them. Returning once more to the `puts` command, it accepts one option, `-nonewline`, which disables appending a newline to the string that `puts` display (puts' default behavior is to append a newline to the string), as shown in the following example (see options.tcl in this chapter's code directory):

```
puts "puts appends a newline to this sentence.";
puts -nonewline "puts doesn't append a newline to this sentence.";
```

The output of this script should look like the following:

```
$ ./options.tcl
puts appends a newline to this sentence.
puts doesn't append a newline to this sentence.
$
```

Notice how the shell's command prompt winds up at the end of the sentence rather than at the beginning of the next line. Demonstrating the `-nonewline` option is not the point, of course, but rather the point is that the `-nonewline` option changes `puts`' default behavior.

Many, perhaps most, of Tcl's commands accept one or more options in addition to the parameters they accept. To further confuse matters, while options are usually, um, optional (that is, not required), many Tcl commands have both required and optional parameters. Failing to specify a required parameter (or a required option, for that matter) generates a syntax error. If you do not use an optional argument (such as `puts`' channel ID argument), you will get the default behavior (in `puts`' case, the default behavior is to display the string argument to stdout).

Arguments, Options, or Parameters?

To keep things simple, I use the term *argument* to refer to both options and parameters unless the distinction between them is important.

Command Substitution

To execute a command, Tcl evaluates the command in two steps or passes: substitution and evaluation. During the first pass, *substitution,* the interpreter parses the command and its arguments (moving left to right), looking for words that need to be replaced with another value. Situations in which words are replaced, or substituted, include substituting variables with their values (hang on, I'll talk about variables later in the chapter) and substituting embedded commands with their results. During the second pass, *evaluation,* the interpreter processes the command and performs the action(s) associated with that command.

One of Tcl's language features that often confuses beginners is that substitution is nonrecursive. That is, only a single round of substitution occurs. If, for example, a variable's value is a second variable, that second variable is passed unmolested to the command; a second round of substitution does not occur (a variable's value can also be a command). Likewise, if an embedded command evaluates to yet another command or to a variable, the second command or the variable will not undergo further substitution.

The Tcl interpreter performs four types of substitutions during the substitution phase:

1. **Variable expansion**: Variables are replaced with their values.
2. **Escape sequence substitution**: Escape sequences (character strings preceded with \) are replaced with their hexadecimal values (see Table 3.1).
3. **Command replacement**: Commands within brackets, what I have referred to as *embedded commands*, are replaced with the results of those commands.
4. **Line continuation**: If a line ends with \newline (that is, a backslash followed by a newline), the \newline is replaced with a space, the current line is merged with the following line, and any leading white space in the following line is discarded.

Although I haven't talked about variables yet, they look like this: $variable. In variable expansion, the value of $variable is replaced by its value. If the variable $name has the value Kurt Wall, the command puts $name; becomes puts "Kurt Wall"; (see varsub.tcl in this chapter's code directory).

With command replacement, embedded commands are evaluated, and their results are substituted. For example, consider the following command (see cmd_repl.tcl in this chapter's code directory):

```
puts "2 + 3 = [expr 2 + 3]"
```

During the substitution phase, the embedded command [expr 2 + 3], which adds 2 and 3, will be replaced by the result of the addition, so after substitution and before evaluation, the statement becomes:

```
puts "2 + 3 = 5"
```

Of all the substitution operations performed, command replacement is the most important because it is the method by which the results of a command are substituted in the command. It is this feature of Tcl that gives Tcl its power and its utility as a glue language. You needn't take my word for it, though. As you read this book, work through the examples, and start writing your own programs, you will see how completely command replacement (widely and somewhat confusingly referred to as *command substitution* in Tcl documentation) pervades the language.

Escape sequence substitution, often referred to as *backslash substitution*, replaces a select set of escape sequences with their hexadecimal equivalent. Generally, escape sequences are used to display special characters, such as tabs or the carriage return character, but Tcl, like other programming languages, also uses escape sequences to display octal and hexadecimal values. The following example (escape.tcl in this chapter's code directory) shows how you can insert tab characters (horizontal tabs, to be specific) into output printed with puts (the escape sequence \t represents a horizontal tab):

```
puts "A\ttab\tseparates\teach\tof\tthese\twords."
```

Here's what the output looks like:

```
$ ./escape.tcl
A       tab     separates       each    of      these   words.
```

Escape sequences make the command slightly more difficult to read, but the output is crystal clear, if oddly formatted. Table 3.1 lists all of the escape sequences Tcl replaces during substitution.

TABLE 3.1: TCL ESCAPE SEQUENCES		
Escape Sequence	**Character**	**Hexadecimal Value**
\a	Bell	\x07
\b	Backspace	\x08
\f	Form Feed	\x0c
\n	Newline	\x0a
\r	Carriage Return	\x0d
\t	Horizontal Tab	\x09
\v	Vertical Tab	\x0b
\ooo	Octal Value	o (values 0 to 7)
\x hh	Hexadecimal Value	h (values 0 to 9 and/or A to F)

Here's a bit of perversity for you. The backslash character is used both to cause characters to be treated specially and to prevent characters from being treated specially. As you just read, \ causes certain characters, the escape sequences shown in Table 3.1, to take on a new meaning. However, you can also escape sequences using \, as it were. If you precede an escape sequence with a backslash, the escape sequence loses it special meaning. So, in the following command, I used \ to inhibit the substitution of the escape sequence \t (see no_escape.tcl in this chapter's code directory):

```
puts "A\\ttab\\tseparates\\teach\\tof\\tthese\\twords."
```

The output is:

```
A\ttab\tseparates\teach\tof\tthese\twords.
```

Now, both the command and its output are difficult to read! The value of escaping escape sequences is that it enables you to use as normal characters, characters that otherwise have special meaning, such as $, which Tcl uses as the operator for obtaining the value of a variable.

Using the \ character to create multi-line comments is an example of line continuation (with the key difference that comments aren't executed). Here's another example of line continuation that uses a command, found in line_cont.tcl in this chapter's code directory):

```
puts "This line is continued below\
but appears as a single line."
```

After the substitution phase, the puts command would look like the following:

```
./line_cont.tcl
puts "This line is continued below but appears as a single line."
```

As you can see, the \newline sequence was replaced by a space. Tcl beginners often make the mistake of adding a space before the \, which creates *two* spaces in the resulting command and ungainly (and probably unintended) spacing in the resulting output:

```
puts "This line is continued below \
but appears as a single line."
```

When executed, the output of this script is:

```
$ ./line_cont_oops.tcl
This line is continued below  but appears as a single line.
```

Notice the two spaces between the words below and but.

If all of this seems confusing, it will make more sense when you start writing programs a little later in this chapter. Think of it like learning a new card game. Someone has to describe the rules to you before you start playing or the actual card play will make little sense. Yet, once you have played a few hands (and, if you're like me, gotten soundly defeated), the rules start making sense. The mechanics of command substitution become more meaningful when you see them in action. Separating this discussion of command substitution from other fundamentals of the Tcl language, particularly grouping, is artificial because in actual practice, command substitution and grouping work together. You don't have much context, yet. Nonetheless, you have to start somewhere, so bear with me.

Grouping

This section will help you grok the previous section's coverage of command substitution. In the simplest terms, *grouping* converts multiple words into a single argument. As you've already learned, Tcl treats multiple words as multiple arguments; grouping alters this behavior. You've already seen how double quotes can be used to group words into a single string argument for the `puts` command. Tcl also uses pairs of braces, { }, to perform grouping. Why use two operators to perform the same operation? Because each operator has different effects on the words or other language elements being grouped.

Grouping with Double Quotes

When you group words with double quotes, the grouped items function as a single argument and will be treated as a single argument during the evaluation phase of Tcl command execution. In addition, double quotes allow any variables that appear in the group to be substituted with their value. If it helps you remember, think of grouping with double quotes as performing *weak grouping*. The grouping is weak because it doesn't prevent variables from being expanded into their values, as you can see in the following example (quotes.tcl on the Web site):

```
set fname Kurt
set mname {Roland}
set lname "Wall"
puts "Full name: $fname $mname $lname"
```

The output of this script shows my full name because the variables $fname, $mname, and $lname are substituted with their values:

```
$ ./quotes.tcl
Full name: Kurt Roland Wall
```

Grouping with Braces

Think of grouping with braces as *strong grouping* because braces inhibit the substitution of variables. They are strong enough to prevent variable substitution. Thus, characters and words grouped with braces are passed to the command exactly as they are written, as you can see in the following example (see braces.tcl):

```
set fname Kurt
set mname {Roland}
set lname "Wall"
puts {Full name: $fname $mname $lname}
```

Unlike quotes.tcl, braces.tcl does not substitute the values of $fname, $mname, and $lname:

```
$ ./braces.tcl
Full name: $fname $mname $lname
```

Backslash or escape sequence substitution is also disabled when the escape sequences are grouped with braces. If you replace the double quotes in quotes.tcl with braces, the \t escape sequence will be left alone, and the output will include the literal characters \t (see brace_esc.tcl in this chapter's code directory):

```
puts {A\ttab\tseparates\teach\tof\tthese\twords.}
```

The output is predictably awful:

```
$ ./brace_esc.tcl
A\ttab\tseparates\teach\tof\tthese\twords.
```

There is one exception to the previous rule, however. An escaped newline at the end of a line is still evaluated as a space, allowing you to use line continuation with brace grouping, as you can see in brace_cont.tcl in this chapter's code samples):

```
puts {This line is continued below\
but appears as a single line.}
```

As you can see in the output, the combination of \ and a newline is replaced by a space, and the two lines are merged into a single line:

```
$ ./brace_cont.tcl
This line is continued below but appears as a single line.
```

You will see many, many examples of grouping with both double quotes and braces in the coming chapters. Like command substitution, grouping is a key feature of Tcl programming.

Variables

Finally, you're going to read about variables. I've already used them several times to highlight the behavior of command substitution, but it's time for a more formal definition. Variables are names that refer to memory addresses, which contain data that a program or script needs. To assign a value to a variable, use the set command. The syntax of the set command is:

```
set varName ?value?
```

This statement assigns *value* to the variable *varName*. *varName* can be a scalar variable or an array. For the time being, I'll focus on scalar variables (Chapter 6, "Creating and Using Arrays," discusses array usage in detail). If you omit the *value* argument, set returns the current value of *varName*. You've already seen several examples of variable assignment. In quotes.tcl, for example, the following commands assign the values Kurt, Roland, and Wall to the variables fname, mname, and lname, respectively:

```
set fname Kurt
set mname {Roland}
set lname "Wall"
```

When you execute this script, you see the following:

```
$ ./quotes.tcl
Full name: Kurt Roland Wall
```

These examples are straightforward. The first command performs no grouping and, because the value is only a single word, it isn't necessary to surround the argument Kurt with double quotes. The second and third examples use brace and double quote grouping.

To obtain a variable's value, known as *dereferencing the variable*, you have two options. The most common method is to use the $ operator in front of the variable name. So, referring back to the previous variable assignments, $fname yields Kurt; $mname yields Roland; and $lname yields Wall. The other method for dereferencing a variable is to use the syntax set *varName*, which omits the value and causes set to return *varname*'s current value. If *varName* hasn't been assigned a value, it is an error to attempt to dereference it via either method, as you can see in the next example:

```
% set min 1
1
% set min
1
% set max
can't read "max": no such variable
```

If you try to put these commands in a script, the script won't execute because the interpreter detects the syntax error in the set max; command. Here's what happens when you execute these commands as a script (see var_set.tcl in this chapter's code directory):

```
$ ./var_set.tcl
can't read "max": no such variable
    while executing
"set max"
    (file "var_set.tcl" line 7)
```

Whether executed interactively or as a script, the error is the same. Because the variable max has not yet been assigned a value, it does not yet exist from the point of view of the Tcl interpreter, so any attempt to dereference it generates an error.

Tcl Creates Variables Dynamically

Although variables have to be assigned a value before you can dereference them, it is not necessary to declare variables before you assign values to them because the interpreter creates variables as they are needed.

What if you want to print text that actually contains a $ character? You escape it, naturally (see print_ref.tcl):

```
set msg "You have won the game!"
puts $msg
puts \$msg
```

Here's the output from the script:

```
$ ./print_ref.tcl
You have won the game!
$msg
```

As mentioned earlier in the chapter, escaping the $ with a backslash causes the Tcl interpreter to ignore $'s special semantics and treat it as it if were a normal, merely mortal character with no special superpowers.

Just as you can use the set command to assign a value to a variable (and, consequently, bring a variable into existence), you can use the unset command to destroy a variable, as the following example, unset.tcl in this chapter's code directory, shows:

```
% set msg "You have won the game!"
You have won the game!
% set msg
You have won the game!
% puts $msg
You have won the game!
% unset msg
% puts $msg
can't read "msg": no such variable
% set msg
can't read "msg" : no such variable
```

As you can see in the example, after you unset a variable name, attempting to dereference it generates an error. You won't be able to execute unset.tcl unless you comment out the last two lines of the script (lines 9 and 10).

A final note before ending this section. The examples in this section use simple expressions to assign values to variables. However, as you might expect, it is common to use command substitutions to generate values for variables. In the following script, for instance (show_rand.tcl in this chapter's code directory), I use the rand() function and the expr command to assign a random integer value between 1 and 20 to the variable randNum, truncate randNum with the round() function, and then pass randNum to puts:

```
set min 1
set max 20
set randNum [expr {round($min + (rand() * ($max - $min)))}]
puts "The random number is $randNum"
```

The output of this script will vary, but it should resemble the following:

```
$ ./show_rand.tcl
The random number is 20
```

The rand() function generates a random number between 0 and 1. The round() function rounds a floating point number (a number that contains a decimal or fractional component) to its nearest integral part. For example, round(10.1) yields 10; round(10.9) yields 11.

Procedures

Tcl procedures (known as subroutines or functions in other languages) are named blocks of code. Procedures enable you to create new commands and to redefine built-in Tcl commands. To define a procedure, use the proc command. The general syntax of the proc command is:

```
proc name args body
```

- *name* is the name you assign to the procedure and by which you invoke it. A procedure name may consist of any combination of valid Tcl characters, but, as you might expect, the name is case-sensitive.

- *args* is a space-separated list of zero or more parameters that you pass to the command. Parameters are optional, meaning that you can define procedures that do not accept any parameters. Later in this book, you will learn how to create procedures that accept variable-length argument lists and how to create procedures that assign default values to parameters.

- *body* is the list of one or more commands that define the procedure. Actually, *body* doesn't really define the procedure. Instead, *body* defines the command or commands that will be substituted (substitution, remember that?) for the name of the procedure when the procedure is invoked. Any valid Tcl language element can be used in the body, including other proc-defined procedures. You cannot, however, have nested procedures, that is, define a procedure within a procedure.

When a procedure terminates (upon reaching the outermost closing brace), the value it returns to the caller is the value of the last statement executed. You could call this a procedure's default return value. Alternatively, you can define the value returned using the return command. My recommendation is to define the return value specifically. Doing so makes your code more readable and reduces the likelihood that later changes in the procedure's definition unintentionally alter the return value.

You'll get into the nuts and bolts of procedures in subsequent chapters, but you probably want to know what one looks like. The following example (from calc_percent.tcl in this chapter's code directory) illustrates defining and using a procedure (the line numbers are not part of the procedure, just explanatory aids):

```
1    proc CalcPercent {part whole} {
2            set retVal [expr {double($part) / $whole * 100}]
3            return $retVal
4    }
```

Line 1 defines the procedure name, CalcPercent, and its formal parameters, part and whole. Tcl syntax requires that the opening brace appear on the same line as the proc command. The expression expr double($part) / $whole * 100 on line 2 calculates the percentage of whole which part represents. Because the outer command is a set command, the result of the calculation is stored in the variable retVal. On line 3, I use return $retVal to pass the result of the calculation back to the caller.

CalcPercent also serves as a good illustration of the importance of grouping. Recall that proc requires three arguments: the procedure's name, its parameters (if any), and the body. In this case, CalcPercent accepts two parameters: part and whole. To present these parameters as a single argument to the proc command, they are grouped with braces. The same reasoning applies to the procedure's body—by enclosing the two lines of code that make up the procedure body in braces, the interpreter parses them and passes them to the proc command as a single argument. In addition, because grouping occurs before substitution, the braces ensure that substitution doesn't result in an unintended result, such as a value appearing in a command where a variable should be. This isn't an issue in this particular procedure, but it can happen.

A Matter of Style

Coding style concerns itself not with the syntax of your Tcl code, but with its appearance, formatting, and structure. White space usage, brace placement, variable and procedure naming, and overall code organization are all elements of coding style. Unlike syntax and grammar rules, which Tcl defines and enforces, nothing in Tcl enforces coding style. Rather, coding style is a matter of convention, personal preference, and, if you work in a software development shop, the company's style guide.

The purpose of coding style is to ensure readability and consistency. It is much easier to find syntax mistakes, typos, and "thinkos" (logical errors) in your code if you adopt a uniform style and use it consistently. Consistently styled code is also easier to read, simpler to maintain, and, to the degree that any programming language has an aesthetic, more aesthetically pleasing.

In this sidebar, I offer three suggestions:

- Regardless of the coding style you ultimately choose to adopt, choose *something* and stick to it. Naturally, I consider my coding style perfectly reasonable, but you are free to use any style you like. The important thing is to use something consistently so that it eventually becomes second nature.

- Begin variable names with lowercase letters and, if the name includes embedded words, use uppercase letters on the first letter of each embedded word. Examples of variable names include start, end, userName, and highScore.

- Begin procedure names with uppercase letters and, if the procedure name contains embedded words, use uppercase letters on the first letter of each embedded word. Examples of procedure names include Save, Login, CalcPercent, and ShowHighScore.

Getting User Input

Tcl has several commands for performing I/O (input/output). For interacting with users, the command is gets, which is the complement to the puts command you have been using. Although gets can be used to get input from files, network sockets, and stdin, this chapter only discusses using gets for stdin. The syntax for gets is:

```
gets channelID ?varName?
```

gets reads a line of input from the input source specified by *channelID*. It reads the entire line of input up to the end-of-line (EOL) character and discards the EOL. For the purposes of this chapter, *channelID* must be `stdin`, which, as you've already learned, is (usually) the keyboard. As you can see in the syntax diagram, *varName* is optional. If you specify *varName*, `gets` stores the input line in *varName* and returns the number of characters it read, not including the EOL. If you omit *varName*, `gets` returns the input line. The following example illustrates `gets`' usage (see gets.tcl in this chapter's code directory):

```
puts -nonewline "Please Player 1's name: "
flush stdout
set count [gets stdin playerName]
puts "Player 1's name is $playerName."
puts "It has $count characters."
```

The output of this program should resemble the following:

```
$ ./gets.tcl
Enter Player 1's name: Bubba
Player 1's name is Bubba.
It has 5 characters.
```

If you don't care how many characters the input line contains, you could rewrite this example as:

```
puts -nonewline "Please Player 1's name: "
flush stdout
set playerName [gets stdin]
puts "Player 1's name is $playerName."
```

The point I want to make is that the following two commands have identical results because both assign `gets`' result to the variable `playerName`.

```
gets stdin playerName
set playerName [gets stdin]
```

You might be wondering what the command `flush stdout` does in these two scripts. Permit me to explain. In short, it is necessary to display a prompt and request input on the same line. Without `flush stdout`, get.tcl would not have prompted for Player 1's name until *after* you entered it and pressed Enter (which generates a newline). Not quite the effect you're looking for.

Why? By default, `puts` *buffers*, or stores, output until it encounters a newline. As you've already learned, though, `puts`' -nonewline option prevents `puts` from appending a newline to the string it displays. As a result, `puts` won't display the requested output. To force the display of a *partial line* (a line of output that doesn't include a newline), use the `flush` command, which does what the name implies, flushes (displays) any buffered I/O. When used on the stdout channel (thus, `flush stdout` in the two examples), the partial line will be displayed, and you get the output you expected.

Basic Mathematical Operators

The Tcl command for performing mathematical operations is `expr`. For as powerful and capable a command as `expr`, its syntax is simple:

```
expr arg ?arg ...?
```

Each *arg* is either a math operator or operand. `expr` concatenates each *arg* (adding spaces for separation as necessary), evaluates the concatenated statement as a Tcl expression, and then returns the result. The result is either a numeric value (an integer or floating point value) or a Boolean value (0 for false and 1 for true). Operands, the values upon which operators work, can be integers, floating point values, variables, or strings. Operators can be one of the mathematical operators shown in Table 3.2 or one of the mathematical functions you learn about in a later chapter.

Tcl supports the standard mathematical operators common to all programming languages. The complete list appears in Table 3.2.

Table 3.2 groups each operator in order of decreasing precedence. Operators that are in the same group have the same precedence.

Operator Groups Don't Really Exist

The operator grouping in Table 3.2 is a device I've used to identify operators that have the same precedence. Tcl lacks this notion. If you're at a cocktail party with other Tcl programmers and refer to "group 5 operators," they probably won't know what you mean.

Operator precedence is the term used to describe the order in which mathematical operators are evaluated when multiple operators exist in an expression. Consider the following `expr` command:

```
set x [expr {21 << 2 * 3 + 4}]
```

Depending on the order of evaluation, x might be assigned 256, 588, 21504, or 344064. Because you (and Tcl) know the relative precedence of the operators, multiplication, then addition, then right-shift, you can reliably predict the answer, 21504. If you need to modify the order of evaluation, use parentheses around the operation(s) that need to occur first. If there are

TABLE 3.2:   TCL MATHEMATICAL OPERATORS

Group	Operator	Description	Float	Integer	String
1	−	Unary minus	Yes	Yes	No
1	+	Unary plus	Yes	Yes	No
1	~	Bitwise NOT	Yes	Yes	No
1	!	Logical NOT	Yes	Yes	No
2	*	Multiplication	Yes	Yes	No
2	/	Division	Yes	Yes	Yes
2	%	Modulus	No	Yes	No
3	+	Addition	Yes	Yes	No
3	−	Subtraction	Yes	Yes	No
4	<<	Left shift	No	Yes	No
4	>>	Right shift	No	Yes	No
5	<	Numeric less than	Yes	Yes	No
5	>	Numeric greater than	Yes	Yes	No
5	<=	Numeric less than or equal	Yes	Yes	No
5	>=	Numeric greater than or equal	Yes	Yes	No
6	==	Numeric equality	Yes	Yes	No
6	!=	Numeric inequality	Yes	Yes	No
7	eq	String equality	No	No	Yes
7	ne	String inequality	No	No	Yes
8	$	Bitwise AND	No	Yes	No
9	^	Bitwise EXCLUSIVE OR	No	Yes	No
10			Bitwise OR	No	Yes	No
11	&&	Logical AND	No	Yes	No
12	||	Logical OR	No	Yes	No
13	x ? y : z	If-Then-Else	Yes	Yes	Yes

multiple parenthetical operations, evaluation proceeds from the innermost parenthesized operations outward, as demonstrated by precedence.tcl in this chapter's code directory:

```
set x [expr {(((21 << 2) * 3) + 4)}]
puts "<< then * then +: $x";

set x [expr {(21 << 2) * (3 + 4)}]
puts "+ then << then *: $x";

set x [expr {21 << 2 * (3 + 4)}]
```

```
puts "+ then * then <<: $x"

set x [expr {21 << 2 * 3 + 4}]
puts "Default (* then + then <<): $x"
```

Executing the program shows the effects of the parentheses:

```
$ ./precedence.tcl
<< then * then +: x = 256
+ then << then *: x = 588
+ then * then <<: x = 344064
Default (* then + then <<): x = 21504
```

If expr's expression evaluator encounters operators that have same precedence in an expression and the order of evaluation isn't modified by parentheses, expr resolves the ambiguity by reading and parsing the expression left to right. For example, given the command [expr {2 * 9 % 5}], the result would be 3 because, absent parentheses to force a specific evaluation order, expr performs the multiplication first, then the modulus. If your program's logic requires the modulus operation to be executed first, you must use parentheses to specify that. Accordingly, the proper expression in this case would be [expr 2 * (9 % 5)], which yields 8.

You will learn more about expr in subsequent chapters. What you've learned in this chapter is enough for you to be productive without bogging you down with subtleties and potential *gotchas*.

CONDITIONAL EXECUTION: THE IF COMMAND

Tcl's if command is used for conditional execution. Most of the scripts you have seen so far have been simple "fall-through" programs. Execution starts the first command and proceeds linearly through each subsequent command until the script terminates after the last command executes. Every command is executed. There are plenty of programming tasks suited to this simple sequential execution model. However, sometimes scripts need to execute a certain command or set of commands multiple times. Likewise, you might need to execute one command or set of commands in one situation, but, in the same script, execute a different set of commands in another situation. Executing commands multiple times is known as *looping* or *repetition* (see "Chapter 4, Strings, Strings, Everywhere Strings!"). Varying the commands executed depending on the situation is referred to as *conditional execution*.

Conditional execution boils down to making a choice and acting on it. You deal with conditionals all the time. If I win the lottery, I won't go to work; otherwise, I'll go to work. If I'm late to work, my boss will be unhappy; if I'm on time to work, my boss will be satisfied; if I'm early to work, my boss will be pleased. Although Tcl has several commands for expressing and dealing with conditionals, the one you'll learn to use in this chapter is the `if` command. It's true that `if`'s general syntax is somewhat imposing to look at in the abstract, but easy to understand in practice:

```
if {expr1} ?then? {
        body1
} elseif {expr2} ?then? {
        body2
} elseif
…
?else? {
        ?bodyN?
}
```

The `if` command starts by evaluating *expr1*. If *expr1* is true, that is, *expr1* evaluates to a non-zero value or a string value of true or yes, then the commands in *body1* are executed. Otherwise, if *expr1* is false (either a numeric value of 0 or a string value of false or no), the `elseif` causes *expr2* to be evaluated. If *expr2* is true, *body2* is executed. If it is false, the next expression will be evaluated, and so forth. If none of the expressions evaluates to true, then the `else` causes the commands in *bodyN* to be executed.

You can have any number of `elseif` clauses, including none at all. The `then` and `else` words are optional; you can include them to make the expressions easier to read (my personal practice is to use `else` but not to use `then`. The opening brace of the body commands must appear on the same lines as their corresponding `if`, `elseif`, and `else` commands. I also *strongly* recommend using indentation and multi-line statements, as shown in the syntax diagram, to make conditional statements easier to read.

Confusing? It isn't, it just sounds that way. In the simplest case, you can have a single `if` command with no `elseif` or `else` clauses

```
set diceValue 5;
if {$diceValue >= 5} {
    puts "You rolled $diceValue. Roll again!"
}

set diceValue 4;
if {$diceValue >= 5} {
    puts "You rolled $diceValue. Roll again!"
}
```

In this command, there is no else clause. If $diceValue is less than five, execution skips to the command immediately following the closing brace. Otherwise, the puts statement executes (see if_simple.tcl). When you execute this script, the second puts statement doesn't execute:

```
$ ./if_simple.tcl
You rolled 5. Roll again!
```

The next simplest case adds the else clause (see if_else.tcl):

```
set diceValue 5;
if {$diceValue >= 5} {
    puts "You rolled $diceValue. Roll again!"
} else {
    puts "You rolled $diceValue. Sorry, you lose!"
}

set diceValue 4;
if {$diceValue >= 5} {
    puts "You rolled $diceValue. Roll again!"
} else {
    puts "You rolled $diceValue. Sorry, you lose!"
}
```

In this case, if $diceValue is greater than or equal to five, the user gets to roll again; otherwise, the puts message informs the user of her bitter defeat. The output is shown in the following example:

```
$ ./if_else.tcl
You rolled 5. Roll again!
You rolled 4. Sorry, you lose!
```

Adding one or more elseif clauses makes it possible to express more than simple either-or choices (see if_elseif.tcl):

```
set diceValue 5;
if {$diceValue >= 5} {
    puts "You rolled $diceValue. Roll again!"
} elseif {$diceValue < 5 && $diceValue > 1} {
    puts "You rolled $diceValue.Lose a turn!"
} else {
    puts "You rolled $diceValue. Game over!"
}
```

```
set diceValue 4;
if {$diceValue >= 5} {
    puts "You rolled $diceValue. Roll again!"
} elseif {$diceValue > 1 && $diceValue < 5} {
    puts "You rolled $diceValue. Lose a turn!"
} else {
    puts "You rolled $diceValue. Game over!"
}

set diceValue 1;
if {$diceValue >= 5} {
    puts "You rolled $diceValue. Roll again!"
} elseif {$diceValue > 1 && $diceValue < 5} {
    puts "You rolled $diceValue. Lose a turn!"
} else {
    puts "You rolled $diceValue. Game over!"
}
```

In if_elseif.tcl, I used an elseif clause to create an option for the case in which the user "rolls" a value greater than one and less than five. The following example shows if_elseif.tcl's output:

```
$ ./if_elseif.tcl
You rolled 5. Roll again!
You rolled 4. Lose a turn!
You rolled 1. Game over!
```

You can have as many elseif clauses as necessary, but if you need very many, you'll probably want to use the switch command, which you'll learn about in Chapter 5, "Working with Lists." More than four or five elseif clauses looks messy and can be difficult to maintain.

if and expr Use the Same Expression Evaluator

The if and expr commands use the same expression evaluator. This means that the rules you learned for using expr also apply when using if. The exception is that you don't have to use expr in if's condition. So instead of writing if {[expr $x < 6]} {...}, you can just write if {$x < 6} {...}.

As I suggested, if looks imposing in a syntax diagram, but is easy to use in practice because its structure neatly mirrors the way you handle decisions.

ANALYZING THE GUESSING NUMBERS PROGRAM

Now that I have described most of Tcl's language features and introduced a number of Tcl commands, this chapter's game, guess_rand.tcl, should be easy to understand. Each of the demonstration game programs in this book is generously commented (perhaps too generously), and significant blocks of code are named Block 1, Block 2, and so forth. Naming the blocks will make it easier for me to refer to them and, hopefully, less confusing for you.

Looking at the Code

Here's the code for guess_rand.tcl.

```tcl
#!/usr/bin/tclsh
# guess_rand.tcl
# Guess a random number between 1 and 20

# Block 1
# Algorithm is "min + (random * (max - min))"
set target [expr {int(1 + (rand() * 19))}]

# Block 2
# Read the user's guess
puts -nonewline "Enter a number between 1 and 20: "
flush stdout
gets stdin guess

# Block 3
# Validate the input
if { $guess < 1 || $guess > 20 } {
    puts "Your guess must be between 1 and 20"
    exit 1
}

# Block 4
# Do we have a winner?
if { $guess == $target } {
    set msg "Correct"
} else {
    set msg "Sorry"
}
puts "$msg! The number was $target."
```

Understanding the Code

Block 1 generates the random number. Strictly speaking, the rand() function generates a pseudo-random number. It is "pseudo" because the random number generator uses the same pattern to generate a random number (it turns out that generating a truly random number is surprisingly difficult). Regardless, I use the rand() function to generate a random number. As you will recall, rand() generates a floating point value between zero and one, so I need a way to scale it (move the decimal point) and convert it to an integer.

While I don't want to get into the mathematics to prove the algorithm, the principle behind my random number generator is just this: to generate a random value between and including the minimum value *min* and the maximum value *max*, use the formula *min + (random * (max − min))*. After generating that number, I use the int() function to truncate the generated number (which is a floating point value) to its integral component and then assign that value to the variable $target.

In Block 2, I use the puts command to create a prompt for the user to input a number. As described earlier, I used -newline option to create a more attractive prompt and the flush stdout command to make sure that the prompt appears. The gets command stores the value the user provides in the variable named guess.

Block 3 performs a basic sanity check to ensure that the user's input is within the range specified (1 and 20 in this case). If the user's input falls outside this range, I display an error message and exit the script.

Otherwise, the script falls through to Block 4, where I compare the user's guess, $guess, to the generated value, $target. This is a comparison ideally suited for conditional execution because, depending on the result of the test $guess == $target, I want to execute different blocks of code (albeit that the "blocks" in this case are each single commands). Specifically, I set the variable $msg. Finally, I display a message, again with the puts command, telling the user whether her guess was correct or not and what the generated value was. Notice how the conditional expression makes it easy to build the string that is displayed with the puts command. This is a typical Tcl technique, one you will see throughout this book, in Tcl code elsewhere, and, as time goes on, increasingly frequently in your own code.

Modifying the Code

Here are some exercises you can try to practice what you learned in this chapter:

3.1. Modify guess_rand.tcl to use variables for storing the upper and lower bounds for the random number generator instead of using "magic numbers" in Block 1.

3.2 Modify the program in Exercise 3.1 to ask the user to input lower and upper bounds for the random number generator rather than hard-coding the values into the script.

3.3 Modify the program in Exercise 3.2 by replacing one or more of the code blocks with a procedure that performs the same task.

Appendix A contains suggested solutions for each exercise.

STRINGS, STRINGS, EVERYWHERE STRINGS!

Now that you know how to do basic math using Tcl, you're ready to learn how to perform a wide variety of string operations. Tcl has a rich set of commands and functionality for manipulating strings, an unsurprising fact when you consider that Tcl is a string-based programming language. *Everything* in Tcl is a string, even numbers. This characteristic of the language sometimes takes beginners by surprise because certain operators behave differently, depending on the context in which they are used, which can lead to unexpected results. If I've done my job properly, though, you'll be able to recognize and avoid these *gotchas*. In this chapter, you will spend some quality time with the `string` command, which is the primary Tcl command for working with strings. The final section continues the discussion of Tcl control structures I started in the previous chapter by introducing two looping commands, `while` and `for`.

MAD LIBS

To play this chapter's game, you provide a word that meets specific criteria, such as an adjective, a verb ending in -ing, or a noun, to create what we called *Mad Libs* when I was growing up. The script takes the words and parts of speech that you provide and plugs them into a story. The result is a silly or nonsense story that is also (hopefully) amusing or at least mildly entertaining. To start the game, execute the script mad_lib.tcl in this chapter's code directory. Here are the results of one execution:

```
$ ./mad_lib.tcl
Enter a verb ending in -ing: swimming
Enter a adjective: enormous
Enter a mythical creature: unicorn
Enter a piece of furniture: coffee table
Enter a noun: sink
Enter a past tense verb: yanked
Enter a noun: shovel
Enter a number: 10
One day while I was swimming in my living room, a enormous unicorn fell through the
roof. It jumped on the coffee table and knocked over the sink. Then it ran into the
dining room and yanked a shovel. After 10 minutes of chasing it through the house I
finally caught it and put it outside. It quickly flew away.
```

Okay, nothing is blowing up, and you're probably not rolling on the floor laughing. Nonetheless, mad_lib.tcl shows you how to do the following programming tasks:

- Repeat a body of Tcl code multiple times.
- Find characters in strings.
- Find substrings in strings.
- Replace one substring with another.
- Incorporate user input into your script.

A significant portion of Tcl programming, indeed, of almost any programming, is reading, writing, and manipulating string-based data. This chapter introduces you to a substantial portion of Tcl's string-handling capabilities. There is a lot to cover in this respect, though too much to stuff into one chapter, so I've saved more advanced string-handling functionality for later chapters.

THE `string` COMMAND

The command you will use most often to work with strings is the aptly named `string` command. As of Tcl 8.4, the `string` command has 21 options that define all of the operations you can perform with it. The general form of the `string` command is:

```
string option arg ?arg? …
```

Each *option* accepts at least one argument, *arg*, but most take more. For convenience and completeness, Table 4.1 lists each of `string`'s options and gives a short description of the option's purpose.

TABLE 4.1: `string` OPTIONS

Option	Description
bytelength	Returns the number of bytes required to store a string in memory.
compare	Tests two strings for lexicographic equality.
equal	Tests two strings for lexicographic equality, returning 1 if the strings are identical, 0 if they are not
first	Returns the index of the first occurrence of a substring.
index	Returns the character that appears at a specified location in a string.
is	Tests whether a string is a member of a given character class.
last	Returns the index of the last occurrence of a substring.
length	Returns the length of a string.
map	Replaces substrings with new values based on key-value pairs.
match	Tests a string for matches against a pattern using shell-style globbing.
range	Returns a substring specified by start and end values.
repeat	Returns a string repeated a specified number of times.
replace	Removes a specified substring or replaces a specified substring with another.
tolower	Converts a string to all lowercase characters.
toupper	Converts a string to all uppercase characters.
totitle	Converts the first character of a string to uppercase.
trim	Removes leading and trailing characters that match a specified pattern.
trimleft	Removes leading characters that match a specified pattern.
trimright	Removes trailing characters that match a specified pattern.
wordend	Returns the index of the end of the word containing a specified character.
wordstart	Returns the index of the beginning of the word containing a specified character.

Table 4.1 should give you a good sense of the breadth of Tcl's string-handling capabilities. I'll show each option's syntax diagram and describe each of the options in the following sections. To structure the discussion, I've arranged the options into three broad groups based on their function: options for comparing strings, options for getting information about strings, and options for modifying strings.

COMPARING STRINGS

Comparing one string to another is a common programming task. Typically, you want to see if one string is the same as another (or not), such as validating a user name or password. Another frequent need is testing a string to see if it contains a given character or sequence of characters. For example, you might want to make sure that user input, say, the number of players in a game, contains only numbers and no letters. The string command has three options for comparing strings: compare, equal, and match. In addition, you can use the operators eq, ne, ==, !=, <, <=, >, and >=.

Kurt's First Rule for Comparing Strings: Use compare, equal, eq, **and** ne **to compare strings.** String comparisons almost always occur in an if, while, or expr command. However, using the logical operators (==, !=, <, and >) is inefficient because of the way that Tcl parses expressions. As you learned in Chapter 3, the expr command has its own expression evaluator that performs substitutions before the main interpreter performs its substitutions. Recall also that the if command (and the while command that you'll see at the end of this chapter) use the same engine as expr. When the expression parser encounters one of the logical operators, it converts the operands to numeric values and then converts them *back* to strings when it detects that a string comparison is being performed. The compare and equal options (and the eq and ne operators) do not perform these internal conversions because they are designed for use with strings.

The following example, rule.tcl in this chapter's code directory, illustrates the point:

```
set hexVal "0xF"
set intVal "15"


# Use compare, equal, eq, and ne to compare strings
if {$hexVal == $intVal} {
    puts "$hexVal equals $intVal"
} else {
    puts "$hexVal does not equal $intVal"
}
if {$hexVal eq $intVal} {
    puts "$hexVal equals $intVal"
} else {
    puts "$hexVal does not equal $intVal"
}
```

If you execute this program, you'll see this odd result:

```
$ ./rule.tcl
0xF equals 15
0xF does not equal 15
```

Since when is "0xF" the same as "15"? The first `if` statement compares the variables `hexVal` and `intVal` using the logical operator `==`. Their values are converted to decimal (integer) numbers, 15 in both cases, and found to be equal. If you intended to compare two strings (by declaring the variables using "" around their values), you would expect this comparison to evaluate to false. The second `if` command uses `eq`, a synonym for the `equal` operator you'll see in the next section, which prevents the expression evaluator from performing the numeric conversion and, even in the absence of quotes in the `if` command, compares the two variables' values as strings.

The `compare` Option

The `compare` option tests two strings for lexicographic equality, where "equality" means the two strings are the same on a character-by-character basis. Its syntax is:

```
string compare ?-nocase? ?-length N? string1 string2
```

string1 and *string2* are the strings to compare. By default, the comparison is case-sensitive, so if you want a case-insensitive comparison, specify the `-nocase` option. To limit the comparison to the first *N* characters, where *N* is an integer, specify `length` *N*. `compare` works the same way as C's `strcmp()` and `strncmp()` functions, so it returns -1 if *string1* is lexicographically less than *string2*, 1 if *string1* is lexicographically greater than *string2*, and 0 if the two strings are equal. The following script (compare.tcl in this chapter's code directory) illustrates how `compare` works:

```
puts -nonewline "Enter player name: "
flush stdout
gets stdin playerName

# Test for strict equality (case-sensitive)
if {![string compare $playerName "Bubba"]} {
    puts "\"$playerName\" is in use."
    puts -nonewline "Please select another name: "
    flush stdout
    gets stdin playerName
}
puts "\"$playerName\" successfully registered."
```

Notice in the last line how I use "\" to cause the name entered to appear in quotes in the output. It's a little ugly to write and to look at, but that's how you have to do it. Executing the script, you might see the following results:

```
$ ./compare.tcl
Enter player name: Bubba
"Bubba" is in use.
Please select another name: Kurt
"Kurt" successfully registered.
$ ./compare.tcl
Enter player name: BUBBA
"BUBBA" successfully registered.
```

Entering the name BUBBA foils the point of the code, which is to make sure that the player name Bubba doesn't get used twice in the same game. This is when the -nocase argument comes in handy, because it disables case-sensitivity when comparing two strings (see compare_nocase.tcl in this chapter's code directory):

```
puts -nonewline "Play again (Y/N): "
flush stdout
gets stdin choice

# Case-insensitive comparison
if {![string compare -nocase $choice "y"]} {
    puts "Excellent! Starting next level."
} else {
    puts "Quitters never win. Exiting."
}
```

compare_nocase.tcl's output should resemble the following:

```
$ ./compare_nocase.tcl
Play again (Y/N): y
Excellent! Starting next level.
$ ./compare_nocase.tcl
Play again (Y/N): Y
Excellent! Starting next level.
```

This script shows how you can make a script slightly more tolerant of sloppy typing using string compare's -nocase argument. Whether the user types "y" or "Y," the game will continue (or it will insult the user if "n" or "N" is entered). Modifying comparte.tcl to ignore case is left as an exercise for the reader.

The `-length` *N* argument enables you to limit the comparison to the first *N* characters of the strings being compared. If *N* is negative, the `-length` argument will be ignored, although I have a hard time imagining a situation in which *N* would be negative, except when it is passed a variable whose range might include a negative value.

The `equal` Option

The `equal` option is almost identical to the `compare` option (the syntax is identical). The difference between the two is that `equal` compares strings for strict equality, returning 1 (true) if the strings are exactly identical or 0 (false) if the strings are not identical. `compare`, you will recall, evaluates whether two strings are lexicographically less than, equal to, or greater than one another. The following example, equal.tcl in this chapter's code directory, rewrites compare.tcl to use `equal`:

```
puts -nonewline "Enter player name: "
flush stdout
gets stdin playerName


# Test for strict equality (case-sensitive)
if {[string equal $playerName "Bubba"]} {
    puts "\"$playerName\" is in use."
    puts -nonewline "Please select another name: "
    flush stdout    gets stdin playerName
}
puts "\"$playerName\" successfully registered."
```

Like I said, `compare` and `equal` have the same syntax; the only difference is the nature of the comparison. As a result, you will most often use the `equal` option because it is rare that you need to determine if one string is less than or greater than another.

The eq operator is a synonym for `string equal` and exists to make tests for string easier to read and write and to make such statements look more like other logical operations. For example, `string equal` requires the awkward looking expressions in the previous examples, such as `string equal $playername "Bubba"`. The eq operator lets you write the more natural expression `$playername eq "Bubba"`. Thus, equal.tcl becomes eq.tcl:

```
puts -nonewline "Enter player name: "
flush stdout
gets stdin playerName
```

```
# Test for strict equality (case-sensitive)
if {$playerName eq "Bubba"} {
    puts "\"$playerName\" is in use."
    puts -nonewline "Please select another name: "
    flush stdout    gets stdin playerName
}
puts "\"$playerName\" successfully registered."
```

Using eq instead of string equal makes the if command much easier to scan and understand, in my opinion. Notice that brackets weren't necessary in this case; I wanted the variable $playerName to be substituted so the comparison would work. In fact, grouping the conditional expression in the if command would result in a syntax error because the interpreter would treat the literal string Bubba as a command.

The match **Option**

The match option compares a string to a pattern and returns 1 if the string matches the pattern and 0 otherwise. The complete syntax is:

```
string match ?-nocase? pattern string
```

Where equal tests for simple equivalence between two strings, match introduces the ability to test for equivalence between *pattern* and *string*. As usual, *string* can be either a literal string or a string variable. Likewise, *pattern* can be a literal string or a variable. The difference is that *pattern* can contain the wildcard characters * and ?. * represents a sequence of zero or more characters and ? represents any one character. The UNIX geeks among you will recognize *pattern* as a glob.

Consider the pattern alpha*, which is the literal string alpha followed by any sequence of zero or more characters. The following list shows a few matching and nonmatching strings:

- alphabet—matches
- Alphanumeric—doesn't match (uppercase A)
- alpha male—matches
- alpha—matches (* matches a sequence *zero or more* characters)
- alpaca—doesn't match
- lambda nalpha—doesn't match (* matches at the end of the string)

Similarly, given the pattern ga?e, the strings game, gate, and gale match the pattern while the strings gayle, glare, and regale do not. match.tcl demonstrates matches using * and ?.

In addition to * and ?, you can specify a pattern that consists of a set of characters using the form [*chars*], where *chars* is a list of characters. *chars* can be specified using the format x-y to indicate a range of consecutive Unicode characters. For example, to see if a one-character string variable input is an uppercase character, one (inefficient) way to write the test is:

```
if {[string match {[A-Z]} $input]} {
    # do something
} else {
    # do something else
}
```

Notice that the expression [A-Z] is enclosed in braces. If you don't use the braces, the interpreter will attempt to execute a command named A-Z and substitute the results into the string match expression. You probably don't have a command named A-Z (Tcl certainly doesn't). The braces prevent this substitution.

 Matching the match **Characters**

If you need to match one of the wildcard characters or the right or left bracket, escape it with a \ (thus, *, \?, \[, \]).

Pattern matching using string match is useful when you need to compare a string to a value that can vary in a regular or systematic way. For example, if you store player scores in files named *name*.scr, where *name* is each player's name, you could use the expression string match "*.scr" $filerName. Another way to use string match is to test whether or not a given string contains characters that might be forbidden. For example, to make sure that player names do not contain uppercase letters, you might write the following bit of code (see no_caps.tcl in this chapter's code directory):

```
if {[string match {*[A-Z]*} $playerName]} {
        puts "Your player name cannot contain uppercase letters"
}
```

The pattern *[A-Z]* matches zero or more characters followed by any single uppercase character followed by zero or more characters. This pattern will match any string that contains a capital letter, regardless of where in the string it occurs.

string's match option gives you a powerful and easy-to-use tool to identify matches that aren't exact. As you gain experience with Tcl, the situations in which pattern matching is an appropriate solution will be clear.

INSPECTING STRINGS

Although comparing strings to one another is a useful thing to be able to do, it is also one of the least interesting things to do. The string options you learn in this chapter let you find out more about a string, such as how long it is, what character is present at a particular location in the string, what is the first or last character in the string, and what kind of characters the strings contain.

The length and bytelength Options

```
string bytelength string
string length string
```

The bytelength option returns the length of *string* in bytes, whereas the length option returns the length of the string in characters. A string's bytelength might not be the same as the number of characters because, as you might remember, Tcl uses Unicode, which can take up to three bytes to represent a character. In this book and in most of your work with Tcl, you will almost always want to use string length *string*, because the situations in which you need to know a string's length in actual bytes are uncommon. For completeness' sake, however, length.tcl shows the use of both:

```
set phrase "®"
puts "Length in bytes of phrase: [string bytelength $phrase]"
puts "Length in characters of phrase: [string length $phrase]"
```

The output shows you the difference between the length and bytelength options:

```
$ ./length.tcl
Length in bytes of phrase: 2
Length in characters of phrase: 1
```

As you can see, the phrase, which translates to *fine quality*, is only 1 character long (count 'em yourself if you wish), but it requires 2 bytes to store (two bytes per character).

The index Option

If you want to find out what character is at a given position in a string, use the string index command. Its complete syntax is:

```
string index string n
```

This command returns the character located at position, or *index*, *n* of *string*. Index values are 0-based (counted from 0). For example, given the string "dice," the command string index "dice" 0 returns d and string index "dice" 3 returns e (see index.tcl):

```
set str "dice"
puts "The character at index 0 of dice is '[string index $str 0]'"
puts "The character at index 1 of dice is '[string index $str 1]'"
puts "The character at index 2 of dice is '[string index $str 2]'"
puts "The character at index 3 of dice is '[string index $str 3]'"
```

The output of this script should look just like the following:

```
$ ./index.tcl
The character at index 0 of dice is 'd'
The character at index 1 of dice is 'i'
The character at index 2 of dice is 'c'
The character at index 3 of dice is 'e'
```

You can specify the index value *n* using an integer, the word end, or the expression end-*int*, where *int* is an integer. If *n* is less than 0 or greater than the length of the string, string index returns the empty string. That's right. Unlike many programming languages, referring to an invalid string index in Tcl does *not* generate an error. The end-*int* syntax for specifying an index makes it trivial to iterate over a string in reverse (that is, to perform an operation on a string starting from its last character and ending at its first). You don't know how to loop over a string in this way (yet!—see "Iterative Loops: The for Command" later in this chapter), but trust me, it's a common operation, so you'll appreciate having a brain-dead easy syntax for doing it.

The first and last **Options**

The first and last options make it possible to find the index value of the first and last occurrences, respectively, of a substring in a string. Their complete syntax is:

```
string first substr str ?start?
string last substr str ?end?
```

string first searches for the first occurrence of the substring *substr* in the string *str* and returns the index of the first letter of *substr*. string last, similarly, returns the index of the first letter of the last occurrence of *substr* in *str*. If the specified *substr* is not found, both options return -1. By default, string first's search starts at index 0 of *str*; if you specify *start*, the search will start at that index rather than at index 0. string last's optional argument, *end*, lets you specify the ending index of the search, meaning that it will only look for *substr* between index 0 and the index specified by *last*.

substr.tcl in this chapter's code directory illustrates how to use `string first` and `string last`. The example is short because it is incomplete. I'm going to build on it in the next two sections.

```
# Original sentence
set old "He was ?verbing? his wife's hair."

set start [string first "?" $old]
set end [string last "?" $old]
puts "start = $start"
puts "end = $end"
```

This script might serve as the start of a routine for performing a search-and-replace operation. The first step is to search for some text. The assumption in this example is that the text you want to replace is surrounded by ? characters. I use `string first` and `string last` to find the index position of the ? characters and then display those indices:

```
$ ./substr.tcl
start = 7
end = 15
```

Remember that index values are zero-based, so ? appears at positions 7 and 15, not 8 and 16 as you might expect. If you were writing a search-and-replace procedure, your next step would be to replace the "found" text with something new, which is precisely what the `string replace` command does.

The `range` Option

The `range` option returns a range of characters, that is, a substring, specified by start and end index values:

```
string range str start end
```

`string range` returns the substring that begins at position *start* and ends at position *end* from the string `str`.

If you're thinking that the *start* and *end* arguments look an awful lot like the return values from `string first` and `string last`, you'd be spot on. In fact, this is a good example of how you'd use Tcl's command nesting. range.tcl builds on substr.tcl from the previous section to extract a ?-delimited substring from another string:

```
# Original sentence
set old "He was ?verbing? his wife's hair."

# Get the starting and end points
set start [string first "?" $old]
set end [string last "?" $old]

# Extract the substring
set substr [string range $old $start $end]
puts "substring is $substr"
```

The output is what you'd expect, the ?-delimited substring:

```
$ ./range.tcl
substring is ?verbing?
```

If you want to use Tcl's ability to nest commands, you could rewrite this script as shown in the following example (range_nested.tcl in this chapter's code directory):

```
# Original sentence
set old "He was ?verbing? his wife's hair."

# Extract the substring
set substr [string range $old [string first "?" $old] [string last "?" $old]];
puts "substring is $substr";
```

The output is identical to the previous example. You can decide for yourself which model you prefer, the sequential method that limits nested commands (illustrated in range.tcl) or the more, um, "Tcl-ish" method that relies upon and takes advantage of command nesting (illustrated in range_nested.tcl). Tcl beginners find code written in the iterative or sequential mode easier to read, but using nested commands results in more idiomatic Tcl. Indeed, the more experienced you become with Tcl, you might find that using nested commands becomes a more natural way to write Tcl code.

The replace Option

The string replace command completes the search-and-replace set of commands you've been exploring in the last few sections. Its complete syntax is:

```
string replace str start end ?newstr?
```

This command removes the substring between and including the indices *start* and *end* from the string specified by *str*. If you include the optional argument *newstr*, the removed text will be replaced with the string specified by *newstr*. replace.tcl in this chapter's code directory illustrates replacing text using string replace.

```tcl
# Source sentence
set old "He was ?verbing? his wife's hair with a ?noun?."
puts "Old sentence:\t$old"

# Find this
set verb "?verbing?"

# Replace with this
set newVerb "washing"

# Get the verb's starting and ending positions
set start [string first "?" $old]
set end [string first "?" $old [expr $start + 1]]

# Replace and display
puts "New sentence:\t[string replace $old $start $end $newVerb]"
```

This script replaces the string ?verbing? with the string washing. Notice in the fourth block of code that I use string first twice. Why? Because string last returns the index of the *last* occurrence of the search string. Using string first with the optional *start* argument lets me reset the starting point of the search. The expression set start [string first "?" $old] found the index of the first ?. The nested expr command, [expr $start + 1], sets the starting point of the next search to the character that *follows* the first ?. This adjustment is necessary because the optional *start* argument for string first (remember, the syntax is string first *substr str ?start?*) begins the search at *start*. If I hadn't incremented the starting index, the second string first command would have returned the position of the first ? instead of the second one.

The last command actually performs the replacement and displays the result. Here's the output of this script:

```
$ ./replace.tcl
Old sentence:  He was ?verbing? his wife's hair with a ?noun?.
New sentence:  He was washing his wife's hair with a ?noun?.
```

I'll leave replacing ?noun? with something else as an exercise for you. As a hint, you can simplify the code if you save the modified sentence produced in replace.tcl.

The is Option

The is option, that is, the string is command, enables you to test whether or not a given string belongs to a character class. A *character class* is a named group of characters that serves as a shorthand notation for the range operator, [*charlist*], introduced earlier in the chapter. For example, the character range for all lowercase characters is specified [a-z] using the range operator. The corresponding character class is lower.

In addition to serving as a shorthand notation, character classes are more general than sets specified using the range operator because character classes are defined over the Unicode character set. At this book's beginning level, the fact that character classes are Unicode-aware won't make a lot of difference. However, if you write a runaway hit game using Tcl and Tk and it gets translated to, say, Tamil, you'll be happy to know that at least the code that uses character classes rather than hand-coded character ranges will work as intended and with no modifications.

The syntax for string is is:

```
string is class ?-strict? ?-failindex varname? str
```

class can be any of the classes listed in Table 4.2 and *str* is the string to test. If *str* is a member of *class*, string is returns 1; otherwise, it returns 0. The empty string, "", is regarded as a member of all character classes unless you specify the -strict option, in which case the empty string is a member of no character class. If a string isn't a member of a given character class, you can specify -failindex *varname* to have Tcl save the index at which *str* fails the comparison to the desired character class. Before you see an example, review the list of possible character classes, shown in Table 4.2.

As you can see from this table, there's a character class for almost every need you might have. A notable exception is octal digits (that is, digits in the base-8 number system). You can see the string is command at work in the following example, which tests the Japanese character □ for membership in each of the classes listed in Table 4.2:

TABLE 4.2: TCL CHARACTER CLASSES

Class	Description
alnum	Any Unicode alphabetic character or digit.
alpha	Any Unicode alphabetic character.
ascii	Any character in the ASCII character set (7-bit characters).
boolean	Any of the forms used for Boolean values.
control	Any Unicode control character.
digit	Any Unicode digit.
double	Any of the forms used to represent double values.
false	Any of the forms used for Boolean values that evaluate to false.
graph	Any Unicode printing character, except a space.
integer	Any of the forms used to represent integer values.
lower	Any lowercase Unicode alphabetic character.
print	Any Unicode printing character, including space.
space	Any Unicode space character.
true	Any of the forms used for Boolean values that evaluate to true.
upper	Any uppercase Unicode alphabetic character.
wordchar	Any Unicode word character.
xdigit	Any hexadecimal digit character.

```
proc TestClass {str class} {
       if {[string is $class $str]} {
               set msg "$str is in class '$class'"
       } else {
               set msg "$str is not in class '$class'"
       }
       puts $msg
}


set symbol "®"


TestClass $symbol alnum
TestClass $symbol alpha
TestClass $symbol ascii
TestClass $symbol boolean
TestClass $symbol control
TestClass $symbol digit
```

```
TestClass $symbol double
TestClass $symbol false
TestClass $symbol graph
TestClass $symbol integer
TestClass $symbol lower
TestClass $symbol print
TestClass $symbol space
TestClass $symbol true
TestClass $symbol upper
TestClass $symbol wordchar
TestClass $symbol xdigit
```

In is.tcl, I use a procedure named `TestClass` to perform the actual test, passing the procedure of the string I want to test and the character class name against which I want to test. Using the `TestClass` procedure makes writing the rest of the script a lot easier, because the balance of the script is a bunch of calls to `TestClass` for each class that interests me. The output of this script should resemble the following:

```
$ ./is.tcl
® is not in class 'alnum'
® is not in class 'alpha'
® is not in class 'ascii'
® is not in class 'boolean'
® is not in class 'control'
® is not in class 'digit'
® is not in class 'double'
® is not in class 'false'
® is in class 'graph'
® is not in class 'integer'
® is not in class 'lower'
® is in class 'print'
® is not in class 'space'
® is not in class 'true'
® is not in class 'upper'
® is not in class 'wordchar'
® is not in class 'xdigit'
```

As you can see, the character ® is a member of the graph and print classes and not a member of the others.

MODIFYING STRINGS

While it's very interesting and even useful to know if a character is a member of a given character class or where in a string a substring appears, it's even more useful to know how to slice, dice, and julienne strings.

Repeating Strings

The simplest string modification is likely repeating a string. Thus, we have the aptly named `string repeat` command:

```
string repeat str count
```

`string repeat` repeats the string *str count* times. It is much easier to write, for example:

```
puts [string repeat "*" 50]
```

than it is to write:

```
puts "**************************************************"
```

Both commands print 50 asterisks, but guess which one is easier to type?

Switching Case

Another frequently used operation is modifying the case of a string. Tcl's string command supports three options for doing so: changing a string to all uppercase (using `string toupper`), changing a string to all lowercase (using `string tolower`), and changing a string to sentence case (using the inaccurately named `string totitle`). Each of the three options shares a common syntax:

```
string toupper str ?start? ?end?
string tolower str ?start? ?end?
string totitle str ?start? ?end?
```

In each case, the string specified by *str* will be returned with all characters modified appropriate to the option requested. By default, the entire string is modified; *start* and *end* (which are both integral values) specify alternative starting and stopping index values. If you specify *start*, the modification begins at that index; if you specify *end*, the modification stops at that index.

For example, given the deliberately perverse string "yOuR gUeSs MuSt Be BeTwEeN 1 aNd 20: ", case.tcl in this chapter's code directory shows how `toupper`, `tolower`, and `totitle` modify it:

```
set str "yOuR gUeSs MuSt Be BeTwEeN 1 aNd 20: "

puts "toupper: [string toupper $str]"
puts "tolower: [string tolower $str]"
puts "totitle: [string totitle $str]"
```

When you execute the script, the output darn well better look like the following:

```
$ ./case.tcl
toupper: YOUR GUESS MUST BE BETWEEN 1 AND 20:
tolower: your guess must be between 1 and 20:
totitle: Your guess must be between 1 and 20:
```

Like I wrote, the `totitle` option seems misnamed because it doesn't render what I consider "title case," capitalizing the first letter of each word. Rather, it capitalizes the first letter of the target string and lowercases the rest. However, it's named `totitle` so that's what we have to use. You're free to write your own `ToTitle` command if you want, of course.

Trimming Strings

Trimming strings refers to deleting unwanted characters from the beginning or end of strings. Tcl's string trimming commands, `string trimleft`, `string trimright`, and `string trim`, are usually used to remove unwanted white space from the beginning or end of user input (those darn users will type anything!) The syntax of these commands is:

```
string trimleft str ?chars?
string trimright str ?chars?
string trim str ?chars?
```

str is the string to trim. By default, white space (spaces, tabs, newlines, and carriage returns) will be removed. If specified, *chars* defines a set of one or more characters that should be removed from *str*. As their names suggest, `trimleft` returns *str* with characters removed from the left end; `trimright` returns *str* with characters removed from the right end; and `trim` returns *str* with characters removed from the left and right ends. If *str* doesn't contain any of the characters listed in *chars*, *str* will be returned unmolested.

TIP

String Operations are Nondestructive

String operations are nondestructive in that they do not modify their string arguments. All of the string operations discussed in this chapter return a *new* string that reflects the changes performed; the original or source string is left alone. This feature is a direct result of Tcl's programming model (grouping and command substitution) and enables you to use the results of string operations without worrying about your source data being modified in some inscrutable fashion. It also means that you must explicitly use the `set` command to assign the results of string operations to variables if you want to keep those results for later use.

Trimming strings is uncomplicated, so I won't discuss it further here. Nevertheless, the script trim.tcl in this chapter's code directory demonstrates the usage of all three string-trimming options.

Appending Strings

Up to now, if you wanted to add text to a string variable, you would use the `set` command:

```
set label "Player Name: "
set label "$label Kurt Wall"
puts $label
```

This approach is functional, but is not the most efficient way to build up a long variable. The easy, efficient way is to use the `append` command. For example, the previous two `set` commands are equivalent to the following command:

```
append label "Player Name: " "Kurt Wall"
```

`append`'s syntax is:

```
append var value ?...?
```

`append` tacks each *value* on to the end of the variable specified by *var*. If *var* doesn't exist, its value will be the concatenation of each *value* specified. Unlike the various `string` commands discussed in this chapter, `append` modifies the value of *var*. It also returns the modified string. The reason that `append` is more efficient than multiple `set` commands is that `append` uses Tcl's internal memory manager to extend the variable being assigned, whereas `set` takes a more roundabout approach. I'll prove this to you in the next section when you learn how to use the `for` command to write an iterative loop.

LOOPING COMMANDS

In the previous chapter, I introduced the notion of control structures, which allow you to write scripts that do more than execute sequentially from the first to the last line of the script. In particular, I showed you how to use the conditional execution command, `if`. In addition to conditional execution, Tcl also supports a number of commands for looping, or executing the same command or set of commands multiple times. I'll cover two of them in this chapter, `while` and `for`. The `while` command creates a loop that executes as long as, or while, a Boolean test expression evaluates to true. When the test expression evaluates to false, control exits the loop and continues with the command immediately following the `while` command. The `for` command creates an iterative loop, that is, a loop that executes a fixed number of times and then terminates (again, with control passing to the command immediately following the `for` command).

Looping with the `while` Command

Loops that use `while` are sometimes referred to as *indeterminate loops* because you don't know how many times they will execute, only that they will (hopefully) eventually terminate when their test condition evaluates to false. The syntax of the `while` command is:

```
while {test} {body}
```

test is a Boolean expression (an expression that has a Boolean result). When the loop starts, *test* is evaluated; if it is true, the command or commands in *body* execute. Otherwise, *body* is skipped and execution resumes with the command immediately following the `while` command. After each pass through *body*, *test* is re-evaluated. If *test* is still true, *body* will execute; otherwise, the loop terminates and execution resumes with the command immediately following the `while` command.

Strictly speaking, the braces I used in the syntax diagram aren't required. However, *test* will almost always need to be enclosed in braces because you need to protect its condition from premature substitution. If you don't use braces, the likely result is either an *infinite loop* (a loop that never terminates) or a loop that never executes at all. The braces are usually necessary because, without them, Tcl interpreter will substitute the value in the *test* condition before the while command evaluates it. Using braces around the *test* condition prevents premature substitution. I suggest enclosing the body of the `while` loop in braces as well. Until you are much more confident of your ability to predict how substitution and grouping will behave, enclosing the body command(s) in braces will result in fewer surprises and unpleasant side effects.

The following script, while.tcl in this chapter's code directory, offers a useful illustration of how `while` loops work:

```
set lineCnt 0
set charCnt 0

while {[gets stdin line] >= 0} {
        incr lineCnt
        incr charCnt [string length $line]
```

```
}
puts "Read $lineCnt lines"
puts "Read $charCnt characters"
```

This simple script reads input typed at the keyboard (or redirected from another file). Each time it encounters a newline, it increments the variable `lineCnt` by 1 and the variable `charCnt` by the number of characters in the line. When it encounters EOF (end-of-file), it drops out of the loop and displays the number of lines and number of characters read.

```
$ ./while.tcl < while.tcl
Read 13 lines
Read 229 characters
```

Recall that `gets` returns -1 when it reads EOF—that means that the test condition `[gets std line] >= 0` will return evaluate to true as long as `gets` receives valid input. When `gets` sees EOF in the input stream, the test condition evaluates to false and the loop terminates.

 Newlines Don't Count

The Linux- or UNIX-using reader (and the obsessive-compulsive reader who counts everything) will notice that while.tcl actually has 242 characters:

```
$ wc -c while.tcl
242 while.tcl
```

So, why does while.tcl say that it only has 229? Because `gets` discards the newline. Accordingly, if you think that newlines should also be counted, change the last line of while.tcl to the following:

```
puts "Read [expr $charCnt + $lineCnt] characters"
```

I cheated by introducing a command you haven't seen yet, `incr`. Briefly, `incr` increments (hence the name) the value of a variable. `incr`'s virtue is that it is easier to write than `set someVar [expr someVar + someValue]`. `incr`'s syntax is simple:

`incr var ?unit?`

By default, `incr` increments *var*, which must be an integer variable, by 1. If you specify *unit*, which must also be an integer value (or an expression that evaluates to an integer value, as in while.tcl), *unit* will be added to *var*. Yes, *unit* can be a negative integer, which would have the effect of decrementing *var*. No, there isn't a separate command `decr` used to decrement a variable, although you could certainly write one if you have a rage for order and symmetry.

Iterative Loops: The for Command

The for command enables you to execute one or more commands a fixed number of times, or *iterations*. Hence, for loops are often referred to as *iterative loops*. Its syntax is:

```
for {start} {test} {next} {body}
```

Again, the braces shown in the syntax diagram aren't required, but I recommend using them to preserve your sanity. *start* is an expression that initializes a *loop counter*, the variable that controls how many times the loop executes. *test* is a Boolean expression that controls whether or not the command(s) in *body* will be executed by testing the loop counter against the *terminating condition*, the value at which the loop exits. *next* is an expression that increments the loop counter.

When a for loop starts, the expression in *start* is executed, which sets the initial value of the loop counter. Then the expression in *test* is evaluated. *test* usually includes the loop counter, but it doesn't have to. If *test* evaluates to false, the for loop will be skipped, and execution resumes with the command immediately following the for command. Otherwise, the command(s) in *body* will be executed. The *next* expression is evaluated after the last command in *body*. *next* increments or decrements or otherwise modifies the loop counter so that the for loop eventually terminates. After the *next* expression is executed, the *test* condition is evaluated. If *test* evaluates to false, the loop terminates and control passes to the command immediately following the for command. If *test* evaluates to true, *body* will be executed, followed by the *next* expression. Wash. Rinse. Repeat.

Confused? The following script (for.tcl in this chapter's code directory) should help:

```
for {set i 1} {$i <= 10} {incr i} {
    puts "Loop counter: $i"
}
```

This script increments the value of a loop counter variable, i, and displays that value. In terms of the syntax diagram I showed at the beginning of this section:

- The *start* condition is set i 1.
- The *test* condition is $i <= 10.
- The *next* expression is incr i, which increments the value of i by 1 on each pass through the loop.
- The *body* command is puts "Loop counter: $i".

The body of the loop executes for each value of i that is less than or equal to 10. The runtime behavior should be unsurprising:

```
$ ./for.tcl
Loop counter: 1
Loop counter: 2
Loop counter: 3
Loop counter: 4
Loop counter: 5
Loop counter: 6
Loop counter: 7
Loop counter: 8
Loop counter: 9
Loop counter: 10
```

You'll use for loops quite a bit in your scripts because for is an easy, natural way to create loops that need to execute a fixed number of times. You'll learn yet another looping construct, foreach, in the next chapter.

COMPARING set AND append

The following script (test_append.tcl in this chapter's code directory) compares the relative performance of the set and append commands (and gives you another example of using the for command to create an iterative loop). The testing methodology is primitive but illustrative:

1. Save a timestamp in millisecond (1000th of a second) units.
2. Execute thousands of set or append commands in a for loop.
3. Save a second timestamp.
4. The difference between the two timestamps represents the time spent executing all of the set or append commands.

```
# Counter
set cnt 100000

# Doing it the hard, ineffecient way
set var1 0
set start [clock clicks -milliseconds]
for {set i 1} {$i <= $cnt} {incr i} {
set var1 "$var1,$i"

}
```

```
set stop [clock clicks -milliseconds]
puts "Elapsed time using set: [expr ($stop - $start) / 1000.0] secs"

# Doing it the easy, efficient way
set var2 0
set start [clock clicks -milliseconds]
for {set i 1} {$i <= $cnt} {incr i} {
        append var2 "," $i
}
set stop [clock clicks -milliseconds]
puts "Elapsed time using append: [expr ($stop - $start) / 1000.0] secs"
```

As you can see in the following table, the runtime performance of set **and** append **differs dramatically:**

Iterations	set **Runtime**	append **Runtime**
100,000	47.884 sec	0.354 sec
200,000	217.359 sec	20.672 sec
500,000	1508.435 sec	1.665 sec
1,000,000	6531.524 sec	3.292 sec

Naturally, the timing results will vary from system to system and my simple test might not reflect real-world usage. Indeed, "real-world" code will probably be more involved than my simple loop bodies. The primary point is the difference in performance, and I think the results speak for themselves. The moral of this story? Don't use set **if you will be doing heavy-duty variable building.** append **is** *far* **more efficient.**

ANALYZING MAD LIBS

As you'll see in the "Looking at the Code" section, mad_lib.tcl doesn't use all of the commands you learned in this chapter. It does illustrate key commands and gives you a fertile base for further experimentation.

Looking at the Code

```
#!/usr/bin/tclsh
# mad_lib.tcl
# Demonstrate string manipulation

# Block 1
```

```
# The source sentence
set line "One day while I was ?verb ending in -ing? in my living room, "
append line "a ?adjective? ?mythical creature? fell through the roof. "
append line "It jumped on the ?piece of furniture? and knocked over the "
append line "?noun?. Then it ran into the dining room and ?past tense verb? "
append line "a ?noun?. After ?number? minutes of chasing it through the "
append line "house I finally caught it and put it outside. It quickly "
append line "flew away."

# Block 2
while {[string first "?" $line] != -1} {
    # Block 2a
    # Find the next ??-enclosed word or phrase
    set start [string first "?" $line]    set end [string first "?" $line [expr
$start + 1]]

    # Block 2b
    # Extract the text between the ??
    set prompt [string range $line [expr $start + 1] [expr $end - 1]]

    # Block 2c
    # Display the prompt and get the user's input
    puts -nonewline "Enter a $prompt: "    flush stdout    gets stdin input

    # Block 2d
    # Update the sentence
    set line [string replace $line $start $end $input]
}

# Block 3
# Print the completed mad lib
puts $line
```

Understanding the Code

The code in Block 1 just sets up the sentence that the rest of the script will be modifying. What
I've done is delimit text I want to replace with ? characters. This makes it easy to find the text
and replace it with the input provided by the user. The other salient point in this block of

code is that I'm following my own advice and using `append` rather than `set` to build up the string. Block 3 is nothing new; it just displays the completed mad lib.

Block 2, which I've subdivided into Blocks 2a through 2d, is where the real work gets done. The test in the `while` loop provides the terminating condition. Recall that `string first` returns -1 if it doesn't find a specified substring. In this case, once I've replaced all the ?-delimited text, there will be no more ? characters for `string first "?" $line` to find, so the command will return -1, the test condition will evaluate to false, and control will drop out of the loop and display the completed silly sentences.

The first step is to find text enclosed in the delimiters, which is handled by Block 2a. I use the same `string first` technique that I described in replace.tcl earlier in the chapter. Once I've found the starting and ending points, which needs to include the delimiters, I save them in the aptly named `start` and `end` variables because I'm going to need these values several times.

Block 2b extracts the text, *without* the ? delimiters, which gives me a ready-made prompt to display to the user. To drop the leading ?, I increment one character into the substring. Similarly, to get rid of the trailing ?, I decrement the ending index value by one character. As I've suggested before, Tcl's ability, even affinity for, nested commands makes this kind of operation easy to express in code, albeit potentially hard to read for Tcl neophytes. However, once you've become familiar with this particular idiom, it will become a natural way to write code.

Block 2c uses the prompt extracted in Block 2b to ask the user to enter a particular word or phrase. The technique for reading user input is the same one I introduced in the previous chapter, so it should look familiar. Whatever the user types gets stored in the variable named `input`.

In Block 2d, finally, I use the `string replace` command to replace the ?-delimited text with the word the user typed. At this point, control returns to the top of the `while` loop, the test condition is evaluated again, and, if it's true, control reenters the loop body. If the test condition is false, control passes to Block 3, and I reveal the completed silly story.

Modifying the Code

Here are some exercises you can try to practice what you learned in this chapter.

4.1 Modify mad_lib.tcl to use a different delimiter in the source string so that the source string can include ? characters.

4.2 Modify Block 2b of mad_lib.tcl to use another method to extract the prompt. Hint: All you're really doing is stripping off leading and trailing characters.

4.3 Modify Block 3 of mad_lib.tcl to format the output such that words don't break across lines. That is, make the printed mad lib fit into lines of approximately 75 characters.

Working with strings is an essential component of most Tcl programs, and Tcl is well-equipped for dealing with strings. In fact, Tcl has such a rich set of commands for dealing with strings that you might not be sure which one to use in a given situation. You can compare strings for equality and for membership in a certain character class. You can also find out how long strings are. Tcl also allows you to find where in a string a certain character or substring of characters is located and, if you need to do so, Tcl even has a command for replacing one substring with another. Miscellaneous functions, such as removing unwanted characters from the ends of a string and changing a string's case, round out the basic string functionality. I'll introduce additional string-handling capabilities in later chapters, but first, you're going to learn about another Tcl strong point, lists.

CHAPTER 5

WORKING WITH LISTS

Lists are one of Tcl's two native or built-in data structures (the second is associative arrays, treated in Chapter 6, "Creating and Using Arrays"). Tcl has a broad set of commands for dealing with lists, and this chapter will get you up to speed with them. I'll finish up the discussion of control structures by introducing the switch command, another command used for conditional execution, and the foreach command, a looping control structure that specializes in iterating over list items. The chapter ends with the two commands you can use to interrupt loop execution, break and continue.

PLAYING BLACKJACK

This chapter's game is a Spartan Blackjack implementation. To play it, execute the script blackjack.tcl in this chapter's code directory.

```
$ ./blackjack.tcl
Queen of Clubs
Ace of Hearts
Deal another card [yn]? n
21: Perfect!
$ ./blackjack.tcl
6 of Spades
8 of Spades
```

```
Deal another card [yn]? n
14: Better luck next time!
$ ./blackjack.tcl
9 of Hearts
4 of Spades
Deal another card [yn]? y
9 of Hearts
4 of Spades
4 of Clubs
Deal another card [yn]? n
17: Tough hand to beat!
```

WHAT IS A TCL LIST?

A Tcl list is nothing more than an ordered sequence of (potentially heterogeneous) values, separated by a space character. I'll use the word *element* to refer to the individual list items. Elements that contain embedded white space need to be grouped (yep, more grouping—I told you that grouping is a pervasive element of Tcl) using braces or quotes. Like strings, lists are accessed by their indices, which are 0-based.

The most cogent example of Tcl lists is a Tcl command. In fact, Tcl lists have the same syntax as Tcl commands. A command is a list, the first element of which is the command itself, and the remaining elements of which are the arguments to that command. Not surprisingly, then, the same rules and considerations that apply to creating Tcl commands (think grouping and substitution here) also apply to creating Tcl lists.

Let me explain my definition of a Tcl list as an ordered sequence of heterogeneous values. *Ordered* in this context doesn't necessarily mean that lists are *sorted*. Rather, lists are ordered because list elements are accessed by their indices, that is, by their position in the list and because list access is idempotent. Each time you access list index N, which must be an integer, you get the same element. For example, given the list of fruits {orange apple pineapple}, element 0 is always orange, element 1 is always apple, and element 2 is always pineapple (provided, of course, you don't change the order).

Tcl lists also consist of potentially heterogeneous elements, which is just a fancy way to say that lists can have elements of mixed data types. Unlike arrays in traditional programming languages (like C), which consist of homogeneous elements such as integers or strings, Tcl lists can contain integers, strings, characters, and even other lists. For example, {a b 893 "Some random string" {Z Y X W}} is a perfectly valid list consisting of five elements: the character a, the character b, the number 893, the string "Some random string", and the embedded list {Z Y X W}.

All Arrays Are Not Created Equal

In older programming languages, arrays do, in fact, consist of elements that all have the same data type. However, many of the newer programming and scripting languages, including Tcl, use associative arrays, in which the array members have both a name and a value and are accessed by their name rather than their index position. You'll learn to use arrays in Chapter 6.

CREATING LISTS

How do you create a list in Tcl? The easiest and by far the most efficient way is to use the list command:

```
list item1 [item2] …
```

The list command creates and returns a list which consists of the arguments *item1*, *item2*, and so forth. Each argument to list must be separated by whitespace. An interesting and useful side effect of this syntax is that when you use list to create a list, the whitespace delimiters between elements make it trivial to resolve quoting and grouping issues—each white-space-delimited argument becomes a single element of the list. The following example shows how to create lists. I used tclsh in this example to show how the list command automatically handles quoting (see list.tcl in this chapter's code directory):

```
$ tclsh
% set faceCards [list Ace King Queen Jack]
Ace King Queen Jack
% set acesBySuit [list {Ace of Hearts} {Ace of Diamonds} {Ace of Spades} {Ace of
Clubs}]
{Ace of Hearts} {Ace of Diamonds} {Ace of Spades} {Ace of Clubs}
% set winningHands [list "Royal Flush" "Flush" {Straight Flush} {Full House} "Three
of a Kind" {Two of a Kind} "Two Pair"]
{Royal Flush} Flush {Straight Flush} {Full House} {Three of a Kind} {Two of a Kind}
{Two Pair}
% set junk [list $faceCards $acesBySuit $winningHands]
{Ace King Queen Jack} {{Ace of Hearts} {Ace of Diamonds} {Ace of Spades} {Ace of Clubs}}
{{Royal Flush} Flush {Straight Flush} {Full House} {Three of a Kind} {Two of a Kind}
{Two Pair}}
```

In the first example, I assign faceCards a list consisting of four elements: Ace, King, Queen, and Jack. In the second example, I create another four-element list, acesBySuit. This time, though, because the elements contain spaces, I use braces to group the items that make up each element. The third list, winningHands, uses both single- and multi- word elements and the multi-word elements are grouped with both braces and double quotes. The feature to notice with winningHands is that list handles the quoting automatically—items that were grouped with double quotes are displayed with brace grouping.

The fourth list, junk, is a list of lists. It consists of three elements, {Ace King Queen Jack}, {{Ace of Hearts} {Ace of Diamonds} {Ace of Spades} {Ace of Clubs}}, and {{Royal Flush} Flush {Straight Flush} {Full House} {Three of a Kind} {Two of a Kind} {Two Pair}}. Of course, each element is a list of its own.

Appending Lists

If you need to add items to the end of an existing list, use the lappend command. Unlike the list command (and most of Tcl's list-related commands), lappend operates on an existing list instead of returning a new list. Its syntax is:

```
lappend listVar item1 …
```

The first argument to lappend is the name of a list variable (listVar in the syntax diagram). The second and subsequent arguments are the items to append to the list.

TIP

lappend **Also Creates a List**

If the variable name passed to lappend doesn't exist, lappend creates it with the value specified. If no values are specified, lappend creates the variable with a null list. Because you can use lappend to create a new list, as well as modify an existing one, I've covered it in this section rather than in the section "Modifying Lists" later in the chapter.

The next section includes an example of using lappend.

Merging Lists

One drawback to lappend is that it maintains the list structure, if any, of appended elements that happen to be lists. In many cases, this is the behavior you want, but not always. The concat command works much like lappend, except that it does not maintain the list structure of appended elements. In addition, concat strips leading and trailing spaces from each of its arguments before concatenating them together. Before I explain, here is concat's syntax:

```
concat ?item1 ...?
```

concat's return value is the concatenated list with one level of list structure removed. To see the difference between lappend and concat, consider the following code, concat.tcl, in this chapter's code directory:

```
set faceCards [list Ace King Queen Jack]
set numberedCards [list 10 9 8 7 6 5 4 3 2]

# lappend creates a list of two lists
lappend suit $faceCards $numberedCards
puts "$suit (length: [llength $suit])"

# concat creates a singe list
set suit [concat $faceCards $numberedCards]
puts "$suit (length: [llength $suit])"
```

You can see the difference in the resulting output:

```
$ ./concat.tcl
{Ace King Queen Jack} {10 9 8 7 6 5 4 3 2} (length: 2)
Ace King Queen Jack 10 9 8 7 6 5 4 3 2 (length: 13)
```

I discuss the llength command in the next section, but I bet you can guess what it does. The lappend command creates a list that consists of two elements: the list of face cards and the list of numbered cards; the list structure of the parent lists has been preserved. The concat command returns a list that consists of 13 elements, having created a single list by splicing together the two constituent lists and removing a single (and, in this case, the only) level of list structure from the parent lists. Neither result is correct or incorrect on its face, as it were. Rather, the correctness depends on the goal you are trying to achieve. If you need a simple list that contains all the elements of the parents, use concat. If you need to maintain list structure, use lappend.

ACCESSING LIST ELEMENTS

So, you've created a wonderful list. What can you do with it? It would probably be nice to know how many elements it contains or what element or elements are present at a given index or indices. llength tells you how many elements are in a list, as you saw in the example in the previous section; lindex returns the element at a given index in the list; and lrange returns the elements between and including a starting and ending index value. Their syntax is:

```
llength listVar
lindex listVar ?index ...?
lrange listVar start end
```

In each case, *listVar* is the list in which you are interested.

Accessing Specific List Elements

You can use lindex and lrange to retrieve one or more elements from a list. If you use lindex, the typical behavior is to specify an index value to retrieve. However, as you can see from its syntax diagram, the *index* value to fetch is optional. If you omit *index*, lindex returns the value of the list. Otherwise, lindex returns the element that corresponds to the specified index. For example, consider the following script:

```
set faceCards [list Ace King Queen Jack]
puts [lindex $faceCards 1]
puts [lindex $faceCards]
```

Executed (see lindex.tcl in this chapter's code directory), the output of this script should be:

```
$ ./lindex.tcl
King
Ace King Queen Jack
```

So, lindex makes it possible to retrieve either a single list element or the entire list. If you request an index greater than the number of elements in the list or less than zero, lindex returns an empty string.

If you specify multiple indices, each index except for the last one returns a sublist of *listVar*. The last index value is the one that returns an actual list element. Before I explain what that means in more detail, let me show you an example (cards.tcl in this chapter's code directory):

```
# Return a random integer between 0 and the number of elements in
# the list specified by cardList
proc Random {list} {
    set index [expr {int(1 + rand() * ([llength $list]) - 1)}]    return $index
}

set values [list Ace King Queen Jack 10 9 8 7 6 5 4 3 2]
set suits [list Clubs Diamonds Hearts Spades]
lappend cards $values $suits

# "Deal" a draw poker hand
for {set i 1} {$i <= 5} {incr i} {
    puts "Card $i: [lindex $cards 0 [Random $values]] of\
        [lindex $cards 1 [Random $suits]]"
}
```

When you execute this script, the output will be a (reasonably) random hand of draw poker:

```
$ ./cards.tcl
Card 1: Queen of Diamonds
Card 2: 3 of Diamonds
Card 3: 9 of Spades
Card 4: 10 of Hearts
Card 5: 5 of Diamonds
```

Yes, this poker hand is a loser. To understand how multi-valued index arguments work, consider the first lindex command in the example, [lindex $cards 0 [Random $values]]. Next, break it down into its components. $cards is the list variable from which I want to extract a value. $cards is a two-element list; the first element is the sublist $values ({Ace King Queen Jack 10 9 8 7 6 5 4 3 2}), and the second element is the sublist, $suits ({Clubs Diamonds Hearts Spades}).

The index values are 0 and the return value of the procedure, [Random $values]. As you can see from the comment above its definition, my Random procedure returns a random integer between 0 and the number of elements in the list passed to it. I only specified two indices, which means that the first index, 0, selects the sublist from which the second index, the return value of [Random $values], selects the desired element.

Given that the sublist of $cards at index 0 is {Ace King Queen Jack 10 9 8 7 6 5 4 3 2}, if [Random $values] returns 2, then the entire expression evaluates to King. To express it another way, the command, [lindex $cards 0 [Random $values]] is equivalent to and a more concise way of writing the following commands:

```
set sublist [lindex $cards 0]
set index [Random $values]
set suit [lindex $sublist $index]
```

I readily concede that specifying multi-valued indices to lindex is confusing. Using multi-valued indices is most appropriate when you are working with nested lists, that is, lists containing elements that are themselves lists. If you are more comfortable using multiple commands to achieve the same result, do so. As you grow more comfortable with Tcl, it will become more natural to use multi-valued indices. More importantly, you might encounter such expressions in *other* people's Tcl code, so you'll need to be able to parse and understand such code, even if you don't like it or use it yourself.

Happily, the command to return multiple consecutive elements from a list, lrange, is much less subtle than lindex. By way of reminder, lrange's syntax is:

```
lrange listVar start end
```

start and *end* indicate the first and last indices, respectively, of the values which lrange should return. lrange returns a new list that consists of the elements between *start* and *end*, inclusive. Consider the following short script (lrange.tcl in this chapter's code directory):

```
set values [list Ace King Queen Jack 10 9 8 7 6 5 4 3 2]
set suits [list Clubs Diamonds Hearts Spades]

puts [lrange $values 5 8]
puts [lrange [list $values $suits] 1 2]
```

The output should resemble the following:

```
$ ./lrange.tcl
9 8 7 6
{Clubs Diamonds Hearts Spades}
```

The first lrange command returns the elements between indices 5 and 8 (remember, list indices are zero-based). The second lrange returns the elements between indices 1 and 2 of the two-element list created by the embedded list command. However, because there is no index 2 (that is, no third element), lrange treats that value as if it were end, which refers to the last element in the list. Similarly, if the starting index is less than zero, lrange will treat it as if it were 0 and return the first element in the list.

Modifying Lists

Your options for modifying lists include lappend, which you've already seen, linsert, lset, and lreplace. linsert inserts one or more new elements into a list, lset sets (changes) the value of one or more specific list elements, and lreplace replaces list elements with new elements.

Inserting New Elements

To insert one or more elements into a list at a specific location, use the linsert command. Its syntax is:

```
linsert listVar index item ?item ...?
```

This command inserts each new element (denoted by *item*) into the list specified by *listVar* immediately before the index specified by *index*. *listVar* itself is not modified. Rather, linsert returns a new list with the inserted values. If *index* is less than zero, the new elements will be inserted at the beginning of the list (at index 0); if greater than the number of elements in the list, the new elements will be appended to the end of the list. You can specify the end of the list using the special index value end.

The following example demonstrates linsert usage (see linsert.tcl in this chapter's code directory):

```
set oldList [list 1 2 3 4 5]
set newList [linsert $oldList 0 0]
set newerList [linsert $newList 2 2.5]
set newestList [linsert $newerList [expr [llength $newerList] + 1] 6]


puts "oldList    : $oldList"
puts "newList    : $newList"
puts "newerList : $newerList"
puts "newestList: $newestList"
```

The second linsert command inserts the element 0 at the front of the list. The third linsert command inserts the element 2.5 in the middle of the list (before index 2). The final linsert command adds the element 6 to the end of the list. In this command, I deliberately set the insertion index to a value greater than the length of the list ([expr [llength $newerList] + 5] evaluates to 10) to show how linsert treats an index value greater than the length of the list.

If you execute this script, the output should match the following:

```
$ ./linsert.tcl
oldList    : 1 2 3 4 5
newList    : 0 1 2 3 4 5
newerList : 0 1 2.5 2 3 4 5
newestList: 0 1 2.5 2 3 4 5 6
```

Notice that the source lists, the lists passed to linsert as arguments, are not modified.

Replacing Elements

To replace one or more list elements with new ones, use the lreplace command. Its syntax is:

```
lreplace listVar start end ?item ...?
```

lreplace returns a new list created by replacing the element or elements between index values start and end in listVar with the elements specified by item. Omitting item has the effect of deleting the corresponding element from the list. If you specify fewer items than there are indices between start and end, the excess elements in listVar will be deleted from the returned list. Similarly, specifying more *items* than there are indices results in inserting the extra elements following the last replaced item, effectively expanding the list at that point. As with other list commands, if *start* is less than zero, it will be treated like zero. If *end* is less than *start*, all of the specified elements will be inserted at the beginning of the list without replacing existing list elements. Finally, if the list specified by *listVar* is empty, all of the specified *items* will be appended to the list. Despite all of the niggling evaluation rules, lreplace behaves the way you would expect it to. The following trivial example illustrates simple lreplace usage (see lreplace.tcl in this chapter's code directory).

```
set oldList [list 1 2 3 4 5]

set newList [lreplace $oldList 0 end one two three four five six]

puts "Original list: $oldList (length: [llength $oldList])"
puts "Replaced list: $newList (length: [llength $newList]);"
```

SEARCHING AND SORTING LISTS

Once you've created, appended, inserted, retrieved, or replaced list elements, chances are pretty darn good that you'll want to be able to search and sort list elements. The commands for doing so are, not surprisingly, lsearch and lsort. I'll discuss lsearch first and then proceed to lsort.

Searching 101

lsearch's general syntax is:

```
lsearch ?option ...? listVar pattern
```

lsearch searches each element of *listVar* for a match with the specified *pattern*. It returns the index of the *first* matching element by default or -1 if there are no matches. The *option* arguments control how the match is performed and the nature of lsearch's return value. The only default option is -glob, which forces a glob-style match using the same rules as the string match command (described in Chapter 4). Table 5.1 lists the permissible *options*.

Don't let the number of options intimidate you. Most of them have to be used in combination with -sorted to even apply. You can perform three types of searches:

- String-style glob searches (-glob, the default)
- Regular expression searches (-regexp)
- Exact match searches (-exact)

TABLE 5.1:   lsearch OPTIONS

Option	Description
-all	Returns all matching indices; cumulative with -inline.
-ascii	Used with -exact or -sorted, compares list elements as Unicode strings.
-decreasing	Used with -sorted, indicates that the search list is sorted in decreasing order.
-dictionary	Used with -exact or -sorted, compares list elements using dictionary-style matches.
-exact	Forces the match to contain exactly the same string as *pattern*.
-glob	Forces a glob-style match following the same rules as string match.
-increasing	Used with -sorted, indicates that the search list is sorted in increasing order.
-inline	Returns all matching values; cumulative with -all.
-integer	Used with -exact or -sorted, compares list elements as integers.
-not	Negates the match, returning the index of the first *non*-matching element.
-real	Used with -exact or -sorted, compares list elements as real numbers (that is, as floating point values).
-regexp.	Treats *pattern* as a Tcl regular expression when evaluating matches.
-sorted	Indicates that the search list is sorted; cannot be used with -glob or -regexp.
-start *index*	Starts the search at the list index specified by *index*.

By default, lsearch returns the index of the first match. If you want the index values of all matches, specify all and lsearch will return a list of matches. If you want the elements themselves rather than their indices, specify -inline. Again, unless you also specify -all, -inline will return only the first match. Finally, to start the search at a specific index, rather than at the beginning of the list, specify -start *index*, where *index* is the index value at which to commence the search.

The balance of the options assume sorted search input, specified with -sort. Why does this matter? As an optimization, if lsearch knows the input is sorted, it can use a search algorithm best suited to the input rather than a general purpose, one-size-fits-all search algorithm. The most interesting option is -not, which inverts the sense of the search and returns the first *non*-matching index or value (or all of them if you also specify -all).

Sort Before Searching

If you need to search a long list, make sure it is sorted first. lsearch does not sort unsorted lists, so you can improve search speed by sorting the list (using lsort) before passing it to lsearch.

I could spend an entire chapter on lsearch alone and not even talk about the -regexp search option. I encourage you to experiment with lsearch and its options to get a better sense of what it can do. To help you out in that respect, programs you encounter later in this book will use a number of lsearch's options, so you will definitely get plenty of lsearch goodness. In the meantime, the following script illustrates basic lsearch usage:

```
# Create a list of cards
set cards [list "Queen of Hearts" "3 of Clubs" "9 of Spades" \
    "Ace of Hearts" "5 of Diamonds"]

# Ask user for what to search
puts -nonewline "Card for which to search (such as King, Spade, or 9): "
flush stdout
gets stdin card

# Loop until user inputs a matching card
while {[set index [lsearch $cards *[string totitle $card]*]] < 0} {
    puts "No such card. Please try again."
    puts -nonewline "Card for which to search (such as King, Spade, or 9): "
    flush stdout    gets stdin card
}

# Show the match
puts "Matched the [lindex $cards $index]"
```

This script creates a list of five cards, asks the user to enter some text that describes a card for which to search, and then searches the list for that card. The prompt-search routine repeats until lsearch finds a match. Upon finding a match, the while loop terminates and the script displays the matching card. Here's how the output might look (see lsearch.tcl in this chapter's code directory):

```
$ ./lsearch.tcl
Card for which to search (such as King, Spade, or 9): 4
No such card. Please try again.
Card for which to search (such as King, Spade, or 9): King
No such card. Please try again.
Card for which to search (such as King, Spade, or 9): queen
Matched the Queen of Hearts
```

I used the string totitle command to uppercase the first letter of the user's input. The search pattern, rather, the search *glob*, is stored in the $card variable. To allow matches to occur in the middle of an element, I added * to the beginning and end of the search pattern so the glob would match the pattern, regardless of where in the element the pattern appears. Finally, notice the loop termination condition. lsearch returns -1 if it doesn't find a match, so the test condition simply checks for a return value that is less than zero. Obviously, you could check for -1, too.

On Naming Variables

In lsearch.tcl, I used the plural noun $cards to refer to the list of cards as a whole and the singular noun $card to denote a specific card. This is a convention, or *idiom*, I use frequently. Most, if not all of my variable names are nouns because, based on my own experience, the "things" that variables represent are usually nouns. When I need to refer to collections (you know, collections like lists) of related values or items, I use the plural form of the noun, such as cards, books, dice, games, and so on. When I need to refer to a particular member or instance of that collection, I use the singular form of the noun (card, book, die, game). The reason I do this is that I can determine at a glance what a variable is and how I'm using it.

Sorting

You probably noticed that a number of lsearch's options involved searching a sorted list. Searching for something, in code and in real life, is much more efficient if the material you're searching is already sorted. To accomplish this in Tcl, use the lsort command. Its general syntax is:

```
lsort ?options? listVar
```

lsort sorts *listVar* and returns a new sorted list. *options* control how the sort is performed. Not surprisingly, lsort and lsearch share a number of options. Table 5.2 lists lsort's options, with bold items representing the defaults when no *options* are specified.

A dictionary sort is handy when the list elements contain mixed alphanumeric values, such as a10 and a2. In the standard (-ascii) sort, a10 would sort before a2 because the first two characters of a10, a1, are "less than" a2. With a -dictionary sort, the numbers are treated as integers, so a2 would sort before a10 because 2 is less than 10.

TABLE 5.2:	lsort OPTIONS
Option	**Description**
-ascii	Performs the sort using Unicode strings.
-dictionary	Performs the sort using dictionary-style sorting.
-integer	Performs the sort by comparing the elements as integers.
-real	Performs the sort by comparing the elements as floating-point numbers.
-command *command*	Performs the sort using *command* (a Tcl command) to compare elements.
-increasing	Sorts the elements in increasing or ascending order.
-decreasing	Sorts the elements in decreasing or descending order.
-index *index*	Sorts sublists on the specified index rather than sorting the entire list.
-unique	Eliminates all but the last set of duplicate elements in the source list.

The -index option needs elaboration. It exists to handle properly sorting lists that consist of sublists. When specified, -index *index* performs the sort by sorting the list as a whole on the *index*th element of each sublist. For example, given the following list of cards, the default sort is by the card value, that is, by index 0:

```
% lsort {{King of Diamonds} {Ace of Hearts} {10 of Clubs}}
{10 of Clubs} {Ace of Hearts} {King of Diamonds}
```

If you want to sort by suit, use the option -index 2 to sort by the third element of each sublist:

```
% lsort -index 2 {{King of Diamonds} {Ace of Hearts} {10 of Clubs}}
{10 of Clubs} {King of Diamonds} {Ace of Hearts}
```

The -unique option is a great way to eliminate duplicates from a list. However, it has a subtlety that might bite you if you also specify -index. If you are sorting a list of sublists, the default sort is to sort by each element of each sublist. If you specify -index and - unique and your list contains two sublists with the same element at the same index, only the last one will appear in the sorted list, regardless of the values of the rest of the elements. To illustrate, compare the results of the following three commands:

```
% lsort -unique {{King of Hearts} {King of Diamonds} {2 of Clubs}
{2 of Clubs} {King of Diamonds} {King of Hearts}
% lsort -unique -index 0 {{King of Hearts} {King of Diamonds} {2 of Clubs}}
{2 of Clubs} {King of Diamonds}
% lsort -unique -index 1 {{King of Hearts} {King of Diamonds} {2 of Clubs}}
{2 of Clubs}
```

The first lsort command shows the default behavior. The second one shows the result if you sort the list on index 0 alone: the resulting list drops the second King (the King of Hearts). As a pathological example, the third lsort sorts on index 1 (the word of in each sublist), which results in dropping the Kings from the sorted list.

The following script, lsort.tcl in this chapter's code directory, shows a simple example of lsort's usage. It uses the rand() function to generate a list of five random numbers and then lsort to sort them, displaying both the unsorted and sorted lists.

```
# Generate a list of 5 floating point numbers
for {set i 0} {$i < 5} {incr i} {
    lappend floats [expr rand()]
}

puts "Unsorted list:"
foreach float $floats {
    puts "\t$float"
}

set s_floats [lsort -real $floats]

puts "\nSorted list:"
foreach s_float $s_floats {
    puts "\t$s_float"
}
```

The only remarkable feature here is that I use the -real option to force the sort to be performed using floating-point comparisons rather than the default Unicode comparisons. Well, I also used the foreach looping command about which you'll read shortly. When you execute this script, you should see output resembling the following (of course, the list elements will differ):

```
$ ./lsort.tcl
Unsorted list:
    0.95407820258
    0.192350764383
    0.839296981617
    0.0643700450027
    0.867346360752
Sorted list:
    0.0643700450027
```

```
0.192350764383
0.839296981617
0.867346360752
0.95407820258
```

ADDITIONAL LIST OPERATIONS

The example scripts in this chapter are contrived in that they create lists specifically for the purpose of demonstrating this or that feature of list manipulation. The code you write will sometimes permit you to do the same. However, in many real-world programs, including games, you won't have the luxury of crafting your data when writing a script. Rather, you have to take the data you're handed and coerce it into the proper format. The last two list operations you need to know are how to convert a plain vanilla string using the `split` command and how to turn a list into a plain vanilla string using the `join` command.

Strings to Lists

Given a string that you want to convert to a Tcl list, the `split` command makes short work of the task. Its syntax is:

```
split $string ?chars?
```

`split` returns a list created by breaking *string* into elements at each occurrence of the split characters specified in *chars*. If you omit *chars*, the default split character is whitespace. Yes, you can specify multiple split characters in *chars*. Each occurrence of adjacent or consecutive *char* results in an empty list element. split also generates an empty list element if the first or last character of *string* matches a split character.

The following command breaks the sentence "A straight flush beats a full house." into a list consisting of each word in the sentence:

```
set words [split $sentence]
```

If, perversely, you want to break the sentence at, say, the letters a and s, the following command would do:

```
set words [split $sentence {as}]
```

Here is the output of both commands. (See split.tcl in this chapter's code directory.) Notice that the result of the second `split` command is grouped with braces. This occurs because the resulting list elements contain embedded whitespace, the default list separator. Tcl does this to protect the spaces and maintain the integrity of the resulting list.

```
$ ./split.tcl
A straight flush beats a full house.
{A } tr {ight flu} {h be} t { } { full hou} e.
```

Be careful when using split on arbitrary input because stray double quotes or braces will cause an error (see bad_split.tcl in this chapter's code directory):

```
% puts [split "A straight {flush "beats a full house."]
extra characters after close-quote
```

Breaking Strings into One-Character Lists

If you want to convert a string into a list of single-character elements, specify the empty list, {}, as the split character:

```
% split {Lots of characters} {}
L o t s { } o f { } c h a r a c t e r s
```

As you can see, split is a command that is easy to understand and use, as well as being capable and powerful.

You Don't Always Need split

In many situations, you don't need to use split to make a list. A string is a list and a list is a string. For example, you can use the list operation lindex on the string "A straight flush beats a full house." without first using split. In fact, history buffs might appreciate the fact that the string length command was added to eliminate the hack of using llength on a string to test whether or not the string was empty.

Lists to Strings

join performs the inverse operation of split, converting a list into a string and return the new string. join's syntax is:

```
join listVar ?chars?
```

join works by converting each element of listVar in a string, with each element separated by the character or characters specified by chars. As with the split command, chars can be a list of multiple characters. For example, in the following example (join.tcl in this chapter's code directory), the first join command splits the list into a single string whose words are separated by newlines, and the second one creates a string whose values are separated by a comma and a space:

```
% join {Ace King Queen Jack 10} "\n"
Ace
King
Queen
Jack
10
% join {{A a} {B b} {C c} d E} ", "
A a, B b, C c, d, E
```

In the second command, the embedded sublists, such as {A a}, were not joined into strings; join only strips off a single level of list structure.

LOOPING WITH THE FOREACH COMMAND

Earlier in the chapter, I sneaked the foreach looping command past you. As promised, I'm following up with a proper explanation. foreach is a specialized form of a loop specially designed for iterating over items in a list. The syntax for the form that you will use most often is:

```
foreach varName listVar {body}
```

foreach iterates over each element in *varList* by assigning an element to *varName* and then executing *body*. The loop terminates after executing *body* for the last element of *varList*. The assumption is that *body* does something with the list elements, but it doesn't have to. The following example shows how you might use foreach (see foreach.tcl in this chapter's code directory):

```
set cards [list Ace King Queen Jack 10]
foreach card $cards {
    lappend newCards [string toupper $card]
}
puts $newCards
```

If you rewrote the foreach loop to use a standard for command, it would be more verbose:

```
for {set i 0} {$i <= [llength cards]} {incr i} {
    lappend newCards [string toupper $card]
}
```

I think you'll find that foreach is more compact to write and much more expressive than the equivalent for loop.

`foreach`'s general syntax is slightly more complex because you can iterate over multiple lists:

```
foreach varName listVar ?varNameN listVarN ...? {body}
```

This is an advanced usage that I won't use in this book, but the basic idea is that on each iteration of the loop, one element from each list is assigned to its corresponding loop variable and then the loop body is executed, presumably using or modifying the loop variables. The potential *gotcha* here is that unless you code defensively, you'll wind up with unexpected results or outright errors. Why? If one of the lists has more elements than the other, the loop variable for the shorter list will be assigned an empty value for each missing element. *Coding defensively* in this case means the loop body must at least accommodate empty values appropriately.

Another commonly used variation of `foreach` loops is to pull multiple elements off a list in a single iteration. This technique is often used to convert lists to arrays and arrays to lists. The following script, pairs.tcl in this chapter's code directory, illustrates a similar use:

```
set cards [list Ace Clubs King Hearts Queen Spades Jack Diamonds 10 Clubs]

foreach {card suit} $cards {
    puts "$card of $suit"
}
```

This script pulls two values off the list variable `$cards` on each iteration, storing the fetched values in the `$card` and `$suit` variables, making it trivial to display nicely formatted card names:

```
$ ./pairs.tcl
Ace of Clubs
King of Hearts
Queen of Spades
Jack of Diamonds
10 of Clubs
```

CONDITIONAL EXECUTION: THE SWITCH COMMAND

Back in Chapter 3, you learned how to use the `if` command to execute a given block of code conditionally. You also learned that you could use as many `elseif` clauses as necessary to handle multiple conditions. At the time, I wrote "If you need very many [`elseif` clauses], you'll probably want to use the `switch` command. More than four or five `elseif` clauses looks messy and can be difficult to maintain." So, about the `switch` command...

switch, like if, branches the flow of control in a program to one of many blocks of code based on the value of an expression. One of the most common situations in which you'll use it is to execute a given code block in response to user input, such as you might get from a menu. Another frequent use of switch is in event-driven programs (such as those you create with Tk). In *event-driven* programs, the main program runs in a loop and waits for an event to occur, such as a mouse click, a keypress, or the completion of a long-running process. When an event occurs, the main program executes code to handle or respond to that event.

switch's general syntax is one of the following (I'll explain why there are two possibilities in a moment):

```
switch ?option ...? value pattern body ?pattern body? ?...?
switch ?option ...? value {pattern body} ?{pattern body}? ?...?
```

switch compares *value* to each *pattern* sequentially and, when it finds a match, executes the corresponding body. Upon completion of the associated *body*, switch returns the result of that *body*. If no matching pattern is found and the last pattern is not the special pattern default, switch returns the empty string. If the last pattern *is* default, it matches *any* pattern. *option*, of which there can be multiple, modifies switch's behavior. It can be one of the following:

- -exact—Uses exact matching when comparing *value* to *pattern* (this is the default).
- -glob—Uses glob-style matching when comparing *value* to *pattern*; this is the same globbing as the string match command supports.
- -regexp—Uses regular expression matching when comparing *value* to *pattern*.
- ---—Signals the end of options; this is necessary so that the *value* argument can begin with a single hyphen and not be interpreted as an (invalid) option.

Why are there two syntax possibilities, one without braces and one with? The first form, the one without braces, allows substitution to occur in the *pattern*s, which is good, but requires backslashes if you want the switch command to span multiple lines, which is a pain. I usually want the switch command to span multiple lines to improve readability. The second form, the one with braces, prevents substitutions from occurring in the *pattern*s, which is potentially bad, but eliminates the need for escaping the newlines.

It's an unfortunate dilemma: Do you want your code to be readable or do you want substitutions in your *pattern* arguments? With careful coding, you might be able to arrange for the patterns to be substituted before you enter a switch block. However, it might be easier to opt for the brace-infested form and put up with unsightly code. As you gain experience reading and writing Tcl code, backslash-escaped newlines will become more familiar and won't be so visually jarring, In addition, my opinion is that the power and expressiveness that command and variable substitution imparts to Tcl is worth the inconvenience of having to escape newlines. Finally, using both syntaxes as the situation requires is preferable to and more practical than being doctrinaire and *always* using one or the other.

Always Group Command Bodies in `switch` Blocks

Regardless of which of the two `switch` syntaxes you use, you should always group the command bodies. This is a matter of efficiency. If all the command bodies are grouped (using braces), no substitutions occur until control enters the body that corresponds to the matching pattern, and substitution will only occur in that body.

Examples? nobrace.tcl in this chapter's code directory shows you how to use the no-brace-ugly-backslashes syntax:

```
# Create menu
set menu [list {S: Save game} {Q: Save game and exit}\
{X: Exit without saving} {N: Start new game} {C: Return to current game}]

# Show the menu
foreach option $menu {
    puts $option
}

# Get user's input
puts -nonewline "Choice \[SQXNC\]: "
flush stdout
gets stdin choice

# Process the input
switch -exact -- [string toupper $choice] \
    S {puts "Game saved"}\
    Q {puts "Game saved. Exiting"}\
    X {puts "Exiting immediately"}\
    N {puts "Starting new game"}\
    C {puts "Returning to current game"}\
    default {puts "Invalid option: $choice"};
```

This script mimics a game menu from which players can save a game, exit the game, and so on. Players simply press a letter corresponding to the option they want:

```
$ ./nobrace.tcl
S: Save game
Q: Save game and exit
X: Exit without saving
N: Start new game
C: Return to current game
Choice [SQXNC]: s
Game saved
$ ./nobrace.tcl
S: Save game
Q: Save game and exit
X: Exit without saving
N: Start new game
C: Return to current game
Choice [SQXNC]: p
Invalid option: p
```

Strictly speaking, this example could have been written to use braces around the *pattern body* pairs because the *patterns* do not use variables.

INTERRUPTING LOOP EXECUTION

When executing a loop, it is sometimes necessary to interrupt execution before the next iteration of the loop. In some cases, you want to exit the loop without executing any more of the loop code. In other situations, you want to start the next iteration immediately. To terminate a loop prematurely, use the break command; to start the next iteration of a loop, use the continue command.

Suppose that you are writing a program to play Blackjack (a/k/a 21) and are using a while loop to handle dealing the cards. If a player draws a Jack and an Ace, that player's hand is an immediate winner, and there is no need to deal more cards. In this case, you would use the break command to terminate the loop because you no longer need to give the player any more cards. The syntax of the break command is just that, a bare break command:

```
break
```

Here's a short script that illustrates the break command:

```
for {set i 1} {$i <= 10} {incr i} {
    # Generate a random number between 1 and 21 inclusive    set num [expr int(1 +
(rand() * 21))]
```

```
    if {$num == 21} {
        break      }
}


if {$num == 21} {
    puts "Got 21 on iteration \#$i"
} else {
    puts "Didn't get 21"
}
```

This script generates a random number between 1 and 21 in a `for` loop that iterates a maximum of 10 times. If the generated number is 21, the `break` command terminates the loop; otherwise, it generates another random number and tries again. If you execute this script (break.tcl in this chapter's code directory), the output should resemble the following. You might have to run it a couple of times before you hit 21:

```
$ ./break.tcl
Didn't get 21
$ ./break.tcl
Got 21 on iteration #7
```

Suppose, on the other hand, you are using a `foreach` loop to iterate over a list of inventory items and are looking for a specific item, say, a knife, and the logic in the loop deals contains code describing what to do with that knife. For each item that *isn't* a knife, you can use the `continue` command to start the next iteration of the loop because there is no need to execute the rest of the code. Like break, `continue`'s syntax is just the command `continue`:

```
continue
```

The script continue.tcl in this chapter's code directory shows `continue` in action:

```
set inventory [list club sword crossbow arrows knife dagger bow]

foreach item $inventory {
    if {$item ne "knife"} {
        continue      }
    puts "Using knife to pry open door to safe"
}
```

Even though the `puts` statement is not protected by an `else` clause, it will only execute when the inventory item is a knife. Each item that isn't a knife causes the `continue` command to execute, which starts the next iteration of the `foreach` loop and skips the `puts` command.

ANALYZING PLAYING BLACKJACK

blackjack.tcl is a good starting point for full-featured Blackjack games. It also demonstrates "real world" usage of the major features of lists and the control structures I introduced in this chapter. It is somewhat long, but that's mostly because there is a lot of repetitive code. Once you learn more about procedures (Chapter 7, "Writing Tcl Procedures"), you'll be able to replace repetitive code blocks with procedures. In the meantime, don't let the length intimidate you.

Looking at the Code

```
#!/usr/bin/tclsh
# blackjack.tcl
# Play a hand of Blackjack

# Return a random integer between 0 and the number of elements in
# the list specified by list
proc Random {list} {
    set index [expr {int(1 + rand() * ([llength $list]) - 1)}]     return $index
}

# Block 1
# Create a deck of cards
set values [list Ace King Queen Jack 10 9 8 7 6 5 4 3 2]
set suits [list Clubs Diamonds Hearts Spades]
lappend deck $values $suits

# Block 2
# Deal 2 cards
for {set i 1} {$i <= 2} {incr i} {
    lappend cards "[lindex $deck 0 [Random $values]] of\
        [lindex $deck 1 [Random $suits]]"
}

# Display the initial hand
foreach card $cards {
    puts $card
}
```

```
# Block 3
# Deal another?
puts -nonewline "Deal another card \[yn\]? "
flush stdout
gets stdin answer
while {[string tolower $answer] eq "y"} {
    lappend cards "[lindex $deck 0 [Random $values]] of\
        [lindex $deck 1 [Random $suits]]"    foreach card $cards {
        puts $card     }
    puts -nonewline "Deal another card \[yn\]? "    flush stdout    gets stdin
    answer
}


# Block 4
# Score the hand
set score 0
foreach card $cards {
    switch -glob -- $card \
        Ace* {set value 11}\
        King* -\
        Queen* -\
        Jack* -\
        10* {set value 10}\
        default {set value [lindex $card 0]}    set score [expr $score + $value]
}


# Block 5
# Display the score
puts -nonewline "$score: "
if {$score > 21} {
    puts "Bust!"
} elseif {$score == 21} {
    puts "Perfect!"
} elseif {$score >= 16 && $score <= 20} {
    puts "Tough hand to beat!"
} else {
    puts "Better luck next time!"
}
```

Understanding the Code

You've already seen the procedure, Random, at the top of the script (refer to the cards.tcl script in the section titled "Accessing Specific List Elements"). It generates a random number between 0 and the number of elements in a list. I use this procedure in Blocks 2 and 3 to deal a reasonably random card. Block 1 just creates a "deck" of cards out of which the script will deal cards—you saw this card in cards.tcl, too. So far, nothing new.

In Block 2, I deal the first two cards, storing them in the list variable named cards. The foreach loop sets the stage for the rest of the game by displaying the player's initial hand of cards.

The game gets going in Block 3. Now that the user has had a chance to examine his cards, I use the standard input sequence I've used throughout the first few chapters of this book to ask the user if he would like another card. If the user types "n," control moves to the code in Block 4. Otherwise, control enters the while loop, which:

1. Deals another card.
2. Redisplays the hand with the new card.
3. Repeats the prompt to deal another card.

The while loop continues until the user types "n." Notice the use of string tolower to make sure that the user can type "y" or "Y" for yes. Another feature of the while loop is the prompt itself. Because I need literal [and] characters, I have to escape them using backslashes. Without the escapes, the interpreter would try to execute a command or procedure named yn and would generate an error that aborts the script.

After all the cards have been dealt in Block 3, Block 4 scores the hand. I use a foreach loop to iterate through the cards list and assign a score to each card using a switch command. The -glob option was necessary because each card has both a denomination (such as Ace or 8) and a suit. For example, the glob pattern Ace* matches "Ace of Spades," "Ace of Clubs," and so forth. The score for each card is stored in the variable value, which is added to the total score, stored in the variable score, at the bottom of the loop.

The scores for Ace and 10 are obvious, but the handling of the other face cards and of the other numeric cards is a little trickier. The command body for a King, Queen, or Jack is -. This means that the body for the following pattern should be used for this pattern. The idea is to share command bodies among several patterns. In this case, the command body for a pattern of 10 will be used for patterns that match King*, Queen*, Jack*, and, of course, 10*. In effect, a body of - allows execution to fall through to a common body.

For the numeric cards, I score them by setting value to the numeric component of the list element (the numeric cards look like "3 of Clubs" or "8 of Spades"). I extract the numeric component using the command `lindex $card 0`. Once again, you see how nested commands and command substitution make it possible, even trivial, to build powerful compound commands with a minimum of code.

After adding the score of the current card to the total score, the scoring process continues with the next element of the list/card in the user's hand. When all cards have been scored, Block 5 displays the score along with a short message and the script exits.

Modifying the Code

Here are some exercises you can try to practice what you learned in this chapter.

5.1 Add code to prevent dealing the same card twice.

5.2 Add code to give the user the choice of scoring Aces as 1 or 11.

5.3 Add code to handle input that isn't `y` or `n`.

5.4 Add code to test for a blackjack and exit the `foreach` loop if it is.

Lists are one of Tcl's two native data structures. The Blackjack game illustrates some of what Tcl's list-related functionality makes possible. Given data that lends itself to arrangement in a list, Tcl has commands for creating the list, accessing particular list elements, sorting the entire list or only part of it, searching a list for elements that match certain criteria, and adding, deleting, or modifying list elements. In addition, you can convert between lists and strings with the `split` and `join` commands. The `foreach` loop control structure is specifically designed to iterate over lists, and you can even control loop execution by using the `break` and `continue` commands. In the next chapter, you'll learn how to use Tcl's other native data structure, the array.

CREATING AND USING ARRAYS

T he lion's share of the work you'll do with data structures will be with lists, introduced in the last chapter, and arrays, introduced in this chapter. Tcl arrays, like Perl's hashes, are *associative*, meaning that they are indexed by strings rather than integers or other numeric types. In addition to learning how to create and use arrays, this chapter also shows you commands and techniques for handling errors. Error handling combines well with material on arrays because common mistakes that occur when using arrays (such as accessing out-of-bounds or non-existent array indices) raise errors that need to be handled gracefully.

WHAT'S THE WORD?

This chapter's game, What's the Word?, introduces you to Tcl arrays using a Jeopardy-like game. It displays the definition of a common word and then prompts you to guess the corresponding word. To play the game, execute the script jeopardy.tcl in this chapter's code directory. The following listing shows one round of the game:

```
$ ./jeopardy.tcl
Tcl command for performing mathematical operations
Your answer: string
Nope. Try again: [expr]
```

```
Nope. Try again: expr
Correct!
expr: Tcl command for performing mathematical operations
```

THE DIFFERENCES BETWEEN ARRAYS AND LISTS

Tcl arrays are variables that store collections of data in a key-value format. Arrays are similar to lists in that both are accessed using an index. With lists, the index is an integer; with arrays, the index can be any string (although I discourage using strings with embedded whitespace as keys for reasons I describe shortly). A more significant difference between arrays and lists is that arrays are unordered collections of values (or elements), whereas lists are ordered sequences of values. In this sense, Tcl arrays are much more like Perl hashes than arrays in third-generation compiled languages like C or C++. If it was even possible to do so, if you tried to access the third element of an array, the value of that element might change because Tcl's arrays are organized for speedy, convenient access, not for orderly, sequential access.

Arrays Are Maintained as Hashes

The reason that Tcl does not guarantee array access order and does not even provide the capability to do reference array elements in sequential order is that, internally, arrays are maintained as hashes. As you add elements to an array, they aren't necessarily put at the "end." Rather, they are arranged and rearranged in a "tree" that provides optimal access to any given element. This is really more than you need to know about Tcl internals, but *someone* is going to ask why arrays work this way. So now you know.

Another significant difference between arrays and lists is the manner in which array elements are referenced. Specific array elements are accessed by enclosing the index in parentheses immediately following the name of the array. To get the value of a particular element, you use $ substitution on the array variable name. For example, suppose that you have a three-element array named roles, which contains the three character classes elf, dwarf, and wizard (yes, this is a dungeon-crawl game). The classes are the indices, and the elements are short descriptions of each class. To set the description of the elf, you might use the following syntax:

```
set role(elf) "Slender humanoids with pointed ears and an affinity for all things
natural"
```

To retrieve the description of the elf role, you would use the following syntax:

```
puts $roles(elf)
```

The following example, array_ref.tcl in this chapter's code directory, shows a more complete example:

```
set role(elf) "\n\tSlender, forest-dwelling humanoid with pointed ears with
    prodigious talent for herbal lore and the healing arts"
set role(dwarf) "\n\tShort, stout, cave-dwelling humanoid, rarely seen in
    sunlight, possessing remarkable gifts for mining and working
    stone and metal"
set role(troll) "\n\tLazy, misshapen creature endowed with extraordinary
    strength and endurance and the unfortunate characteristic of
    turning to stone when exposed to sunlight"

puts "Troll: $role(troll)\n"
puts "Elf: $role(elf)\n"
puts "Dwarf: $role(dwarf)\n"
```

Here's the output:

```
$ ./array_ref.tcl
Troll:
    Lazy, misshapen creature endowed with extraordinary
    strength and endurance and the unfortunate characteristic of
    turning to stone when exposed to sunlight

Elf:
    Slender, forest-dwelling humanoid with pointed ears with
    prodigious talent for herbal lore and the healing arts

Dwarf:
    Short, stout, cave-dwelling humanoid, rarely seen in
    sunlight, possessing remarkable gifts for mining and working
    stone and metal
```

With these few pieces of information, you're ready to dive into the particulars of using arrays.

WORKING WITH ARRAYS

Much like the string command, you work with arrays using the array command and one of 11 options or subcommands. Table 6.1 lists and briefly describes each array option.

TABLE 6.1: ARRAY OPTIONS	
Option	**Description**
array anymore *arrayVar id*	Returns 1 if more elements exist in the search of *arrayVar* specified by *id*, 0 otherwise.
array donesearch *arrayVar id*	Ends the search of *arrayVar* specified by *id*.
array exists *arrayVar*	Returns 1 if *arrayVar* is an array variable, 0 otherwise.
array get *arrayVar ?pattern?*	Returns a list of index-value pairs from *arrayVar*; specify *pattern* as a glob-style match to limit the returned elements to indices which match *pattern*; returns the empty list if there are no matches or *arrayVar* is empty.
array names *arrayVar ?mode? ?pattern?*	Returns a list of indices in *arrayVar* which match *pattern* (all if *pattern* not specified); *mode* specifies the type of match, defaulting to glob-style matching if omitted.
array set *arrayVar list*	Initializes *arrayVar* to the elements in *list*.
array size *arrayVar*	Returns the number of indices defined in *arrayVar*.
array startsearch *arrayVar*	Returns a search ID for a search of *arrayVar*.
array statistics *arrayVar*	Returns interesting statistics about *arrayVar*.
array unset *arrayVar ?pattern?*	Deletes all elements of *arrayVar*; if *pattern* is specified, delete only elements matching the glob denoted by *pattern*.

Of the 10 options in Table 6.1, four deal with searching arrays and three provide information. The other three do real work.

Getting Information About Arrays

Array variables look like any other variable in Tcl and, in most cases, act like them. However, it is an error to try to assign a *scalar* (single) value to an array variable. Once a variable has been assigned to an array-type value, you cannot use it a as a scalar. You can use the array exists command to see if a variable is an array before you access it using array syntax (see array_exists.tcl in this chapter's code directory):

```
array set nums {one 1 two 2 three 3 four 4}
set chars [list {a c e g b d f h}]

if {[array exists nums] == 1} {
    puts "nums is an array"
```

```
} elseif {[info exists num]} {
    puts "nums exists but is not an array"
} else {
    puts "nums doesn't exist"
}

if {[array exists chars]} {
    puts "chars is an array"
} elseif {[info exists chars]} {
    puts "chars exists but is not an array"
} else {
    puts "chars doesn't exist"
}
```

First, I set up a couple of variables, nums, which is an array variable, and chars, which is a list variable. Then each if block tests to see if the variable is an array or if it even exists (using the info exists command discussed at the end of the chapter—see the section titled "Examining Variables"). Based on the result of these tests, I print an appropriate message:

```
$ ./array_exists.tcl
nums is an array
chars exists but is not an array
```

Once you know that an array exists, you might be interested in how many elements it contains. The array size command will tell you how many indices have been defined in an array, which doesn't necessarily correspond to the number of elements:

```
array size arrayVar
```

If *arrayVar* is undefined, array size returns 0. The script array_info.tcl in this chapter's code directory shows both the array size and the array statistics in action:

```
array set nums {one 1 two 2 three 3 four 4}
array set chars {}
array set roles {elf {} dwarf {} troll {}}

puts "nums has [array size nums] elements"
puts "chars has [array size chars] elements"
puts "roles has [array size roles] elements"
```

Here's the output of this script (array_size.tcl in this chapter's code directory):

```
$ ./array_info.tcl
nums has 4 elements
chars has 0 elements
roles has 3 elements
```

Notice that the `roles` array has three indices but no values. Well, it has values, but they are all empty. For this reason, your array-handling code should not assume that the number of indices is the same as the number of elements.

If you are interested in the internal structure of an array, and you shouldn't be, you can use the `array statistics` command to find out a little bit about the hash table used to maintain the array. The syntax is simple:

```
array statistics arrayVar
```

That said, the `array statistics` command is useful to Tcl developers debugging problems with the `array` command's implementation, but not to mere mortals like you and me. You can safely ignore it, which is precisely what I'm going to do for the rest of the book.

Converting Lists to Arrays

As Table 6.1 showed, you can initialize an array from a list using the `array set` command. Each pair of values in the list becomes an index and value in the resulting array. At the risk of stating the obvious, `array set` is the command to use to convert a list to an array. Key facts to bear in mind when using `array set` are:

- The initializing list must have an even number of elements.
- The odd-numbered elements in the list become the array indices.
- The even-numbered elements become the corresponding array values.

If your initializer list has an odd number of elements, `array set` returns an error, as shown in the following short example (array_error.tcl in this chapter's code directory):

```
array set nums {one 1 two 2 three 3 four}
puts "nums has [array size nums] elements"
```

The initializer in this example only has seven elements. As a result, you'll get the following error when you execute this script:

```
$ ./array_error.tcl

list must have an even number of elements
```

```
    while executing

"array set nums {one 1 two 2 three 3 four}"

    (file "./array_error.tcl" line 6)
```

You've already seen `array set` in several scripts (for example, array_size.tcl), so I won't belabor it any further.

Converting Arrays to Lists

To convert an array to a list, or simply to retrieve elements from the list, the command to use is `array get`. It returns a pair of elements; the first item in each pair is the index and the second is the value corresponding to that index. The syntax is:

`array get arrayVar ?pattern?`

If you omit *pattern*, you'll get all of the elements in *arrayVar* or an empty list if *arrayVar* doesn't contain any elements (that is, if it's empty) or if *arrayVar* isn't an array. If specified, *pattern* limits the return lists to those elements whose indices match the glob-style *pattern*. If there are no matches, again, the return value is an empty list. The script array_get.tcl in this chapter's code directory illustrates `array get`'s behavior:

```
set roles(elf) "\n\tSlender, forest-dwelling humanoid with pointed ears with
    prodigious talent for herbal lore and the healing arts"
set roles(dwarf) "\n\tShort, stout, cave-dwelling humanoid, rarely seen in
    sunlight, possessing remarkable gifts for mining and working
    stone and metal"
set roles(troll) "\n\tLazy, misshapen creature endowed with extraordinary
    strength and endurance and the unfortunate characteristic of
    turning to stone when exposed to sunlight"

puts "Number of elements in array of roles: [array size roles]"
puts "Number of elements in list of roles: [llength [array get roles]]"
puts "dwarf, n.: [array get roles dw*]"
puts "wizard, n.: [array get roles wizard]"
```

After initializing three elements in an array named `roles`, I first use `array size` to show the number of elements in the array. Next, I use `llength` to illustrate that the three elements of the array convert to six elements in a list. The first `array get` command uses a search glob, dw* to retrieve any matching elements from the roles array. The second `array get` command shows when a matching index (to `wizard`, in this case) doesn't exist. The output of this script shouldn't surprise you:

```
$ ./array_get.tcl
Number of elements in array of roles: 3
Number of elements in list of roles: 6
dwarf, n.: dwarf {
    Short, stout, cave-dwelling humanoid, rarely seen in
    sunlight, possessing remarkable gifts for mining and working
    stone and metal}
wizard, n.:
```

Retrieving Array Elements

The problem with `array gets` is that it returns both the index and the value and, as you can see in the output of array_get.tcl, the output retains the list grouping (the {} characters). Sometimes, or perhaps most of the time, you are only interested in either the index or the value. To access the values, you can use the $ substitution method I showed you earlier in the chapter. For example, to access the value corresponding to the `dwarf` index, you could say `$roles(dwarf)`:

```
puts $roles(dwarf)
    Short, stout, cave-dwelling humanoid, rarely seen in
    sunlight, possessing remarkable gifts for mining and working
    stone and metal
```

Of course, using $ substitution assumes you know the indices of the array. If you don't, you need to use the `array names` command, which returns a list of all the indices defined in an array. Its syntax is:

```
array names arrayVar ?mode? ?pattern?
```

As usual, *pattern* specifies a pattern to match. *mode* can be either `-glob` (the default) for glob-style matching, `-exact` to require an exact match, or `-regexp` to request a regular expression match. If you specify neither *-mode* nor *-pattern*, all indices will be returned. Otherwise, only indices that match *pattern* and match according to the matching rule specified by *-mode* will be returned. Given the definition of the `roles` array in array_get.tcl, the following `array name` commands illustrate the corresponding return values:

```
puts "All indices: [array names roles]"
puts "Glob '*r*': [array names roles *r*]"
puts "Exact 'd': [array names roles -exact d]"
```

These commands produce, respectively:

```
All indices: dwarf troll elf
Glob '*r*': dwarf troll
Exact 'd':
```

Once you have the indices, a `foreach` loop makes trivial work of accessing the corresponding values (remember, `foreach` is specifically designed for iterating through lists, and the `array names` command returns a list):

```
foreach role [array names roles *r*] {
        puts "$role: $roles($role)"
}
```

The output corresponding to this code fragment is:

```
dwarf:
        Short, stout, cave-dwelling humanoid, rarely seen in
        sunlight, possessing remarkable gifts for mining and working
        stone and metal
troll:
        Lazy, misshapen creature endowed with extraordinary
        strength and endurance and the unfortunate characteristic of
        turning to stone when exposed to sunlight
```

The script array_names.tcl in this chapter's code directory contains all of the snippets of code used in this section.

Names or Indices?

The Tcl documentation uniformly refers to the index of an array as its *name*. I prefer to use the term index because it avoids the possible confusion that might arise when one uses the phrase *array name*, which might refer to the name of the array variable or the name used to index a particular value in the array. Neither term is incorrect, but the Tcl documentation is pretty consistent in its use of name, so you need to be aware of this matter of diction.

Searching Arrays

The final array-related functionality I should cover is how to search arrays using `startsearch`, `nextelement`, `anymore`, and `donesearch`. However, I'm not going to do so because you can obtain the same results using an appropriately crafted `array get` or `array names` command and a `foreach` loop. In addition, the processor and memory overhead of accessing very large arrays is, shall we say, suboptimal at this time. From the man page for the `array` command, "It is currently more efficient and easier to use either the `array get` or `array names` [commands], together with `foreach`, to iterate over all but very large arrays." If Tcl's maintainers recommend eschewing the array search commands, that's good enough for me. If you insist, the man page (`man 3tcl array`) describes the syntax of the search commands and also includes examples. I think you'll find that they are awkward and unintuitive to use, and, IMNSHO, very un-Tclish.

Grace Under Pressure

One of the hallmarks of high-quality code, regardless of the language in which it is written, is its *robustness*, that is, how it behaves in the face of unexpected conditions, invalid data, errors, and the other digital disasters that plague computers and computer users. The worst scripts and programs just crash or terminate without warning, without giving users a chance to save their work or possibly to recover from the situation, and without providing any clue regarding what happened. These are the programs about which some wit said, "If it breaks, you get to keep both pieces."

At the opposite end of the spectrum are those programs that just seem to keep chugging along and, when errors do occur, degrade gracefully. *Degrading gracefully* means that when errors do occur (and they will), the application does more than just throw up its hands and abruptly terminate. Rather, it provides the user with information about errors, offers suggestions about how to recover, or tries to recover on its own without soliciting user input. Better still are those programs that attempt, to the degree it is possible, to anticipate potential problems and code around them, or at least provide meaningful diagnostic information.

Robustness is partially the result of seasoned programmers building their experience into the code they write and partially the result of taking advantage of language features designed to facilitate dealing with errors and exceptions. This section introduces you to some of Tcl's built-in capabilities for responding to unanticipated situations and degrading gracefully in the face of unrecoverable errors.

Dealing with Exceptions: The `catch` Command

If you've been a diligent reader and tried the exercises at the end of each chapter, you've likely already experienced how Tcl (well, the Tcl interpreter) behaves when it encounters errors in a script: It terminates the script and displays a stack trace that begins at the point at which the error occurred. Errors include calling commands with the wrong number or type of arguments, such as calling the `puts` command with four arguments or attempting to use an array variable in a scalar context. Tcl commands all have command-specific errors, that is, errors that aren't general Tcl runtime errors but peculiar to the implementation of a given command.

The Tcl command for trapping such errors and, if you wish, doing something other than bailing out, is catch. Its general syntax is:

```
catch script ?resultVar?
```

script consists of one or more Tcl commands that might generate errors you want to catch. *resultVar*, if specified, stores script's return value (that is, the result of the last command executed) or, if an error occurs, an error message. If script raises an error, catch itself returns 1. If *script* does not raise an error, catch returns 0.

To execute *script*, catch invokes the Tcl interpreter. As a result, you should always protect (group) *script* with braces rather than double quotes because if you use double quotes, *script* will go through a second round of substitution. catch itself always returns without raising an error, although the commands it is executing might raise errors.

I'll start with a simple example, catch_1.tcl in this chapter's code directory:

```
catch {[puts $str]}
```

Ordinarily, puts $str would raise an error, and the script would terminate because the variable str is undefined:

```
$ ./catch_1.tcl
can't read "str": no such variable
    while executing
"puts $str"
    (file "./catch_1.tcl" line 7)
```

However, if you use the catch command as shown, the error will be ignored. Comment out the line puts $str in catch_1.tcl before executing it a second time:

```
$ ./catch_1.tcl
$
```

As you can see in the second example, the invalid puts command does not terminate the script. The Tcl interpreter didn't really "ignore" the error, though. Rather, the catch command trapped the error and modified the normal behavior.

If you're trapping errors using catch, you'll want to do something other than just eating the error and continuing. A more typical use is to embed the catch command in an if or switch command so you can test catch's return value and decide how to proceed based on the error that occurred. Here's a slightly more involved example, catch_2.tcl:

```
if {[catch {[puts $str]} retVal]} {
    puts "An error occurred: $retVal"
} else {
    puts "Nope, no errors here!"
}
```

The `if` condition tests `catch`'s return value, which will be 0 or 1, and then executes the corresponding block of code:

```
$ ./catch_2.tcl
An error occurred: can't read "str": no such variable
```

In this case, instead of the stack trace, the output simply states the nature of the error. If you're so inclined, you can provide a definition for the string variable `str` to see how catch_2.tcl works if `catch` returns 0. But I bet you can figure it out yourself.

The idea with `catch` is to handle errors without your script or program unceremoniously crashing. For example, suppose that your script is supposed to open a file that contains a saved game. If it can't find the file, the script can either give up and quit, or it can prompt the user for another filename. Guess which behavior will give users a more pleasant experience?

Raising Errors: The `error` Command

You've seen that you can trap errors raised by the Tcl interpreter and by Tcl commands using the `catch` command. You can also raise your own errors, which can in turn be caught by `catch`. The rationale here is to provide one or more custom error handlers to replace or supplement Tcl's built-in error handling. The command to raise an error is, you guessed it, `error`. Its syntax is:

```
error msg ?info? ?code?
```

`error` returns 1 to the calling procedure or command. *msg* is the string that describes what went wrong. The *info* argument is used to initialize a special Tcl global variable, `errorInfo`, which, in turn, is used to store a *stack trace*, the chain of commands that led up to the error you raised with `error`. If you don't specify *info*, *msg* will be displayed, followed by the stack trace. *code* is a machine-readable and succinct error description. If you use it, code will be stored in (yet another) special global Tcl variable, `errorCode`, and it should adhere to the format described in the `tclvars` man page (`man 3tcl tclvars`) for the `errorCode` global variable. If you don't specify *code*, the Tcl interpreter sets it to NONE. To keep things simple, I recommend not using *code* in your scripts.

The following two scripts show how to raise errors with the error command. The first script (error_msg.tcl in this chapter's code directory) sets only the *msg* parameter. The second example (see error_info.tcl) sets both *msg* and *info*:

```
set numerator 9;
set denominator 0;

# Just set the error message
if {$denominator == 0} {
    error "Dude! Division by zero is undefined"
}
```

The output of this script is:

```
$ ./error_msg.tcl

Dude! Division by zero is undefined
    while executing
"error "Dude! Division by zero is undefined""
    invoked from within
"if {$denominator == 0} {
    error "Dude! Division by zero is undefined"
}"
    (file "./error_msg.tcl" line 9)
```

As you can see, error still generates a stack trace, but the first entry is the message passed to it in *msg*:

```
set numerator 9;
set denominator 0;

# Set the error message and initialize errorInfo
if {$denominator == 0} {
    error "Dude! Division by zero is undefined" "Undefined"
}
```

When you execute the second script, it is the *info* parameter that is displayed at the top of the stack trace, rather than the *msg* parameter:

```
$ ./error_info.tcl
Undefined
    invoked from within

"if {$denominator == 0} {
    error "Dude! Division by zero is undefined" "Undefined"
}"
    (file "./error_info.tcl" line 9)
```

Which style should you use? Continuing with my theme of keeping things simple, I suggest using the format error *msg* because it has the virtue of preserving the complete stack trace created by the Tcl interpreter while displaying the error message you specify. You usually want to use the second form if you have a need to set or modify the stack trace.

EXAMINING VARIABLES

Earlier in the chapter, I used the `info exists` command to see if a variable existed before I tried to print its value. This technique is very handy as both a debugging tool and as part of making your code a little sturdier. Its syntax is:

```
info exists varName
```

This command returns 1 if the variable *varName* exists *and* has been defined (given a value). Otherwise, it returns 0. The array_info.tcl script contains an example, so I won't repeat it here.

Another useful `info` command is `info vars`, which returns a list of the names of all of the variables visible in the current scope. Its syntax is:

```
info vars ?pattern?
```

If specified, *pattern*, which is a `string match`-style glob, limits the return list to those variables matching *pattern*. `info vars` might not seem terribly useful just now, but after you learn how to organize your scripts into modules and store each module in a separate file, it will be very useful. You will be able to load an arbitrary file of Tcl code and find out exactly what variables it contains. Yes, I still need to show you how to do that, too. Patience, grasshopper, I'm getting there. Chapter 7, "Writing Tcl Procedures," shows you how to load Tcl code from one file into another.

In a newly `started` `tclsh` instance, there are a number of predefined variables that you might find useful:

```
% info vars
tcl_rcFileName tcl_version argv0 argv tcl_interactive auto_oldpath errorCode auto_path
errorInfo auto_index env tcl_pkgPath tcl_patchLevel argc tcl_libPath tcl_library
tcl_platform
```

To find out what these variables are, have a look at the tclvars man page (`man 3tcl tclvars`).

Similar to `info vars` is `info procs`, which displays a list of all the procedures defined in the current scope. Again, in a fresh `tclsh` instance, there are a number of predefined procedures. These won't be much use to you at this stage of your Tcl programming, but later on you might find them useful:

```
% info procs
auto_load_index unknown auto_import auto_execok auto_qualify auto_load history tclLog
```

Unlike the predefined Tcl variables, these procedures have their own manual pages, which you can view using the command `man 3tcl` *proc_name*, replacing *proc_name* with the name of the procedure in which you are interested.

ANALYZING WHAT'S THE WORD?

Although it is simple, jeopardy.tcl combines features from several of the preceding chapters. In addition to using an array to store questions and answers, it uses list commands to access the list objects returned by array operations, mathematical calculations for selecting an array element to use, and string commands to massage user input and evaluate the user's guess. In short, it exhibits a key characteristic of "real" Tcl programs, using a variety of commands and techniques to solve a programming problem.

Looking at the Code

```tcl
#!/usr/bin/tclsh
# jeopardy.tcl
# Play a simple Jeopardy-like game

# Block 1
# Words and their definitions
array set words {
    "Tcl" "Programming language originally designed as a glue language"
    "Ousterhout" "Surname of the person who originally wrote Tcl"
    "expr" "Tcl command for performing mathematical operations"
```

```
    "HTML" "The 'language' of the World Wide Web"
    "9" "The Arabic numeral equivalent to the Roman numeral IX"
    "25" "The missing value in the sequence of numbers 4, 9, 16, 36"
    }

# Block 2
# Select a random word and definition
set i [expr {int(rand() * 6))}]
set word [lindex [array names words] $i]
set def $words($word)

# Block 3
# Show the definition and prompt for the word it defines
puts $def
puts -nonewline "Your answer: "
flush stdout
gets stdin input
set guess [string trim $input]

# Block 4
# Evaluate user's guess, prompt for new answer until correct
while {[string tolower $guess] ne [string tolower $word]} {
    puts -nonewline "Nope. Try again: "    flush stdout    gets stdin input
set guess [string trim $input]
}

# Block 5
puts "Correct!"
puts "$guess: $def"
```

Understanding the Code

Blocks 1 and 2 set up the game. Block 1 creates an array of words (with the wonderfully imaginative name $words) and their definitions using array set and a list. $words is indexed by the word I want to define, and the value of each index is the corresponding definition. Nothing terribly remarkable, but a necessary step. In Block 2, I use my (by now) familiar routine for generating a random number between 0 and 5 so I can select a random term and its associated definition from the $words array. The second set command in Block 2 uses the list operator lindex on the list returned by array names to select the word I want to define. The third set command uses a simple array reference ($words($word)) to retrieve the definition.

Game play begins in Block 3. Here, I show the definition and then prompt the user to type a word. The user's answer gets stored in the variable $input, which I store in $guess after using the trim command to remove leading and trailing whitespace, if any. Trimming input is a technique I often use to clean up user input before using it in comparisons. In this case, my goal is to reduce the likelihood of stray characters incorrectly causing a correct answer to be considered incorrect.

Block 4 uses a while loop to compare the player's answer to the correct answer. If the answer is correct, the loop exits and control passes to Block 5. If the player guessed incorrectly, I ask for another guess, performing the same trim operation as described for Block 3. The loop condition, [string tolower $guess] ne [string tolower $word], converts both the player's input and the correct answer to lowercase. I do this to enhance the game's playability—it seems unfair to assert, for example, that HTML and html are not the same answer in the context of the game.

Block 5 ends the game, showing the player the guess and its definition.

Modifying the Code

Here are some exercises you can try to practice what you learned in this chapter:

6.1 Modify Block 1 to use a different set of six words and definitions.

6.2 Modify Block 4 to give users the option to play another round instead of exiting the game after guessing the correct answer.

6.3 Modify the loop condition in Block 4's while loop to use a different string operation to compare the player's guess to the correct answer.

Arrays are the second most important data structure (the *most* important is lists). Although arrays and lists share a number of characteristics and you can easily convert between arrays and lists, their syntax is different. Arrays also have a smaller range of natively supported operations that you can perform. This chapter also introduced you to the catch command, which allows you to handle runtime errors more gracefully than simply exiting the script abruptly. Robust, fault-tolerant programs are a hallmark of professional, skilled developers. The next chapter, "Writing Tcl Procedures," introduces you to another characteristic of high-quality programming, which is modularization.

## CHAPTER 7

WRITING TCL PROCEDURES

Procedures enable you to replace a commonly used sequence of commands with a single new command. Known as *subroutines* or *functions* in other programming languages, Tcl procedures can be called with or without arguments. You will also learn about variable and procedure scope, which determines when and where variables and procedures are visible. Together, procedures and an understanding of variable and procedure scope give you the tools you need to start implementing your Tcl scripts in a more modular and easy-to-maintain manner.

FORTUNE TELLER

This chapter's game, Fortune Teller, is a poor man's implementation of the classic UNIX game, fortune. Primarily a vehicle for demonstrating the use of Tcl procedures, Fortune Teller also uses Tcl's list functionality discussed in Chapter 5. To play this game, execute the script fortune.tcl in this chapter's code directory. Although the fortunes you see might differ, the output should resemble the following:

```
$ ./fortune.tcl
Everything that you know is wrong, but you can be straightened out.
$ ./fortune.tcl
Your supervisor is thinking about you.
$ ./fortune.tcl
Live in a world of your own, but always welcome visitors.
```

What Is a Procedure?

Tcl procedures replace and parameterize a commonly or frequently used collection of commands with a single command. Procedures enable you to create your own Tcl commands and, if you are so inclined, to replace core Tcl commands with your own implementations (not recommended when you're starting out, but certainly possible). Procedures eliminate blocks of repetitive code, making scripts easier to edit, read, and understand. Programs using procedures are easier to edit because if you change a procedure, you only edit a single block of code; blocks of repetitive code, on the other hand, require multiple edits, introducing the possibility of typos and, more than likely, bugs. Procedures make programs easier to read because repeated blocks of code in a program not only make it longer, but they also create what amounts to distracting visual noise. In the absence of this visual noise, I find it easier to understand what a script is doing.

Procedures separate use of a command from its implementation, making it possible to modify the implementation without having to edit multiple files. While this simplifies editing (I'd rather edit one file than, say, ten), it also simplifies debugging. I don't know about you, but I don't want to grovel through a bunch of code blocks to track down a typo or *thinko*. It's much simpler to modify a single procedure. Yet another virtue of procedures is that you can use them in multiple scripts. After you have written and debugged a procedure, you can reuse it in multiple programs.

Logical Errors

A *thinko* is the mental or logical equivalent of a typo. For an interesting discussion of the origin of this geeky idiom, see its entry in the Jargon File at http://www.catb.org/esr/jargon/html/T/thinko.html.

A number of the example scripts in the previous chapters generated a random number between a minimum and maximum value, inclusive. I've had to write (well, cut-and-paste) the code several times and have hard-coded the minimum and maximum values. For example:

- From guess_rand.tcl: `set target [expr {int(1 + (rand() * 19))}]`;
- From blackjack.tcl: `set index [expr {int(rand() * [llength $list])}]`;
- From break.tcl: `set num [expr int(1 + (rand() * 21))] `;
- From cards.tcl: `set index [expr {int(rand() * [llength $list])}]`;
- From jeopardy.tcl: `set i [expr {int(1 + (rand() * 5)) }]`;

Without going into detail about why and how it works, the algorithm underlying all of these commands is, in pseudo-code:

```
random_num = minimum_val + (rand() * (maximum_val - minimum_val))
```

If your random number generator returns values between 0 and 1 inclusive, you can use this algorithm as is. However, if your random number generator does not return 1, which is the case with Tcl's `rand()` function, you need to add 1 to the expression `maximum_val - minimum_val`. Thus, the algorithm becomes:

```
random_num = minimum_val + (rand() * (maximum_val - minimum_val + 1))
```

It would be much simpler and more general to create a procedure (call it `RandomInt`) that accepts two parameters specifying a minimum value and a maximum value and that returns a random integer between (and including) those parameters. After I show you the syntax for defining procedures, that's exactly what I'll do.

But I'm getting ahead of myself. In addition to abstracting a block of code into a single, possibly parameterized command, Tcl procedures have two other features that you'll grow to appreciate: They can have default parameters, and they can accept a variable number of arguments. *Default parameters* are formal parameters which assume a predefined value if you omit the corresponding argument when you call the procedure. In the case of `RandomInt`, for example, I could define it so that the minimum value defaults to 1 unless specified, so that instead of writing `RandomInt 1 100`, I can write `RandomInt 100`. If I want a random number between 10 and 20, I would write `RandomInt 10 20`.

Procedures that accept a variable number of arguments add an additional level of generality to your procedures. Suppose that you have a procedure that formats and prints its two arguments in a particular manner. Later on, you discover that you need a similar procedure to format and print three arguments. Later still, you realize you need to do the same with four arguments. Rather than write three separate procedures to handle each case, you can write a single procedure that accepts at least two arguments but can accept an arbitrary number of arguments in excess of two. And, before you ask, yes, you can write procedures which have default parameters *and* which accept a variable number of arguments.

DEFINING PROCEDURES

The syntax for creating a procedure is:

```
proc name params body
```

The `proc` command creates a new Tcl procedure named *name* with the formal parameters specified by *params*. The commands specified in *body* are executed each time *name* is invoked. If *name* already exists as a command or procedure, the new procedure replaces it. The *params* argument is required in the procedure definition, but can be an empty list (`{}`), so it is possible to create a procedure that doesn't accept any arguments. If the *params* argument isn't empty, each argument is a list consisting of one or two elements, the first of which is the argument's name and the second of which, if present, is that argument's default value. If the last item in *params* is the keyword args, then each actual argument in excess of the defined formal parameters will be assigned to a list variable named args (which is local to the procedure).

I'll start with a simple procedure, the RandomInt procedure I promised (see random_int.tcl in this chapter's code directory):

```
proc RandomInt {min max} {
    set i [expr int($min + (rand() * ($max - $min + 1)))];
    return $i;
}


puts "Number between 0 and 100: [RandomInt 1 100]";
puts "Number between 1 and 4: [RandomInt 4]";
puts "Number between 1000 and 2000: [RandomInt 1000 2000]";
```

RandomInt accepts two arguments: min and max, which generate a random integer between and including those values, and return the generated value. Here's RandomInt in action:

```
$ ./random_int.tcl
Number between 0 and 100: 86
Number between 1 and 4: 3
Number between 1000 and 2000: 1805
```

Defining Procedures with Default Values

The rule for using default parameter values is:

Parameters with default values must appear after all parameters that do not have default values.

Default parameters must appear at the end of the parameter list because the interpreter assigns actual arguments to formal parameters sequentially. If the first parameter has a default value and subsequent ones don't, there is no way for Tcl to determine to which formal parameter to assign a given argument.

The next version of RandomInt uses a default value, defining min to have a default value of 1 (see random_def.tcl in this chapter's code directory):

```
proc RandomInt {max {min 1}} {
    set i [expr int($min + (rand() * ($max - $min + 1)))];
    return $i;
```

```
}
```

```
puts "Number between 0 and 100: [RandomInt 100 0]";
puts "Number between 1 and 4: [RandomInt 4]";
```

The difference with this definition of RandomInt is that min is defined as {min 1}, which means that if you call RandomInt with a single argument, that argument will be assigned to max, while min will be assigned the default value of 1. The other difference is that min is the second parameter, resulting in an ugly, counterintuitive calling interface for cases that need to specify the (non-default) minimum value.

Here's the output of random_def.tcl:

```
$ ./random_def.tcl
Number between 0 and 100: 98
Number between 1 and 4: 3
```

Defining Procedures with Variable Arguments

To create a procedure accepting a variable number of arguments, specify args as the final element of the formal parameter list. You must write code in the procedure body to process the arguments that are not assigned to formal parameters. Arguments not assigned to formal parameters are assigned to the procedure-local args list variable. I'll explain variable and procedure scope in the next section, "Understanding Variable and Procedure Scope." Again, I'll start with a simple procedure that prints its arguments one argument per line:

```
proc PrintArgs {args} {
    foreach arg $args {
        puts $arg;
    }
}
```

```
PrintArgs "5 arguments" Ace King Queen Jack;
PrintArgs "11 arguments" 1 2 3 4 5 6 7 8 9 10;
PrintArgs;
```

The body of PrintArgs consists of a simple foreach loop that iterates through the args list and prints each element. It doesn't specify a return value, so the default return value is the value of the last executed command, which in this case is the empty string (puts' return value). The argument list is the special parameter args, so you can pass zero or more arguments to

PrintArgs. Here's an example of PrintArgs at work (see print_args.tcl in this chapter's code directory):

```
$ ./print_args.tcl
5 arguments
Ace
King
Queen
Jack
11 arguments
1
2
3
4
5
6
7
8
9
10
```

Notice that the PrintArgs invocation that has an empty argument list results in no output. Another feature to notice is the list-oriented nature of the arguments. Specifically, the first arguments of the first two PrintArgs calls are the two-element sublists 5 arguments and 11 arguments; the foreach loop handles these sublists as a single element, as you would expect.

A slightly more useful procedure is ReverseArgs, which returns its argument list in reverse order:

```
proc ReverseArgs {args} {
proc ReverseArgs {args} {
    for {set i [expr [llength $args] - 1]} {$i >= 0} {incr i -1} {
        lappend reversed [lindex $args $i]
    }
        return $reversed;
}
puts [ReverseArgs Ace King Queen Jack];
puts [ReverseArgs 1 2 3 4 5 6 7 8 9 10];
#puts [ReverseArgs];
```

The ReverseArgs procedure's argument is the special parameter args, which means that it accepts zero or more arguments. However, because of the way the procedure body is defined, you must invoke ReverseArgs with at least one argument or else the return command will raise an error that the reversed variable you are trying to return doesn't exist. The reversal is accomplished by iterating backward through the list. The for loop does the bulk of the work, iterating from the end of the args list (using the expression end-$i and incrementing the counter variable i on each iteration) to its beginning. On each iteration, I use the lindex command to peel the next element off the end of the list. I use lappend to assign the value to the reversed list. After grabbing element 0 (which is actually the *last* element in this case), ReverseArgs returns the reversed list, which can then be printed or otherwise used by the calling command.

The output that follows shows how ReverseArgs works (see reverse_args.tcl in this chapter's code directory):

```
$ ./reverse_args.tcl
Jack Queen King Ace
10 9 8 7 6 5 4 3 2 1
```

I leave discovering what happens if you call ReverseArgs with no arguments as an exercise for you.

Understanding Variable and Procedure Scope

In general, *scope* determines where and when variables and procedures are visible. When referring to variables, scope controls the range of commands and procedures in which a given variable can be accessed. For procedures, the default scoping rules are simple:

- Procedure names not defined in a user-defined namespace have global scope which means that you can use a procedure anywhere in your script.
- Procedure names and variables names exist in different namespaces, which means you can have a variable named count and a procedure named count in the same script.

I don't discuss user-defined namespaces in this book, but you should be aware that Tcl procedures can have non-global scope if they are defined in user-defined namespaces.

Although Tcl's grammar allows you to have procedures and variables with the same name, I don't recommend taking advantage of this feature in practice unless you have a compelling reason to do so. The Tcl interpreter can easily and efficiently disambiguate identically named procedures and variables; your mental interpreter might not be so readily adept.

For variables, scoping rules are slightly more complicated, but only slightly:

- Variables defined outside of any procedure are global variables and can be used any-where in the script, except inside procedures. Global variables are not, by default, visible inside procedures.

- Variables defined inside a procedure are said to be local to that procedure. That is, a variable named count in the procedure FooProc is different from a variable named count in BarProc.

- To use a global variable inside of a procedure, you must use the global command to make that variable visible to the procedure.

So much for the theory and rules. Practically speaking, consider a script that defines a variable named count. Suppose that this same script has a procedure which *also* defines a variable named count and a procedure named count:

```
proc SetCount {} {
    set count 9;
    puts "In SetCount, count is $count";
}

proc count {} {
    set count 0;
    puts "In count, count is $count";
}

set count 10;
puts "Before count, count is $count";
count;
puts "After count, count is $count";

puts "Before SetCount, count is $count";
SetCount;
puts "After SetCount, count is $count";
```

The procedure SetCount sets a variable named count to 9; the count procedure sets its count variable to 0; the script itself sets the global count variable to 10. When control returns to the main script after the procedures terminate, the global count variable retains its original value of 10 (see local.tcl in this chapter's code directory):

```
$ ./local.tcl
Before count, count is 10
In count, count is 0
After count, count is 10
Before SetCount, count is 10
In SetCount, count is 9
After SetCount, count is 10
```

As you can see, the value of the global variable count is unaffected by either count or SetCount. Similarly, the Tcl interpreter has no problem distinguishing between the two variables named count and the procedure named count.

If your intent is to modify the global count, use the global command *inside the procedure* to add the global variable to the procedure's scope. The script global.tcl in this chapter's code directory shows you how to use global. The only change from the previous script is the definition of SetCount:

```
proc SetCount {} {
    global count;
    set count 9;
    puts "In SetCount, count is $count";
}
```

At the top of the procedure body, I inserted the command global count;, which adds the global variable named count to SetCount's scope. The effect is clear in the script's output:

```
$ ./global.tcl
Before count, count is 10
In count, count is 0
After count, count is 10
Before SetCount, count is 10
In SetCount, count is 9
After SetCount, count is 9
```

global's syntax is:

global *varName* ?...?

global adds each *varName* specified to the current scope. The global command *must* be used inside a procedure—using it in the top-level code has no effect—so if you need to modify a global variable in multiple procedures, you need to use the global command with that variable in each procedure.

Tcl Variables Are Passed by Value

Those readers with a programming background, particularly C, are no doubt wondering whether Tcl passes variables by reference or by value. By default, Tcl passes variables by value. Moreover, Tcl lacks a notion of passing a variable by reference, that is, of passing the memory address of a variable to a procedure, because Tcl lacks (fortunately or otherwise) pointers. Tcl *does* support an effectively equivalent operation, *pass by name*. If you need to pass a variable's name to a procedure, use the upvar command. upvar is more advanced a topic than I'm covering in this book, though, so I refer curious readers to the man page (man 3tcl upvar) for the gory details on upvar.

Analyzing Fortune Teller

Honestly, Fortune Teller is a simple game. You learned everything you need to know to write it yourself in the previous six chapters, except for the use of procedures. Its sole purpose in life is to illustrate the most salient features of defining and using Tcl procedures.

Looking at the Code

```
#!/usr/bin/tclsh
# fortune.tcl
# Display a randomly selected fortune

# Block 1
# Return a random integer between min and max, inclusive
proc RandomInt {min max} {
    set i [expr int($min + (rand() * ($max - $min + 1)))];
    return $i;
}

# Block 2
# Show the fortune at the specified index
proc ShowFortune {index} {
    global fortunes;
    puts [lindex $fortunes $index];
}

# Block 3
# A list of fortunes to get started
set fortunes [list {Avert misunderstanding by calm, poise, and balance.} \
```

```
{Day of inquiry.  You will be subpoenaed.} \
{Everything that you know is wrong, but you can be straightened out.} \
{Good news.  Ten weeks from Friday will be a pretty good day.} \
{Live in a world of your own, but always welcome visitors.} \
{So you're back... about time...} \
{Tomorrow will be cancelled due to lack of interest.} \
{You are fairminded, just and loving.} \
{You have a deep interest in all that is artistic.} \
{You may get an opportunity for advancement today.  Watch it!} \
{You will be divorced within a year.} \
{You will contract a rare disease.} \
{You will live to see your grandchildren.} \
{You'll be sorry...} \
{Your supervisor is thinking about you.}];

# Block 4
# A single command shows the fortune
ShowFortune [RandomInt 0 [llength $fortunes]];
```

Understanding the Code

Block 1 reuses the `RandomInt` procedure to return a randomly selected integer between two numbers. Nothing new here. Block 2 defines a gratuitous procedure named `ShowFortune`, which shows the user his fortune. `ShowFortune` accepts a single argument, `index`, which specifies the element from the `fortunes` array to display. `ShowFortune` uses the `global` command to access the global variable `fortunes`, which is necessary because the `fortunes` array is a global variable. Speaking of the global `fortunes` array, Block 3 defines it with 15 quips. A significant improvement, which will be possible after you read the next chapter (Chapter 8, "Accessing Files and Directories"), would be to read the list of fortunes from a file rather than tediously defining them inline.

After all of the set-up work is complete, actually displaying the user's fortune is anti-climactic, being reduced to a single command that calls both of the procedures defined at the beginning of the program. Here again, I took advantage of Tcl's command substitution and nested command capabilities: the result of the command `[llength $fortunes]` becomes the second argument to the `RandomInt` procedure, whose own result becomes the `index` argument to `ShowFortune`, which displays the fortune selected by the index.

Modifying the Code

Here are some exercises you can try to practice what you learned in this chapter:

7.1 Modify the RandomInt procedure to throw an error if min is greater than or equal to max. Test the behavior.

7.2 Modify block 4 of fortune.tcl to display fortunes until the user indicates to stop by pressing a key, such as "q" for quit or "x" for exit.

Procedures eliminate blocks of repetitive code, making scripts easier to edit, read, and understand. Procedures and variables reside in different namespaces, so it is possible, although not necessarily advisable, to have procedures and variables with the same name. By default, variables in Tcl have global scope but are not visible inside procedures. To make global variables visible inside a procedure, you must use the global command with that variable inside the procedure. Variables inside procedures are local to the procedure and thus do not clash with global variables, or like-named variables in other procedures.

ACCESSING FILES AND DIRECTORIES

Most non-trivial programs involve interacting with the host filesystem. In this chapter, you'll learn how to open, close, delete, and rename files. The chapter also shows you how to perform file I/O using the `puts` (output) and `gets` (input) commands and how to use the `format` command to "pretty print" output. Finally, you'll learn how to navigate the filesystem programmatically and work with file and directory names in a platform-neutral manner.

WORD SEARCH

This chapter's game, word_search.tcl in the code directory, is a simplified version of the classic bus and plane game. It shows you a grid of space-delimited litters. Each row of letters contains an embedded word that you have to find. Each row has one word oriented left to right; there are no words (at least deliberately) oriented on vertical or diagonal axes. As a hint, the words you have to find are commands used or introduced in this chapter. You start the game executing the script. Review the game grid and when you find a word in one of the rows, type the row number, press Enter, and then type the word you found and press Enter. After the script evaluates your input, it shows you the result and asks if you want to play again. To keep the screen tidy, I use the hoary UNIX command `tput clear`; on Windows, you will probably have to use the old DOS command `cls` unless you are using a UNIX emulator like Cygwin. Here are a few iterations of word_search.tcl:

```
$ ./word_search.tcl
1   e o p e n u g r i v c
2   n l v n j c l o s e d
3   j b p u t s s z m h i
4   s q n i d g g e t s t
5   h e r r e a d e r s e
6   z o t z g v a n e r s
7   f o r m a t a l b m c
8   d h n p s e e k p g e
9   a m a j y r a t e l l
Select a line (1-9): 2
What word do you see: closed
player: 'closed' puzzle: 'closed'
Correct!
Play again (Y/n)?  y
1   e o p e n u g r i v c
2   n l v n j c l o s e d
3   j b p u t s s z m h i
4   s q n i d g g e t s t
5   h e r r e a d e r s e
6   z o t z g v a n e r s
7   f o r m a t a l b m c
8   d h n p s e e k p g e
9   a m a j y r a t e l l
Select a line (1-9): 7
What word do you see: mat
Sorry.
Try again (Y/n)? y
1   e o p e n u g r i v c
2   n l v n j c l o s e d
3   j b p u t s s z m h i
4   s q n i d g g e t s t
5   h e r r e a d e r s e
6   z o t z g v a n e r s
7   f o r m a t a l b m c
8   d h n p s e e k p g e
9   a m a j y r a t e l l
Select a line (1-9): 1
What word do you see: open
Correct!
Play again (Y/n)? n
```

You've already seen and used many of the commands used in word_search.tcl. The file handling commands are new, though, as are some of the ways I've combined the commands. The balance of the chapter will fill in the gaps.

OPENING AND CLOSING FILES

Before you can do much else with a file, you have to open it. When you're done with a file, it is good practice, but not necessarily required, to close it. The syntax for opening a file is:

```
open name ?access? ?perms?
```

name identifies the name of the file to open. If specified, *access* defines the type of file access you want (see Table 8.1). Similarly, if *perms* is specified, it defines the UNIX-style file permissions to set on newly created files.

open returns a *channel ID*, a unique identifier or handle used to refer to the file in subsequent operations on it. Although you might not have realized it, you've already used channel IDs with the puts and gets commands. Recall that puts writes to stdout by default (that is, puts "foo" and puts stdout "foo" are identical commands). stdout is a channel ID. Similarly, when you use gets to read keyboard input, you have to write gets stdin. stdin is another channel ID.

The *access* argument indicates whether you want to read a file, write to a file, read *and* write a file, or append to a file. If not specified, Tcl assumes you merely want to read the file. Table 8.1 lists the possible values for *access*.

TABLE 8.1: FILE ACCESS MODES

Argument	Mode	Description
r	Read-only	Open for output: *name* must exist.
r+	Read/write	Open for input and output: *name* must exist.
w	Write-only	Open for output: If *name* exists, truncate it; otherwise create it.
w+	Read/Write	Open for input and output; If *name* exists, truncate it; otherise create it.
a	Append	Open for output, appending data to *name*; create *name* if it doesn't exist.
a+	Read/Write	Open for input or output, appending data to *name*; create *name* if it doesn't exist.

File permissions control who can do what to a file. I'm going to skip a tedious, detailed excursus on UNIX file permissions. Any good UNIX or Linux reference (and most bad ones, too) can get you up to speed on UNIX-style file permissions. What you most need to know is that unless otherwise specified, open commands that result in creating files apply a default mode of 0666, which means that they are readable and writable by everyone. As a matter of habit and security, I prefer to create files with mode 0644, which means that I can read and write them, but everyone else can only read them. If you are extremely paranoid, you can use a mode of 0600, which means that you can read and write the file but no one else can.

To close a file, the syntax is quite simple:

```
close id
```

id must be a channel ID returned by a previous open (or socket) command. One would think that closing a file is a simple operation, but the reality is slightly more complicated. When you issue the close command, several tasks occur before the file is really, truly closed:

- Any buffered output is flushed to disk.
- Any buffered input is discarded.
- The associated disk file or I/O device is closed.
- The channel ID is invalidated and cannot be used for subsequence I/O operations.

Although not strictly necessary, I vigorously encourage you to close files explicitly. When your script exits, any files that you opened will be closed. In the nominal case, this is fine. However, long-running scripts or scripts that open lots of files might use up operating system resources (on UNIX and UNIX-like systems, for example, file descriptors are a finite resource), so get into the habit of closing your files.

The following short script (open.tcl in this chapter's code directory) illustrates opening and closing a text file. The text file, sonnet20.txt, is Shakespeare's Sonnet XX and is also included in this chapter's code directory:

```
set fileId [open sonnet20.txt r]
puts "opened 'sonnet20.txt' with channel ID '$fileId'"
close $fileId

if {[catch {set fileId [open sonnet21.txt r+]} err]} {
    puts "open failed: $err"
    return 1
} else {
    puts "opened 'sonnet21.txt' with channel ID '$fileId'"
    close $fileId
}
```

Here's what the output should look like when you execute this script:

```
$ ./open.tcl
opened 'sonnet20.txt' with channel ID 'file5'
open failed: couldn't open "sonnet21.txt": no such file or directory
```

The first block of code opens the file sonnet20.txt in read-only mode, storing the returned ID in the $fileId variable. After opening the file, I promptly close it.

The second block of code *attempts* to open sonnet21.txt in read-write mode. However, because this is a cooked-up example and I knew that sonnet21.txt didn't exist, I embedded the open command in a catch statement to illustrate how to handle file access errors. If open fails for some reason, it raises an error. In the absence of the catch command, you'd see the standard, ugly Tcl stack trace followed by an abrupt, graceless exit. My error handler is only slightly more graceful and attractive, but the point I want to emphasize is that in real-world code, you need to code defensively and try to anticipate possible or common errors (such as files not existing).

I Don't Follow My Own Advice

The code samples in this book set a bad example. For clarity and brevity, most of the scripts in this book don't include error handling. Do as I say, not as I do!

If you review Table 8.1, you'll see that most of open's access modes will create files if they don't exist (w, w+, a, and a+). The key difference is that write operations (w and w+) will truncate a file that already exists (provided you have write permissions for the file), whereas append operations (a and a+) don't truncate an existing file. Rather, when you append to an existing file, it is opened for writing, and the file pointer is positioned at the end of the file so that write operations don't overwrite existing data. The following scripts, trunc.tcl and append.tcl in this chapter's code directory, illustrate the difference. trunc.tcl opens an existing file, junk, for writing, and then closes it:

```
set fileId [open junk w]
puts "opened 'junk' with channel ID '$fileId'"
close $fileId
```

Before you run this script, make sure a file named junk exists in the directory from which you execute the script. On Linux, UNIX, and Mac OS X, you could execute the command touch junk to create an empty, zero-length file named junk.

Using ls -l before and after running the script, you can see what happens:

```
$ touch junk
$ ls -l junk
-rw-r--r-- 1 kwall kwall 110622 2007-08-03 01:39 junk
$ ./trunc.tcl
opened 'junk' with channel ID 'file5'
$ ls -l junk
-rw-r--r-- 1 kwall kwall 0 2007-08-03 01:42 junk
```

You'll need a file named "junk" for this script to work and, naturally, the output of the ls commands will be different.

append.tcl, on the other hand, opens junk in append mode, which preserves its contents:

```
set fileId [open junk a]
puts "opened 'junk' with channel ID '$fileId'"
puts $fileId [info vars]
close $fileId
```

As you can see from the following commands, appending a file for appending leaves its existing contents remain intact and adds new data to the end of the file:

```
$ date > junk
$ cat junk
Sat Sep  1 20:04:05 EDT 2007
$ ./append.tcl
opened 'junk' with channel ID 'file5'
$ cat junk
Sat Sep  1 20:04:05 EDT 2007

tcl_rcFileName tcl_version argv0 argv tcl_interactive fileId errorCode auto_path error-
Info env tcl_pkgPath tcl_patchLevel argc tcl_libPath tcl_library tcl_platform
```

First, I redirect the output of the date command to the file named junk and then cat junk's contents. After I execute the append.tcl script, I cat junk a second time to show the the data I added was put at the end of the file and that its existing contents untouched.

CAUTION

R Means W and W Means R, Sometimes

In an unfortunate bit of perversity, the access modes r+ and w+ open a file for both reading and writing. In the case of r+, the file must exist. If you specify the w+ mode, the file will be created if it doesn't exist. The perversity to which I refer is not that there are two modes that do (almost) the same thing, but that the "r" in r+ mnemonically suggests reading, not reading and writing. Likewise, the "w" in w+ mnemonically suggest writing, not writing and reading.

The moral of this story is to be careful when opening files for writing. If you need to preserve the existing data, use the a or a+ mode and append data. If you don't care about the existing contents, use w or w+ as the situation requires.

READING FILES

I'm going to go out on a limb here and guess that you want to do more than just open and close files. Reading and writing them will probably be helpful. Fair enough. You have at least three options for reading a file for input: the `gets` command, which you've already seen; the `read` command; and the `scan` command. Which one should you use? Here are three rules of thumb:

1. Use `gets` to read and process one line of input at a time.
2. Use `read` if you want to read blocks of input without regard to end-of-line markers.
3. Use `scan` to read formatted input.

The following subsections cover the specifics of using each of these three input commands.

Using `gets` for File Input

So far in this book, you used `gets` to read input from stdin (the keyboard), using a command such as one of the following:

```
set line [gets stdin]
get stdin line
```

The first `gets` command reads input from stdin, discards the terminating newline, and returns the fetched line, which the `set` command stores in the variable `$line`. If a blank line had been read, `gets` would have returned the empty string, which would have been stored in $line. To differentiate between a blank line and the end-of-file, you have to use the EOF command on the I/O channel (stdin in this case). If EOF returns 1, end-of-file has been reached; if EOF returns 0, `gets` has not reached end-of-file.

The second `gets` command also reads input from stdin but, in this case, stores the input in the variable `$line` itself after discarding the trailing newline. In this form, `gets` returns the number of characters it read (*not* counting the newline). If it reads a blank line, then `gets` returns 0. If it encounters the end-of-file, `gets` returns -1. For file I/O, I think this form of `gets` is easiest to use because it automatically detects end-of-file, saving you from having to check for end-of-file conditions with an EOF call. This is the form of the command I'll use for the rest of the book when dealing with input from a file. For keyboard input, I'll continue to use the first form of the `gets` command.

Applying what you learned in the previous section about I/O channels, if you replace stdin with a channel ID returned by the open command, you can read from a file. The following script, gets.tcl in this chapter's code directory, demonstrates opening and reading a file:

```
set fileId [open sonnet20.txt r]
set totalChars 0
set totalLines 0

while {[set cnt [gets $fileId line]] != -1} {
    puts "($cnt chars) $line"
    incr totalChars $cnt
    incr totalLines
}
puts "read $totalChars chars"
puts "read $totalLines lines"

close $fileId
```

The first command opens sonnet20.txt for reading. The next two commands set a couple of counter variables I use while reading the input file. The most complicated part of the script is the while loop. In English, it simply means, "Read a line of input from the file, store the input text in the variable named line and the number of characters read in cnt. Keep doing this until you encounter end-of-file." Inside the while loop, for each line read, I display the number of characters read (not counting the terminating newline) and the text of the line; then I increment the number of characters read (incr totalChars $cnt) and the number of lines read. When gets hits the end-of-file, control drops out of the while loop, at which point I display the total number of characters and lines read, close the input file, and exit the program.

If you execute gets.tcl, the output should look like the following:

```
$ ./gets.tcl
(2 chars) XX
(0 chars)
(46 chars) A woman's face with nature's own hand painted,
(45 chars) Hast thou, the master mistress of my passion;
(42 chars) A woman's gentle heart, but not acquainted
(50 chars) With shifting change, as is false women's fashion:
(54 chars) An eye more bright than theirs, less false in rolling,
(39 chars) Gilding the object whereupon it gazeth;
```

```
(43 chars) A man in hue all 'hues' in his controlling,
(50 chars) Which steals men's eyes and women's souls amazeth.
(40 chars) And for a woman wert thou first created;
(48 chars) Till Nature, as she wrought thee, fell a-doting,
(36 chars) And by addition me of thee defeated,
(42 chars) By adding one thing to my purpose nothing.
(54 chars)    But since she prick'd thee out for women's pleasure,
(53 chars)    Mine be thy love and thy love's use their treasure.
(0 chars)
read 644 chars
read 17 lines
```

Using read for File Input

If you don't want or need to read and process an input file line-by-line, you can use the read command, which reads a specific number of characters or the entire file. read's syntax is:

```
read ?-nonewline? id
read id numChars
```

id is the file to read and *numChars*, if present, indicates how many characters to read from *id*. read's return value is the data read from *id*. In the first form of the command, read reads the entire file and, if -nonewline is specified, discards the last character of the file if it is a newline. In the second form of the command, read reads exactly *numChars* characters, unless it encounters EOF before reading the specified number of characters. In the latter case, read returns the data it was able to read.

Before explaining why you might want to use read instead of gets, have a look at the following script, read.tcl in this chapter's code directory. The source file, wssnt10.txt, is the complete text of Shakespeare's sonnets, courtesy of Project Gutenberg (http://www.gutenberg.org/etext/1041), and is also included in the code directory:

```
# Read the entire file
set fileId [open wssnt10.txt r]
set input [read $fileId]
puts "Read [string length $input] characters"
close $fileId

# Read the file 1024 characters at a time
set fileId [open wssnt10.txt r]
while {![eof $fileId]} {
```

```
        set input [read $fileId 1024]
        puts "Read [string length $input] characters"
}
close $fileId
```

In the first block of code, I read the entire file and then closed it. The second block of code reopens the file, reads it in 1024-character blocks, and then closes it. First, I have to close the input file explicitly and then reopen it before trying to read it a second time. Why? After the first read command completes, the file pointer is positioned at the end of the file. Accordingly, the next read or gets command has nothing to read. Closing and reopening the file resets the file pointer to the beginning of the file. As it happens, there's a smarter way to move the file pointer, the seek command, which you'll meet in the section, "Moving the File Pointer: Random Access I/O," later in this chapter.

Second, notice that the while condition uses the EOF command to test for an end-of-file condition on $fileId. Unlike the gets command, read does not return a special value (referred to as a sentinel value, or just a sentinel) to indicate it's at the end of the file. In fact, in the absence of the EOF command, read would happily continue to "read" the file, it just wouldn't return anything, so the script would be stuck in an infinite loop.

When you execute this script, the output should look like the following. I'll only show the first and last three lines of the output here to preserve space:

```
$ ./read.tcl
read 107701 characters
read 1024 characters
read 1024 characters
...
read 1024 characters
read 1024 characters
read 181 characters
```

Hardly riveting output, but the last line bears discussion. Although the read command requested 1024 characters, there were only 181 left in the input file, so read returned what was available.

Why use read instead of gets? Suitability is one reason, but the primary reason is efficiency. In this context, *suitability* just means that the task you are trying to perform might not require processing a file line-by-line or that the data itself isn't appropriate for line-by-line input. For example, a binary file can contain embedded newline characters that aren't used for line breaks *per se*. In such a case, read is the right command to use.

Although reading and processing input line-by-line with gets is convenient and easy, it is inefficient for large files because multiple small disk read operations are much slower than a single large read that takes advantage of the disk's read-ahead functionality. How inefficient? Consider Table 8.2. It shows the time required to read a 1GB text file using gets, using read to slurp up the entire file in one large read, and using read with various block sizes.

TABLE 8.2: I/O TIMES FOR GETS AND READS ON A 1GB FILE			
Command	**Read Size (chars)**	**Elapsed Time (secs)**	**MB/sec**
gets	N/A	65.9	15.5
read	N/A	25.9	39.5
read	64	68.4	15.0
read	128	37.4	27.4
read	256	22.4	45.7
read	512	14.7	69.6
read	1024	10.9	93.3
read	2048	9.2	111.8
read	4096	8.8	116.9
read	8192	8.3	122.8
read	16384	8.3	123.0
read	32768	8.4	121.7

As you can see in Table 8.2, read is *much* more efficient than gets. If you want to try this experiment yourself, create a 1GB file named bigfile and execute the script readtest.tcl in the readtest subdirectory of this chapter's code directory. Of course, the performance you see will be different on your system.

This Is *Not* a Rigorous Benchmark!

The I/O speeds reported by readtest.tcl are relative. The results are influenced by CPU speed, available memory, the other processes running on the system, the type and speed of your hard disk, the amount of on-disk cache, the filesystem type, the phase of the moon, and what you ate for lunch today. Use readtest.tcl to gain insight into the performance of gets and read, not to establish whether your computer is an I/O speed machine or a boat anchor.

WRITING FILES

Now that you've seen how to get data *in* to your program, I'll show you how to get data *out* of it. The two workhorse Tcl commands for output are puts, which you've already seen and used a good deal, and format. puts is great if you don't care about how the output looks, don't have any requirements for precisely formatted output, or if you are in a hurry. The format command is the tool to use if you *do* care how the output looks, do have requirements for carefully formatted output, and can take a little bit longer to write your script (but only a little bit longer).

Using puts for Output

As explained and shown in previous chapters, puts writes data to an output channel. So far, the output "channels" have been the screen, specifically, standard output and standard error (stdout and stderr, respectively) and, as you saw earlier in this chapter, disk files. In the general case, though, a *channel* is any stream capable of receiving output. So, in addition to stdout, stderr, and file IDs returned by the open command, puts can also write a network socket created by the socket command (I don't discuss network I/O in this book) or an output medium created by a Tcl extension. For example, you can use puts to send data to a printer or to a serial device (such as a mouse or a modem) if you have an output channel that has been set up for such a purpose.

To simplify the presentation, I've glossed over some of puts' subtleties because they are fine points that would obscure the point I am trying to make. For example, Tcl buffers output, so data you want to print using puts won't appear until the buffer is full or the buffer is specifically flushed (using the flush command). Buffering is handled by the underlying operating system, although you can modify buffering behavior using special-purpose Tcl commands.

Another issue I haven't addressed is how puts handles newlines. For better or worse, each of the major operating systems uses different end-of-line *(EOL)* sequences differently. Linux, UNIX, Macintosh OS X, and related systems use a linefeed character (\n) to indicate EOL; Macintosh systems before OS X use a carriage return (\r); and Microsoft Windows (and MS-DOS and OS/2) use a carriage return followed by a linefeed (\r\n). In large part, you don't have to concern yourself with this because Tcl handles the EOL translations for you automatically, converting EOLs to the character sequence appropriate for the host operating system. However, you can modify this behavior using the fconfigure command. Again, this is an advanced topic I won't cover in this book.

The point to take away from this discussion is that Tcl and puts by and large do the right thing with respect to output. If you find you need greater control, the capability is there. In the meantime, you can use puts for output and be blissfully ignorant of its under-the-covers details.

Formatting Output with `format`

If you have ever written C, chances are very good that you have used C's `printf()` function to print formatted output. Tcl's `format` command is much like `printf()`. The biggest difference is that `format` doesn't print the string it formats, it just returns the formatted string. Printing the formatted string is handled with the `puts` command. `format`'s syntax is:

```
format spec ?val …?
```

`format` formats one or more values, specified by *val* in the syntax diagram, according to the format specification defined by *spec*. The format specification can consist of up to six parts:

- A position specifier
- Zero or more flags
- A field width
- A precision specifier
- A word length specifier
- A conversion character

I'm going to focus on the items on the flags: field width, precision specifier, and conversion character. The position and word-length specifiers are less commonly used and are used in situations this book won't cover. Each argument of the format specifier begins with a percent sign, %, followed by zero or more modifiers, and ends with a conversion character.

Conversion characters indicate how to print, or convert, the corresponding argument in the value list. Although conversion characters appear last in the format specification, I cover them first so you'll know what you're trying to format. Table 8.3 lists the most frequently used conversion characters.

TABLE 8.3: COMMON FORMAT CONVERSION CHARACTERS

Character	Description
c	Displays an integer as the ASCII character it represents.
d	Signed integer.
f	Floating point value in *m.n* format.
s	String.
u	Unsigned integer.
X	Unsigned hex value in uppercase format.
x	Unsigned hex value in lowercase format.

A complete list of conversion characters is available in the `format` man page (man 3tcl format). For example, to format a string, you would use the command, `format "%s" "string to format"`. The command `format "%d:%x" int_val hex_val` would format a signed integer, followed by a literal colon, followed by a lowercase hexadecimal value. Although not specifically necessary, I use double quotes around the format specifier as a matter of habit. If the format specifier or the value to format contains embedded spaces, the quotes would be necessary.

Flags are modifiers used to specify padding and justification of the formatted output. Table 8.4 lists the valid flags.

TABLE 8.4: VALID FORMAT FLAGS

Flag	Description
–	Left-justify the field.
+	Right-justify the field.
0	Pad with zeros.
#	Print hex numbers with a leading 0x, octal numbers with a leading 0.
space	Precede a number with a space unless a sign is specified.

After the flags, you can specify a minimum field width and an optional precision value. For example, to format the floating point value 1.98, you could use any of the following commands (see format.tcl in this chapter's code directory):

```
puts [format "%f" 1.98]
puts [format "%5f" 1.98]
puts [format "%5.2f" 1.98]
```

The first command uses the default floating point formatting (`%f`). The second command uses a field width of 5 (`%5f`). The third command uses the same field width and adds a precision specifier (`%5.2f`). These commands correspond to the following output:

```
1.980000
  1.980000
 1.98
```

On my OS X system, the second line of output was not indented as it should have been. This is known as A Bug. Most of the example scripts in this chapter use `format` commands, so you can refer to these scripts for more examples of using the `format` command. The man page has complete details.

PARSING INPUT WITH scan

Neither gets nor read **exhaust Tcl's ability to process input. You can use Tcl's** scan **command to read input, much as the C language function** sscanf() **formats input.** scan**'s general syntax is:**

scan *str spec* ?*varName* …?

Unlike read, **which is ideal for reading from files, and** gets, **which is suitable for reading from stdin or the keyboard,** scan **excels at parsing strings. You can use it for raw keyboard or file input, but it is easier if you use** gets **or** read **to grab your input and then parse it using** scan. **You can use the same types of format specifiers with** scan **as you can with the** format **command.**

The reason I don't discuss scan **in the main body of the chapter is because I believe that Tcl's string commands and regular expression support provide the same functionality in a more powerful package.**

MOVING THE FILE POINTER: RANDOM ACCESS I/O

Earlier in this chapter, I noted that a read operation advances the file pointer through an I/O channel. In an example, I closed and reopened the input file to reposition the file pointer at the beginning of the file. While this type of sequential I/O is a common operation, you often want or need to read from arbitrary file locations or need to be able to reposition the file pointer without closing and reopening the file. Tcl's seek and tell commands provide this ability, which is referred to as *random access I/O*.

As an I/O operation proceeds, the file pointer's current position in the file, known as the *seek offset*, can be determined by using the tell command. tell's syntax is:

tell *channelID*

tell returns an integer string that indicates the current seek offset. If the specified I/O channel does not support seeking (process pipelines, for example, do not support seeking), tell returns -1.

To move the file pointer (change the seek offset), use the aptly-named seek command. Its syntax is:

seek *channelID offset* ?*origin*?

This command moves the file pointer *offset* bytes forward or backward relative to *origin* in the file referred to by *channelID. origin* must be one of start, end, or current and defaults to start if not specified. *offset* can be negative or positive. It is an error to seek backward (using a negative offset) from the beginning of a file but not to seek forward from the end of a file.

The following script, randread.tcl in this chapter's code directory, shows how you might use the seek and tell commands:

```
set fileId [open wssnt10.txt r]

seek $fileId 10 start
set input [read $fileId 10]
puts "Text between bytes 10 and 20: =>$input<="
puts "File pointer at byte: [tell $fileId]"

seek $fileId -25 end
set input [read $fileId 25]
puts "Last 25 characters: =>$input<="
puts "File pointer at byte: [tell $fileId]"

if {[catch {seek $fileId -5 start} err]} {
    puts "seek back from start: $err"
} else {
    puts "seek back from start: [tell $fileId]"
}

if {[catch {seek $fileId 5 end} err]} {
    puts "seek forward from end: $err"
} else {
    puts "seek forward from end: [tell $fileId]"
}

seek $fileId 0 end
puts "file size: [tell $fileId] bytes"

close $fileId
```

After opening the file, the first block of code moves the pointer 10 bytes into the file, reads the next 10 characters, and then displays the text it read between => and <= and the current position of the file pointer. The second code block positions the file pointer 25 bytes from the end of the file, reads 25 characters, and then displays the text it read and the current position of the file pointer.

The next two sections of code attempt to seek backward from the beginning of the file and forward from the end of the file. I use the `catch` command so an error during either operation won't abort the script. Notice in the output that reading backward from the beginning of the file causes an error but that reading forward from the end of the file moves the file pointer five characters forward, to offset 107706.

Positioning the file pointer past the end of the file works for several reasons. First, `seek` simply reports the position of the file pointer, an operation independent of reading or writing. `seek` has no idea whether you are going to read or write the underlying file. Secondly, while no filesystem of which I'm aware supports the notion of adding data to the front of a file, most (if not all) permit data to be appended to the end of a file. Accordingly, you have to be able to position the pointer past the end of the file to do so.

Finally, most filesystems allow you to create *sparse files*, or files that have holes in them. Such a file will have a length of N bytes, yet will contain fewer than N bytes of data. Byte ranges of files that contain no data are known as *holes*, and files that contain such holes are referred to as *sparse files*.

The last section of code shows you a trick for finding out a file's size in bytes: `seek` to the end of the file and then use `tell` to get the location of the file pointer. Unfortunately, you can't use this trick to determine the length of sparse files.

When executed, the script's output should look like the following:

```
$ ./randread.tcl
Text between bytes 10 and 20: => Project G<=
File pointer at byte: 20
Last 25 characters: =>ented as Public Domain.

<=
File pointer at byte: 107706
Seek back from start: error during seek on "file5": invalid argument
Seek forward from end: 107706
File size: 107701 bytes
```

You can also use `seek` and `tell` with output operations, as demonstrated in the following script (see randwrite.tcl in this chapter's code directory):

```
set fileId [open output.txt r+]
seek $fileId 0 end;
set oldSize [tell $fileId]
```

```
seek $fileId 10 start
puts "Offset before puts: [tell $fileId]"
puts -nonewline $fileId [string repeat * 10]
puts "Offset after puts: [tell $fileId]"

seek $fileId [expr $oldSize - 25]
puts "Offset before puts: [tell $fileId]"
puts -nonewline $fileId [string repeat * 10]
puts "Offset after puts: [tell $fileId]"

seek $fileId [expr $oldSize + 800]
puts "Offset before puts: [tell $fileId]"
puts $fileId [string repeat * 10]
puts "Offset after puts: [tell $fileId]"

seek $fileId 0 end
puts "New file length: [tell $fileId] bytes"

close $fileId
```

Perhaps the first question you'll ask when you look at this script is why I open the file I want to write in r+ mode (read/write), rather than for writing or appending. To insert new data or overwrite existing data, you must read the existing data before adding new data. If I open the file in w or w+ mode, I'll truncate the existing file. Similarly, if I open the file in a or a+ mode, data written to the file will wind up appended to the end of the file, regardless of where I position the file pointer before starting the write. The behavior in the append modes is somewhat counterintuitive, but if you think about it, it *is* called append mode. If it really bothers you, you could write a procedure that adds insert and overwrite modes to the open command, but that would just result in all the other Tcl programmers teasing you.

After opening the file, I seek to the end and then store its original size (actually, its byte length) in the variable $oldSize. I'll explain why in a moment. Next, I seek 10 bytes into the file and write 10 asterisks starting at that offset.

The next code block scribbles 10 more asterisks 25 bytes from the end of the file. In this case, though, I use the expression $oldSize - 25 to calculate the offset. I do this because I want to insert data at the *original* EOF; after the first puts command, the EOF has moved from byte 661 to byte 671. Schlepping around the original EOF offset enables me to write in the correct location.

The last write adds another 10 asterisks 800 bytes past the original EOF. Again, I use $oldSize as the reference point for the offset. After all the writing is done, I calculate and display the length of the modified file and close the file.

To execute this script and verify for yourself that it behaves as I've described, use the following sequence of commands:

```
$ cp sonnet20.txt output.txt
$ ls -l sonnet20.txt output.txt
-rw-r--r-- 1 kwall kwall 661 2007-08-08 03:18 output.txt
-rw-r--r-- 1 kwall kwall 661 2007-08-06 23:30 sonnet20.txt
$ ./randwrite.tcl
Offset before puts: 10
Offset after puts: 20
Offset before puts: 636
Offset after puts: 646
Offset before puts: 1461
Offset after puts: 1469
New file length: 1469 bytes
$ ls -l sonnet20.txt output.txt
-rw-r--r-- 1 kwall kwall 1472 2007-08-08 03:13 output.txt
-rw-r--r-- 1 kwall kwall  661 2007-08-06 23:30 sonnet20.txt
$ diff -a sonnet20.txt output.txt
3c3
< A woman's face with nature's own hand painted,
---
> A woma**********ith nature's own hand painted,
16c16
<   Mine be thy love and thy love's use their treasure.
---
>   Mine be thy love and thy lov**********eir treasure.
17a18
> **********
```

The cp command creates a copy of sonnet20.txt. The ls command verifies that the two files are identical. After executing randwrite.tcl, the second ls command shows that the two files have different sizes. The diff command, finally, shows the actual differences between the original file and its modified copy.

CAUTION   Bytes Versus Characters

The seek and tell commands calculate file positions in terms of bytes, or, rather, *byte offsets*. However, the read command operates in terms of *character offsets*. In most situations, this distinction doesn't matter because in the ASCII character set, each character is one byte long. Thus, reading five characters grabs five bytes of data. The distinction becomes important when you work with multibyte character sets (such as Asian language character sets), which use multiple bytes to encode a single character. For the purposes of this book, one byte equals one character; just be aware that this is not always the case.

WORKING WITH DIRECTORIES

Like any proper programming language, Tcl enables you move around in the filesystem and create, delete, and rename directories. When a Tcl script begins executing, its working directory is the directory from which it was invoked. To change your working directory, use the cd command. If you want to find out the current working directory, use the pwd command. The syntax of these commands is:

```
cd ?dirName?
pwd
```

If you omit *dirName*, cd sets the script's working directory to the directory specified by the $HOME environment variable. If $HOME is not set or the directory it references does not exist, cd raises an error and the script aborts. After successful execution, cd returns the empty string.

pwd returns the absolute pathname of the current directly. The short script that follows illustrates cd and pwd (see dirs.tcl in this chapter's code directory):

```
puts "Current directory: [pwd]"
cd /tmp
puts "Current directory: [pwd]"
cd
puts "Current directory: [pwd]"
```

The output from this script is what you would expect:

```
$ pwd
/home/kwall/tclbook/08
$ ./dirs.tcl
Current directory: /home/kwall/tclbook/08
Current directory: /tmp
Current directory: /home/kwall
```

```
$ pwd
/home/kwall/tclbook/08
```

As you can see, after the script terminates, the working directory of my shell is unchanged. This is because the Tcl script executes in a subshell, so when the subshell terminates, any changes it made to its execution environment (such as the initial working directory) are destroyed.

ANALYZING WORD SEARCH

As I noted at the beginning of the chapter, what's new in word_search.tcl is the file handling and the way commands are combined to get the desired results.

Looking at the Code

```tcl
#!/usr/bin/tclsh
# word_search.tcl
# Find words embedded in a string of letters stored in a text file


#
# Block 0
#
# Read the puzzle data from a file
proc ReadPuzzle {srcFile} {
    global starts stops lines

    # Open the puzzle file
    set fileId [open $srcFile r]

    # Read the source file
    while {[gets $fileId input] > -1} {
        lappend starts [lindex $input 0]
        lappend stops [lindex $input 1]
        lappend lines [lrange $input 2 end]
    }

    # Close the source file
    close $fileId
```

```tcl
}

# Clear the screen and redraw the puzzle
proc DisplayPuzzle {} {
    global starts lines

    # Display the puzzle
    exec clear >@ stdout
    for {set i 0} {$i < [llength $starts]} {incr i} {
        puts [format "%-4d%s" [expr $i + 1] [lindex $lines $i]]
    }
}

# Get the line on which the player wants to work
proc GetPlayerLine {min max} {
    puts -nonewline "\nSelect a line (1-9): "
    flush stdout
    set playerLine [gets stdin]

    # Did player choose a valid line number?
    if {$playerLine < $min || $playerLine > $max} {
        puts "Select a line number between $min and $max"
        exit 1
    }
    return $playerLine
}

# Get the word the player found
proc GetPlayerWord {} {
    puts -nonewline "What word do you see: "
    flush stdout
    set playerWord [gets stdin]
    return $playerWord
}

# Compare the player's guess to the correct answer
proc GuessCorrect {playerLine playerWord} {
    global starts stops lines
```

```
# Did user guess correctly?
set start [expr [lindex $starts [expr $playerLine - 1]] - 1]
set stop [expr [lindex $stops [expr $playerLine - 1]] - 1]
set line [lindex $lines [expr $playerLine - 1]]
set puzzleWord [join [lrange $line $start $stop] ""]
if {[string match -nocase $puzzleWord $playerWord]} {
    return true
} else {
    return false
}
}
#
# Block 1
#
# Main game loop
ReadPuzzle puzzle.txt
set continue "y"
while {$continue ne "n"} {
    DisplayPuzzle
    set playerLine [GetPlayerLine 1 9]
    set playerWord [GetPlayerWord]
    if {[GuessCorrect $playerLine $playerWord] == true} {
        puts "Correct!"
        puts -nonewline "Play again (Y/n)? "
    } else {
        puts "Sorry."
        puts -nonewline "Try again (Y/n)? "
    }
    flush stdout
    set continue [string tolower [gets stdin]]
}
```

Understanding the Code

Most of the code is in Block 0, the procedure definitions. The first procedure, ReadPuzzle, opens the puzzle data file passed as an argument and splits the data into three lists. To make sense of the data parsing, have a look at a sample data line from puzzle.txt:

2 5 e o p e n u g r i v c

Each row of data translates to a single row in the game grid. The data points are space-delimited. The first two values contain the starting and ending locations of the word in that row, and the rest of the data (11 letters) constitutes the row to display on the game grid. For example, in the record above, the word of interest begins in the second column and ends in the fifth column of the row. The columns are numbered from one, so the word in this row is "open." The while loop reads the data file line-by-line and uses lappend to create three ordered lists of starting and stopping locations and the text lines (starts, stop, and lines, respectively).

DisplayPuzzle uses a UNIX-specific command, clear, to clear the screen between each round. Because clear is an external command, not a Tcl built-in, I use the Tcl exec command to execute and redirect clear's ouput to stdout. The balance of the procedure is a simple for loop that uses the format command to display a nicely formatted line, consisting of the row number and the letters. I use the length of one of the lists as the loop control value; each of the three lists has the same length, so I could have used any of them.

GetPlayerLine solicits the row number in which the player is interested. The min and max arguments set the minimum and maximum values for the row number. If the player inputs a number outside of that range, the script terminates after printing a short usage message. Otherwise, GetPlayerLine returns the line number the user entered. GetPlayerWord asks the player to type in the word and returns it to the calling procedure.

The GuessCorrect procedure is word_search.tcl's workhorse. It accepts two arguments, the line number entered in GetPlayerLine and the word entered in GetPlayerWord, and then it compares the player's guess to the target word embedded in the data line. It returns true if the player's word matches the puzzle's word and false otherwise. I use list manipulation to extract the target word from the puzzle data. Recall that lists are indexed from zero. The line number displayed to the player and the starting and ending points for each word in the data file, however, are indexed from one. Accordingly, to extract the correct data, I have to subtract 1 from both $playerLine and from the index value passed to the lindex commands. I use the join command to convert the list of discrete letters returned by the lrange to a proper string. This step is necessary because lrange returns a list of elements that are separated by spaces, and I need a string to perform the comparison in the string match command.

Block 1, as you can see, is short and to the point. It invokes ReadPuzzle, sets the game loop control variable to y, and then enters the game play loop. The while loop displays the game grid, calls GetPlayerLine and GetPlayerWord to set up the comparison, and then calls GuessCorrect to evaluate the guess. It displays the result and then asks the player to play again. The way the enclosing while loop is written, gameplay terminates if the player enters anything but Y or y.

Modifying the Code

Here are some exercises you can try to practice what you learned in this chapter:

8.1 Modify the GetPlayerLine procedure to loop until the player enters a line number between min and max, inclusive, rather than terminating.

8.2 Modify the while loop in Block 1 so that only N or n will cause the game to exit.

8.3 Modify the code to support keeping score. The score should include how many words players guess correctly and incorrectly and how many total guesses the players made. Show a scoring percentage in addition to the raw scores for right and wrong guesses.

You won't get very far in your Tcl programming before it will become desirable, if not downright necessary, to read and write files. Use open and close to create I/O channels, the essential first step for performing file I/O. The gets and read commands can be used to read files, while the puts command works for writing files. If you prefer attractive, easy-to-read output, you'll spend quality time with the format command. Sequential file I/O is often the appropriate way to access files, but there are many situations in which you know exactly where in a file you need to be. In other cases, you might want to update a particular piece of data in a file. In such situations, random file access, brought to you by seek and tell, are the tickets to file I/O happiness.

This chapter concludes your whirlwind introduction to Tcl programming. With the material in these first eight chapters, and plenty of practice, you have everything you need to get started writing GUI programs using Tcl's graphical counterpart, Tk.

UNDERSTANDING TK PROGRAMMING

This chapter introduces you to the fundamental concepts of programming in Tk. Unlike the previous chapters, I'm not going to use a game program to illustrate the text. Instead, I'm falling back to that most ubiquitous of all programs, "Hello World," to illustrate Tk programming. As an introductory chapter, this chapter will be light on code and long on text, as it discusses topics including event-driven programming and widget attributes and operations. Covering this information here simplifies my job in the rest of the chapters because most Tk programming assumes familiarity with material presented in this chapter. The chapter closes with a description of each of the widgets available to Tk programs.

HELLO, TK WORLD!

The following script demonstrates most of the features of a Tk program (see hi.tcl in this chapter's code directory):

```
label .l -width [string length "Hello, Tk World!"] \
        -text "Hello, Tk World!";
button .b -text "Exit" -command exit;
pack .l -padx 40 -pady 10;
pack .b -padx 40 -pady 10;
```

Tk Programs Need wish

Unlike text-mode Tcl programs, which use the tclsh interpreter, Tk programs need to be interpreted using wish, the Tk interpreter (short for *windowing shell*). If you try to execute Tk scripts using tclsh, you'll get errors about invalid commands:

```
$ tclsh hi.tcl
invalid command name "label"
    while executing
"label .l -width [string length "Hello, Tk World!"] \
        -text "Hello, Tk World!""
    (file "hi.tcl" line 5)
```

When executed, hi.tcl displays the screen shown in Figure 9.1.

FIGURE 9.1

Hello World using Tk.

Left-clicking the Exit button closes the window and terminates the application.

Tk consists of about 45 Tcl commands that create user-interface widgets. *Widgets* are user-interface items such as windows, text boxes, drop-down boxes, scrollbars, and buttons that provide a particular type of functionality in a graphical user interface. For example, in Figure 9.2, the Hello World! application has two user-interface (*UI*) widgets: a label widget that contains the "Hello, Tk World!" text and a button widget that serves as the Exit button.

FIGURE 9-2

Tk widgets.

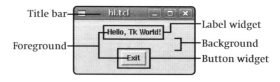

Tk programs are event-driven. In this context, an event can be keyboard activity; mouse movement or clicks; window creation, destruction, resizing, or movement; or I/O completion (both local and network I/O). Fortunately, Tk widgets handle most events automatically, so all you have to do is write the code specific to your application. If you want, you can use the bind command to associate commands and events. The reason you might do this would be to exercise greater control over the control flow in your Tk program or to override or supplement Tk's default event handling.

COMPONENTS OF A TK APPLICATION

The Hello World program in the previous section contains all of the components a Tk application needs, for example, UI widgets for receiving input and displaying output, the graphical conventions of the host platform, and the application-specific code that provides the functionality you want.

As you can see in Figure 9.2, Hello World sports two Tk-specific widgets, a text label and a button. The button, naturally, creates an on-click event when it is pressed and released, causing the command associated with that button to execute. The label is the canvas, if you will, on which our cheery message displays (Tk also has a canvas *widget*, but that is the subject of Chapter 15, "The Canvas Widget"). Figure 9.2 also calls out the foreground and background areas. These are not widgets themselves, but they *are* widget attributes that you can set, for example, by changing their color.

The other graphical elements of the window shown in Figure 9.2, such as the title bar and the control buttons on the left and right sides of the title bar, are *not* Tk widgets. Rather, they are created and managed by the underlying graphical system in use. I captured Figure 9.2 on a Linux system (Ubuntu 7.04, to be precise) using the GNOME window manager. For comparison, have a look at Figure 9.3, which shows the Hello World application running on Mac OS X, while Figure 9.4 shows Hello World running on a Windows XP system.

FIGURE 9.3

Hello World on
Mac OS X.

FIGURE 9.4

Hello World on
Windows XP.

For the record, I didn't modify the code at all to run on OS X or Windows. I just copied the script file to the appropriate system and used each platform's native wish executable to run the script. Notice that Tk readily adapts to the UI conventions (the "look-and-feel") of the host operating system or graphical system.

The other component of any Tk application is the application-specific Tcl (or Tk) code you write that provides the desired functionality. Hello World's code is pretty simple. The first line creates a label named .l containing the text Hello, Tk World! I use a plain vanilla Tcl command, string length, to set the width of the label, but this is not strictly necessary because Tk automatically sizes the label to contain the specified text. The second line of code creates a button named .b with the word Exit on it that invokes Tcl's exit command when the button is activated.

The final two commands use the pack geometry manager to arrange the specified widgets in the parent widget. I'll discuss geometry managers in later chapters (the pack geometry manager in particular is covered in the next chapter), but they are responsible for laying out and managing the widgets in a window. In this case, I use the pack command to position the text label at the top of the window with 40 pixels of space, or *padding*, on either side and 10 pixels of padding above and below the label. Next, I place the button below the label, again using 40 pixel pads on the sides and 10 pixel pads on the top and bottom. Order matters—if I had reversed the two pack commands, the button would appear above the label. More about pack in the next chapter.

Geometry managers serve another important function: They *register* widgets with the windowing system so they will be visible. Just defining a widget isn't enough; it must be activated by asking the geometry manager to map it into a window.

NAMING TK WIDGETS

Tk widgets are arranged in a hierarchy which establishes a parent-child relationship. The top-level widget is named . (period), which corresponds to the main application window. The initial period in the name is *required*. Subsequent periods denote that the widget to the right of the period is a child of the widget whose name appears to the left of the period. Accordingly, widget names cannot contain embedded periods.

The main application window is the parent of all other widgets in the application. Thus, the .l label widget and the .b button widget are children of the main application window. Similarly, if I create two smaller labels inside the .l label named top and bottom, they would be named .l.top and .l.bottom. This means, for example, that the label named top is the child of the label named l, which in turn is the child of the top-level or root widget, which is named...

Widget names must begin with either lowercase letters or numbers, an artifact of Tk's origins in UNIX and the X Window System. Without going into the gory details, the X resource database is a configuration system for X applications and their constituent widgets. The resource database uses initial uppercase letters in its resource names, so Tk uses lowercase letters (and digits) to avoid conflicts with the resource database and to provide an easy, mnemonic method to relate Tk's widget configuration items to X's configuration items.

To summarize, the following rules apply to Tk widget names:

- The initial period is required.
- Names cannot include embedded periods.
- Names must begin with a lowercase letter or a digit.

UNDERSTANDING EVENT-DRIVEN PROGRAMMING

Although it sounds intimidating, event-driven programming is simple from the application programmer's perspective. After widgets are initialized and an application is running, Tk-based programs enter an event loop. Consider the event loop to be a big `switch` command (as discussed in Chapter 5, "Working with Lists"). Each widget in the application can generate one or more unique events. In terms of the `switch` command as described in Chapter 5, each event corresponds to a pattern. When an event occurs, such as a key press, Tk searches for the matching pattern in its list of possible events to find the *event handler* (the body of code that needs to be executed) corresponding to that event and executes it. After executing the handler, control reenters the main event loop and waits for another event to occur. In most applications, multiple events can occur nearly simultaneously, so the event loop includes a queue onto which pending events are enqueued until they are handled.

The good news for you is that Tk handles the event loop and the event queue for you. Your mission is to decide to which events you want to respond. For example, in my Hello World program, when the Exit button is clicked, I want the `exit` command invoked. Tk's button widget is already "wired" to invoke a handler (you can tell this is the case because it supports the `-command` option); all I had to decide was what the handler would be. In Hello World, I used Tcl's `exit` command, but I could have invoked any built-in Tcl command or written a procedure of my own.

WIDGET OPTIONS

If all you could do with Tk was create widgets using their stock appearance and default behaviors, Tk's usefulness would be limited. However, all of Tk's widgets support a common set of attributes and options that considerably extend their capabilities. In addition to the standard options and attributes (see Table 9.1), each individual widget has its own unique attributes and options that enable it to function and enable developers to customize and control that widget. Instead of repeatedly listing the standard options and attributes that all Tk widgets support, Table 9.1 lists them once. Subsequent chapters will introduce only options and attributes unique or specific to the widgets under discussion.

TABLE 9-1: STANDARD TK WIDGET OPTIONS

Option	Description
-activebackground	Sets the background color of the active element; the *active element* is the element over which the cursor is positioned or on which a mouse button is pressed.
-activeborderwidth	Sets the width in pixels of the border of the active element.
-activeforeground	Sets the foreground color of the active element (see -activebackground).
-anchor	Sets the position of text in a widget (one of n, ne, e, se, s, sw, w, nw, or center).
-background	Sets the background color.
-bd	Alias for -borderwidth.
-bg	Alias for -background.
-bitmap	Specifies the bitmap to display in the widget.
-borderwidth	Sets the width of border around (outside) a widget.
-compound	Indicates whether a widget should display both text and a bitmap simultaneously and the position of the bitmap relative to the text (one of bottom, top, left, right, or center).
-cursor	Sets the mouse cursor used when the cursor is positioned over the widget.
-disabledforeground	Sets the foreground color used for disabled widgets.
-exportselection	Toggles whether or not the selected text in a Tk widget should also be the X selection.
-fg	Alias for -foreground.
-font	Sets the font used to draw text on a widget.
-foreground	Sets the foreground color for a widget.
-highlightbackground	Sets the background color of a highlighted region of a widget that has the input focus.
-highlightcolor	Sets the color of a highlighted region of a widget that has the input focus.
-highlightthickness	Sets the width of the highlighted region of a widget that has the input focus.
-image	Sets the image displayed in a widget, overriding -bitmap and -text.
-justify	Sets the alignment of text in a multi-line text widget; must be one of left, right, or center.
-padx	Sets the amount of padding to the right and left sides of a widget.
-pady	Sets the amount of padding above and below a widget.

Option	Description
-relief	Sets the 3D effect of a widget; must be one of flat, groove, raised, ridge, sunken, or solid.
-repeatdelay	Sets the delay in milliseconds a button or key must be depressed before it starts to autorepeat, used with -repeatinterval.
-repeatinterval	Sets the number of milliseconds between auto-repeated key and mouse button presses; used with -repeatdelay.
-selectforeground	Sets the foreground color used for selected items.
-text	Sets the string displayed in a widget.
-textvariable	Sets the variable whose value is the string to display in a widget; when the value changes, the widget text updates automatically.
-underline	Sets the character index of a character to underline in a widget.
-wraplength	Specifies the maximum length of a line of text before it will be wrapped.

That an option is considered *standard* does not also mean that all widgets support the option. For example, the option -activeborderwidth is standard, but in practice, only those widgets that display multiple elements simultaneously, such as menus or top-levels, support it. Menus, for example, only display a single submenu at a time, so they do not support the -activeborderwidth option.

But Wait! There's More!

Despite its length, Table 9.1 is not an exhaustive list of all of Tk's standard widget options. The options manual page (man 3tk options) lists all options that are considered standard in any given release of Tk. As of Tk 8.4.14, I counted 42 so-called standard options. I recommend browsing the list to see the complete list.

SURVEYING TK'S WIDGETS

Table 9.2 lists the widgets supported in Tk 8.4 and the chapter in this book where they are discussed. There are "only" 18 widgets, but when you consider the attributes and options they support, you'll quickly realize that the Tk toolkit is rich and full-featured.

Strictly speaking, the widget names listed in Table 9.2's first column are actually the *commands* that create the corresponding widget. The distinction is subtle and not important in practice, but if you need to be precise, well, there you are. In this chapter, I won't describe the listed widgets because I cover all of them in subsequent chapters.

TABLE 9-2: TK WIDGETS

Widget	Chapter	Description
button	10	Creates a command button.
canvas	15	Creates a canvas on which graphic primitives and widgets can be drawn.
checkbutton	10	Creates a checkbox or toggle button.
entry	12	Creates an editable, one-line text-entry box.
frame	11	Creates a container for positioning other widgets.
label	11	Creates a read-only, multi-line text box.
labelframe	11	Creates a frame that also has label-like features.
listbox	13	Creates a scrollable, line-oriented list.
menu	10	Creates a menu.
menubutton	10	Creates a menu item that displays a menu.
message	11	Creates a read-only, multi-line text box in a dialog box.
panedwindow	11	Creates a container for displaying other widgets in a pane-like manner.
radiobutton	13	Creates one of a set of radio buttons for setting a variable's value.
scale	15	Creates a slider widget that can scale the value of a variable.
scrollbar	14	Creates a widget that scrolls the viewport of another widget.
spinbox	12	Creates a text-entry widget that adjusts a variable's value using spinner buttons.
text	14	Creates a general-purpose text-entry widget.
toplevel	11	Creates a frame that becomes a new top-level window.

Tk programs are more than just Tcl programs with a layer of eye candy applied. Tk implements a full event-driven programming model for graphical applications and includes a rich set of highly configurable UI elements, called widgets, to give Tcl applications the same smooth, easy-to-use graphical interface as other graphical toolkits. Although Tk's widgets are its own, Tk applications adopt the look and feel of the host platform's native windowing system, freeing Tk developers to focus on functionality instead of emulating an interface.

Like many graphical toolkits, the Tk programming model arranges widgets in a hierarchical, parent-child relationship. This arrangement makes it easy to manage groups of widgets at once. Although Tk relies heavily on event-driven programming, application developers rarely need to be concerned with the mechanics of the event loop; rather, developers only need to select or write the handler for a given event generated by a widget. Tk takes care of the rest of the event model automatically, again, freeing Tk developers to focus on their application.

Tk 8.4 defines 18 widgets for programmers to create and use. This might seem like a small number, but the range of available widgets covers the gamut of standard graphical UI elements (buttons, frames, text entry and display, list boxes, and scrollbars). Between the variety of widgets available and their flexibility, you could write a lot of Tcl programs and never need anything more than what's available in the standard Tk toolkit.

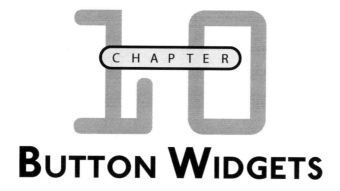

BUTTON WIDGETS

U nless you've been living in an unelectrified cave for the last decade, you are accustomed to clicking buttons. After providing more information about the first of Tk's three geometry managers, pack, this chapter looks at Tk's button widgets. In addition to learning how to use buttons, I'll show you how to use color in a Tk application and how to bind buttons to commands and events.

MEMORY TEST

This chapter's game, Memory Test, flashes buttons arranged in a grid in a given sequence (see Figures 10.1-10.4) and then asks you to repeat that sequence from memory, much like the game Simon (except there are no musical tones to accompany the flashing buttons).

FIGURE 10.1

Click the Play button to begin the game.

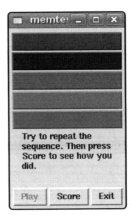

FIGURE 10.2

Remember the order in which the colored buttons flash.

FIGURE 10.3

Click the buttons in the correct sequence to win.

FIGURE 10.4

Click the buttons
out of order, and
you'll lose.

PACKED AND READY: THE PACK GEOMETRY MANAGER

As I remarked in Chapter 9, geometry managers arrange widgets on the screen, register them with the underlying windowing system, and manage their display on the screen. Of the three geometry managers Tk uses, pack, grid, and place, pack and grid are general-purpose. I start with pack because it is the one I use most often and because it was the first geometry manager Tk used. I'll discuss the grid geometry manager in Chapter 11, "Windows, Frames, and Messages."

The first thing to understand is that pack is constraint-based, meaning that rather than specifying precise placement information for widgets, you tell pack in general terms how you want widgets placed, that is, you define limits or *constraints* on widget placement, and then allow pack to work out the placement details itself. The upside to this method is that pack is easier to use precisely *because* you don't have to fuss with placement details; the downside to this placement model is that if you don't understand how pack's algorithm works, the results you get will surprise you or might not be what you wanted or expected.

NOTE Masters, Slaves, Parents, and Children

Recall that widgets are arranged hierarchically. As I use them in this book, the terms *master* and *parent* are equivalent and refer to widgets that contain other widgets. Likewise, *slave* and *child* are equivalent and refer to widgets that are contained within master or parent widgets.

The packer works from an ordered list of slaves referred to as the *packing list*. When you use -in, -before, and -after, you are inserting new slaves into specific positions in the packing list. Otherwise, as widgets are packed, they are added to the end or bottom of the packing list. After creating a cavity into which to place widgets, the packer processes the packing list in order, doing the following:

1. Assigns a rectangular area, or *parcel*, of the cavity to the widget on the side of the cavity specified by -side (the bottom if -side is not specified).
2. Dimensions the slave, which is its requested width plus twice the sum of -ipadx and -padx and its requested height plus twice the sum of -ipady and -pady.
3. If -fill is x or both, the width is expanded to fill the parcel width minus twice the value -padx, if specified. Likewise, if -fill is y or both, the height is expanded to fill the parcel height minus twice the value of -pady, if specified. If -fill is all, both the width and height are expanded to fill the parcel.
4. If the widget is smaller than the parcel, the value of -anchor, if specified, controls where the widget will be placed, offset by the value(s) of -padx and/or -pady, if specified.
5. The size of the parcel is subtracted from the cavity, leaving the remaining cavity space for the next slave.
6. If the size of the parcel isn't large enough to contain the slave, the slave gets the remaining space.
7. If the cavity space shrinks to zero, remaining slaves will be unmapped (removed from the screen) until the master window is large enough to hold them.
8. After all slaves have been placed, remaining cavity space, if any, is evenly allocated to all slaves for which the -expand option was set. Horizontal space is evenly allocated to expandable slaves whose -side option, if any, specified left or right; and vertical space is evenly allocated to expandable slaves whose -side option, if any, specified top or bottom.

Figure 10.5 illustrates the layout of a widget on the screen.

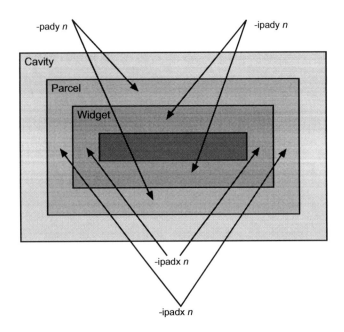

FIGURE 10.5

Widget layout.

To get you over the initial hump, here are some tips for using `pack`:

- The parent must be created before you can pack widgets into it.
- Pack vertically or horizontally, but not both.
- Use `-in`, `-before`, and `-after` to specify a slave's master widget.

Table 10.1 shows the arguments that `pack` supports.

TABLE 10.1: PACK ARGUMENTS	
Option	**Description**
`-after` *other*	Inserts the slave window in the packing order after the window specified by *other* and uses *other*'s master as the slave's master.
`-anchor` *position*	Places each slave window at *position* in its parcel (defaults to center).,
`-before` *other*	Inserts the slave window in the packing order before the window specified by *other* and uses *other*'s master as the slave's master.
`-expand` *Boolean*	Expands the slave to consume extra space in the master if true; defaults to 0 or false.
`-fill` *style*	Defines the fill behavior of a slave that is smaller than its parcel; must be one of none, x, y, or both.
`-in` *other*	Inserts the slave window into the packing order of the master specified by *other*.
`-ipadx` *n*	Specifies *n* as the amount of internal horizontal padding of the slave.
`-ipady` *n*	Specifies *n* as the amount of internal vertical padding of the slave.
`-padx` *n*	Specifies *n* as the amount of horizontal padding to add outside the widget.
`-pady` *n*	Specifies *n* as the amount of vertical padding to add outside the slave.
`-side` *side*	Packs the slave against *side* of the widget; must be one of left, right, top, or bottom (defaults to bottom).
`configure`	Sets the configuration options for slave widgets.
`forget`	Removes specified slaves from the packing list, removing them from the screen.
`info`	Returns the configuration of the specified slave.
`propagate`	Disables/enables propagation of a master's geometry settings to its slaves.
`slaves`	Returns a list of slaves in a specified master's packing order.

BUTTON, BUTTON, WHO'S GOT THE BUTTON?

Tk's buttons come in the three flavors listed below:

- `button`—Creates `button` widgets.
- `checkbutton`—Creates `checkbutton` widgets.
- `radiobutton`—Creates `radiobutton` widgets.

Actually, there's a fourth button widget, the `menubutton`, but I cover it in the section, "A Smörgåsbord of Menus," because it makes more sense to discuss `menubuttons` in the context of the menu widget. Figure 10.6 shows what each of these buttons looks like in its default, unconfigured state.

FIGURE 10.6

Basic Tk button
widgets.

Sure, they're not much to look at just now, but as you'll see in the rest of this section, Tk's button widgets are highly configurable and support most, if not all, of the options and capabilities sophisticated GUI users have come to expect.

Plain Vanilla Buttons

I'll start with the simplest of Tk's buttons, the eponymously named `button` widget. Its syntax is:

```
button name ?args?
```

This command creates a button whose *name* is name with the attributes and command options specified by *opts*. Table 10.2 lists the arguments the `button` command supports.

TABLE 10.2: BUTTON ARGUMENTS

Option	Description
-command	Specifies the command to execute when the button is pressed.
-default	Defines the state used for the default appearance, which must be one of `normal`, `active`, or `disabled`.
-height	Sets the button's height.
-overrelief	Specifies a non-default relief when the cursor hovers over the button.
-state	Specifies the button's current state, which must be one of `normal`, `active`, or `disabled`.
-width	Sets the button's width.
cget	Returns the value of the specified option.
configure	Returns or sets the button's configuration options.
flash	Flashes the button by alternating between its active and normal colors.
invoke	Executes the Tcl command associated with the button, if one is defined.

Tk's widget commands support two kinds of arguments: options and commands. *Options* are prefixed with a hyphen, and each option is usually followed by an argument. The -command option, for example, specifies a Tcl command to execute when the widget is executed, while the -height option specifies the widget's height. *Commands* perform operations on the widget, such as the configure command, which modifies or queries the widget's current configuration, and the flash command, which causes the widget to flash. Some commands accept no arguments, others accept a single argument, and still others accept multiple arguments.

In the case of the button command, you'll usually want to modify the width or height, the command it executes, or click it programmatically by using the invoke command.

The following script, button.tcl in this chapter's code directory, gets you started with buttons:

```
proc FlashButton {b} {
    # Save the original color
    set ocolor [$b cget -activebackground]       $b configure -activebackground red
$b flash      # Restore the original color
    $b configure -activebackground $ocolor
}

set lFlash [label .flash -width 20 -text "Flash Activate button"]
set lActivate [label .activate -width 20 -text "Activate Exit button"]

set bExit [button .e -width 8 -text "Exit" -state disabled \
    -command exit]
set bActivate [button .a -width 8 -text "Activate" \
    -command {$bExit configure -state normal}]
set bFlash [button .f -width 8 -text "Flash" \
    -command {FlashButton $bActivate}]

pack $lFlash
pack $bFlash -pady {0 20}
pack $lActivate
pack $bActivate -pady {0 20}
pack $bExit
```

When you execute this script, the initial screen should resemble Figure 10.7.

Basic Tk command
buttons.

The FlashButton procedure accepts a single argument, the name of a button to flash (using the button widget's flash command). Because the flash is so quick, I use the configure command to change the active background color to red (-activebackground red) before flashing the button. That way, when the button flashes, it is easier to see. After flashing the button, FlashButton restores the original background color, which is stored in the ocolor variable using the cget command at the beginning of the procedure.

Next, I create two labels to provide some descriptive text for their associated buttons. As a convention, I use an initial lowercase l (ell) to indicate that the variables (lFlash and lActivate) refer to label widgets. As with most coding conventions, it matters less *what* the convention is than it does that you choose and use one. This is mostly for your own sanity, but it helps other people who read your code to understand it, too. Similarly, for readability, I assigned easily recognized pathnames to the label widgets, .flash for the Flash button's label and .activate for the Activate button's label.

The next step is to create the buttons (I use an initial b for variables that refer to button widgets). The Exit button, a reference to what is stored in the bExit variable, is initially disabled (-state disabled), as you can see in Figure 10.7. When enabled and clicked, it executes the Tcl exit command to terminate the script.

The Activate button (accessed through the bActivate variable) comes next. When clicked, it changes the state of the Exit button to normal, meaning that the Exit button is enabled. I defined the Activate button *after* the Exit button because I needed to refer to $bExit when specifying $bActivate's -command option. Similarly, the Flash button ($bFlash) had to be defined after $bActivate because $bFlash's -command invokes the FlashButton procedure with an argument of $bActivate.

Click the Flash button to flash the Activate button. When you're done amusing yourself with that, enable the Exit by clicking the Activate button. Finally, click the newly enabled Exit button, shown in Figure 10.8, to terminate the script.

FIGURE 10.8

One Tk button can modify another button's state.

Okay, so it isn't a mind-numbingly awesome program, but it does demonstrate some of the key features of Tk's `button` widget.

Check Buttons

Tk's `checkbutton` widget is equivalent to what are known as *option buttons* in other windowing toolkits. Its syntax is identical to the `button` widget's syntax:

`checkbutton` *name* ?*args*?

In addition to all the functionality of plain vanilla Tk buttons, `checkbuttons` also have a variable associated with them. When you select a `checkbutton`, the indicator is set (or "on"), and its linked variable's value is set to 1 (the default) or the value specified by the `-onvalue` attribute. Deselecting or clearing a `checkbutton` clears or unsets the indicator and sets the variable's value to 0 by default or the value specified by the `-offvalue` attribute. You can also use a `checkbutton` widget's `-command` option to execute a Tcl command when the widget is clicked with the left mouse button.

Check buttons are often used in windows or tabs that set multiple options for program behavior. Unlike radio buttons, discussed in the next section, multiple `checkbutton` widgets can be set at once (radio buttons are linked together and only one can be set at a time). When used in this way, script code interrogates the value of the associated variable and sets the program's behavior based on that value.

Tk's `checkbutton` widget supports a wider array of options than does the plain `button` widget, as you can see in Table 10.3.

TABLE 10.3:	CHECKBUTTON ARGUMENTS
Options	**Description**
-command	Specifies the command to execute when the checkbutton is pressed.
-height	Sets the checkbutton's height.
-indicatoron	Determines if the indicator is on (true) or off (false).
-offrelief	Specifies the relief if the indicator is not drawn and the checkbutton is off.
-offvalue	Sets the value of the associated variable when the checkbutton is off (defaults to 0).
-onvalue	Sets the value of the associated variable when the checkbutton is on (defaults to 1).
-overrelief	Specifies a non-default relief when the cursor hovers over the checkbutton.
-selectcolor	Specifies the checkbutton's background color when it is selected.
-selectimage	Specifies the image to display when the checkbutton is selected and -image is also specified.
-state	Specifies the checkbutton's current state, which must be one of normal, active, or disabled.
-variable	Sets the name of the variable associated with the checkbutton.
-width	Sets the checkbutton's width.
cget	Returns the value of the specified option.
configure	Returns or sets the checkbutton's configuration options.
deselect	Unselects the checkbutton and sets its associated variable to the value specified by the -offvalue attribute.
flash	Flashes the checkbutton by alternating between its active and normal colors.
invoke	Executes the Tcl command associated with the checkbutton, if one is defined.
select	Selects the checkbutton and sets its associated variable to the value specified by the -onvalue attribute.
toggle	Toggles the checkbutton's selected state and sets the value of the associated variable to its "on" or "off" value as appropriate.

The following listing, ckbutton.tcl in this chapter's code directory, shows how you can use checkbuttons and regular buttons together:

```
proc DoButton {action ckbuttons} {
    foreach ckbutton $ckbuttons {
        switch $action \
            toggle { $ckbutton toggle } \
            clear { $ckbutton deselect } \
            set { $ckbutton select }     }
}
```

```
proc ShowStatus {ckbuttons} {
    foreach ckbutton $ckbuttons {
        set var [$ckbutton cget -variable]        global $var        set val
[set $var]        puts "$var = $val"      }
}

set ckTop [checkbutton .cktop -text "Top checkbutton" \
    -command {ShowStatus .cktop}]
set ckMid [checkbutton .ckmid -text "Middle checkbutton" \
    -command {ShowStatus .ckmid}]
set ckBot [checkbutton .ckbot -text "Bottom checkbutton" \
    -offvalue "OFF" -onvalue "ON" -command {ShowStatus .ckbot}]

set ckbuttons [list $ckTop $ckMid $ckBot]

set bExit [button .eb -width 8 -text "Exit" \
    -command exit]
set bToggle [button .toggle -width 8 -text "Toggle All" \
    -command {DoButton toggle $ckbuttons}]
set bClear [button .clear -width 8 -text "Clear All" \
    -command {DoButton clear $ckbuttons}]
set bSet [button .set -width 8 -text "Set All" \
    -command {DoButton set $ckbuttons}]
set bShow [button .show -width 8 -text "Show All" \
    -command {ShowStatus $ckbuttons}]

pack $ckTop $ckMid $ckBot -anchor w
pack $bToggle -pady 5 -padx 5 -side left
pack $bClear $bSet $bShow $bExt -pady 5 -padx {0 5} -side left
```

The first procedure, DoButton, takes two arguments: an action to perform and a list of checkbuttons on which to perform the requested action. action corresponds to one of three command buttons: toggle (for the Toggle All button), clear (for the Clear All button), and set (for the Set All button). Toggling the checkbuttons means reversing their selected status; clearing them means calling each checkbutton's deselect command; setting them means invoking their select command. I use a foreach loop to iterate through each button and perform the requested operation.

The second procedure, ShowStatus, displays the value of each checkbutton's associated variable. It accepts a single argument, a list of checkbuttons over which to iterate. Again, using a foreach loop, I iterate over each checkbutton, performing the following steps:

1. Retrieve the name of the widget's associated variable.
2. Declare that variable name as a global variable so I can access its value.
3. Retrieve the *value* of the widget's associated variable.
4. Display both the variable's name and its value.

Step 3, fetching the value of the widget's linked variable, is a bit of a trick. Recall that the set command called with just a variable name (for example, set $var) returns the value of that variable. So the code set val [set $var] evaluates the nested command [set $var] and assigns the result of that command, the value of $var, to the variable $val. Although this might seem a bit obscure, you will appreciate being able to build a variable name and extract its value this way as you progress in your Tcl-writing avocation.

Notice that ShowStatus uses the puts command, which displays its output to stdout. I just want to be clear that even in a GUI program, you still have access to stdout and that the puts command does *not* scribble on the GUI, but on a plain old terminal session. If you start ckbutton.tcl from an icon without an underlying terminal session, the output generated by puts would be lost (unless you puts it to a file, of course).

The next section of code creates three checkbutton widgets. Nothing really extraordinary in this code block, but do notice that I give each widget a -command option, {ShowStatus *name*}. When you click the corresponding checkbutton, it will display its value *after* the click. For example, if you click the top checkbutton (see Figure 10.9), that click first selects the widget, setting its linked variable to its -onvalue (which defaults to 1), and then executes ShowStatus .cktop, which displays the new value. As a final twist, I define alternative values for the bottom checkbutton ($ckBot) selected and unselected states, OFF and ON, respectively, to demonstrate that you aren't limited to using simple numeric values.

Don't Forget about Grouping!

The -command option expects a single string argument, so you have to use braces to group arguments that include embedded spaces.

The last bit of setup code involves defining the command buttons that provide most of the application's functionality. There are five buttons: an Exit button ($bExit); a Toggle All button ($bToggle) that invokes each checkbutton's toggle command; a Clear All ($bClear) button that deselects each checkbutton; a Set All button ($bSet) that selects each checkbutton; and a Show All button ($bShow) that displays each checkbutton's current selection status.

Finally, I'm ready to arrange and display the widgets. The first `pack` command arranges the three `checkbuttons` in the upper-lefthand corner of the window. I use the `anchor w` option to fix the `checkbuttons` against the "west" or left edge of the window. All of the buttons are laid out relative to the left side of the window using the `-side left` attribute. First, I place `$bToggle` with five pixels of padding on all sides. Next, I place `$bClear`, `$bSet`, `$bShow`, and `$bExit` with five pixels of padding on the top and bottom, zero padding on the left side, and five pixels of padding on the right. I don't pad the left side of these four buttons because the padding on the right side of the previous button provides the spacing I need.

Figure 10.9 shows this script in action. Play around with the buttons while looking at the associated code so you can see how all the parts connect and interact.

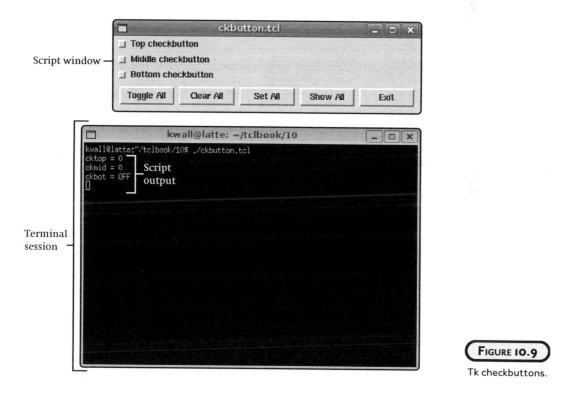

FIGURE 10.9

Tk checkbuttons.

Figure 10.9 shows the ckbutton.tcl script and the output created by clicking the Show All button. I ran this ckbutton.tcl from a terminal so you could see the output when you click the Show All button or one of the `checkbuttons`.

Radio Buttons

Unlike checkbuttons, radio buttons are usually used to select one item from a set of mutually exclusive set of items. Suppose that you want to allow users to select a color scheme, often called *themes* or *skins*, for your application. You can only apply a single color scheme at a time, so it makes sense to use radio buttons for the scheme selection interface. When a user selects one color scheme, the other color scheme radio buttons will be automatically unselected. The nice thing about Tk's radiobutton widget is that it monitors the value of its associated variable and when the value of that variable changes, the widget automatically updates its selection status to reflect the current value of the linked variable. If, for example, the radiobutton for the Raspberry Red color scheme is selected and the user, in a fickle moment, selects the Passionate Purple radiobutton, the radiobutton for the Raspberry Red scheme automatically unselects itself. You'll see this in action in just a moment.

Table 10.4 shows the arguments that Tk's radiobutton widget supports.

TABLE 10.4: RADIOBUTTON ARGUMENTS	
Option	**Description**
-command	Specifies the command to execute when the radiobutton is pressed.
-height	Sets the radiobutton height.
-indicatoron	Determines if the indicator is on (true) or off (false).
-selectcolor	Specifies the radiobutton's background color when it is selected.
-offrelief	Specifies the relief if the indicator is not drawn and the radiobutton is off.
-overrelief	Specifies a non-default relief when the cursor hovers over the radiobutton.
-selectimage	Specifies the image to display when the radiobutton is selected and -image is also specified.
-state	Specifies the radiobutton's current state, which must be one of normal, active, or disabled.
-value	Defines the value to store in the radiobutton's associated value when the radiobutton is selected.
-variable	Sets the name of the variable associated with the radiobutton (selectedButton by default).
-width	Sets the radiobutton's width.
cget	Returns the value of the specified option.
configure	Returns or sets the radiobutton's configuration options.
deselect	Unselects the radiobutton and sets its associated variable to the value specified by the -offvalue attribute.
flash	Flashes the radiobutton by alternating between its active and normal colors.
invoke	Executes the Tcl command associated with the button, if one is defined.
select	Selects the radiobutton and sets its associated variable to the value specified by the -onvalue attribute.

The following script, radio.tcl in this chapter's code directory, uses Tk's radio buttons to implement a simple color section interface (you'll learn more about Tk's color handling later in this chapter):

```
proc SetColor {newColor} {
    . configure -background $newColor

    global lColor    $lColor configure -background $newColor

    global radButtons    foreach w $radButtons {
        $w configure -background $newColor \
            -activebackground $newColor \
            -highlightbackground $newColor    }

}

set rRed [radiobutton .rred -text "Red" -value red]
set rBlue [radiobutton .rblue -text "Blue" -value blue]
set rGreen [radiobutton .rgreen -text "Green" -value green]
set rYellow [radiobutton .ryellow -text "Yellow" -value yellow]
set rPurple [radiobutton .rpurple -text "Purple" -value purple]

set radButtons [list $rRed $rBlue $rGreen $rYellow $rPurple]

set lColor [label .lcolor -text "Select color scheme"]

set bSet [button .bset -width 8 -text "Set Color" \
    -command {SetColor $selectedButton}]
set bExit [button .bexit -width 8 -text "Exit" -command exit]

$rPurple select
$bSet invoke

pack $lColor -anchor w
pack $rRed $rBlue $rGreen $rYellow $rPurple -pady 0 -padx {2 0} -anchor w
pack $bSet -pady {10 2} -padx 5
pack $bExit -pady {2 10} -padx 5
```

radio.tcl uses five Tk `radiobutton` widgets from which you can select a color. When you click the Set button, the background color of the main window, the label, and the buttons change to the color you selected. Figure 10.10 (in black and white, so the color change is difficult to see) illustrates how it looks.

FIGURE 10-10

Using
`radiobutton`
widgets.

The `SetColor` procedure takes a single argument: the new color for the main window, the label, and the buttons. The first command sets the background color of the main window. After declaring the `lColor` global variable, I set its background color. I use a `foreach` loop to set the background color for each of the `radiobutton` widgets. Rather than passing in a list of widgets like I did in ckbutton.tcl, I declare the `$radButtons` variable as a global. I set three background attributes for each `radiobutton` to ensure that the color is correct, regardless of its state. The `-background` attribute covers the normal state, enabled but not active. It will come as no surprise that `-activebackground` covers the state when the `radiobutton` is active, that is, when the mouse is hovering over the button and clicking (selecting, in this case) the button. The `-highlightbackground` attribute colors the rectangle that appears around a widget when it is active.

After I define the `SetColor` helper procedure, I start laying out the widgets. First, I define five `radiobutton` widgets, one each for red, blue, green, yellow, and purple and a list of `radiobutton` widgets (`$radButtons`). For each button, I use the `-value` *color* attribute. This attribute sets the value that is assigned to the linked variable when the `radiobutton` is selected. You'll no doubt notice that I don't specify the name of the linked variable. If no variable name is specified (using `-variable` *varname*), the name defaults to `selectedButton`. While one could argue that it would be better to use a special variable name for uniqueness and easy identification, this script is short enough that using the default name is acceptable.

I then create a label, $lColor, to give users a hint what the radio buttons do, followed by two buttons, $bset and $bExit, to set the selected color or exit the script, respectively. The Exit button needs no comment. The Set Color button simply invokes the SetColor procedures, passing the $selectedButton variable to the procedure. *Be careful here!* Although the variable's name is $selectedButton, the value it holds is the name of the color that will be set. It is precisely this potential confusion that makes defining my own variable instead of using the default variable a good idea. I kept the default name for a pedagogical reason (not to mention plain laziness), namely, I wanted you to know that radiobutton widgets have a default variable and what it is named.

Before displaying the widgets, I set a bit of initial state. The $rPurple select command sets the state of the purple radiobutton to be selected, which means that $buttonSelected has the value purple. $bSet invoke programmatically clicks the Set Color button to set the color to the one I just selected, which is purple. Bear in mind that the results of these commands won't be visible until I explicitly draw the window with pack.

To display my GUI masterpiece, I first draw the label, anchoring it to the left side of the window. Next, I stack the five radiobutton widgets one on top of the other, again, anchoring them to the left side of the parent window. When I pack the Set Color button, I use a large amount of vertical padding to visually separate it from the radio buttons above it. For a similar but inverse reason, I pack the Exit button with very little vertical padding between it and the Set Color button. The purpose of this visual grouping is to relate the two command buttons to each other and to distinguish them from the radio buttons.

A Smörgåsbord of Menus

A GUI without menus is like a day without sunshine. Or not. Regardless, menus are an important part of any graphical application, and Tk has excellent support for the full range of menu operations. To create a menu, you use the menu widget to create a menu entry and then use additional commands to add entries to the menu widget. Tk supports a variety of menu features, including:

- Cascading menus, which allow you to display sub-menus.
- Check entries, which resemble checkbutton widgets.
- Command entries, which resemble button widgets.
- Option menus, which display a set of choices using radiobutton widgets.
- Pop-up menus, normally displayed in response to a right-click.
- Radio entries, which resemble radiobutton widgets.
- Separators, providing visual separation between menu entries.

- System menus, which add entries to the existing Windows system menu, the Macintosh Apple menu, and the Help menu on any supported platform.
- Tear-off entries, which allow users to detach, or *tear off*, a menu from its parent.

To do full justice to Tk's menu support would require a full chapter and more space than I have, so I'll focus in this section on creating a menu bar that contains commands and separators. This should meet your immediate menu-creation needs, provide a template for creating complete, full-featured menus, and give you a sense of Tk's capabilities with respect to menus.

Creating a Basic Menu Bar

The following script, basic_menu.tcl in this chapter's code directory, shows the steps you need to follow to add a menu to your application:

```
set mainMenu [menu .mainmenu]

. configure -menu $mainMenu

set mFile [menu $mainMenu.mFile -tearoff 0]
$mainMenu add cascade -label "File" -menu $mFile

$mFile add command -label "Open" -command {DoCmd Open}
$mFile add command -label "Close" -command {DoCmd Close}
$mFile add command -label "Save as" -command {DoCmd "Save as"}
$mFile add command -label "Save" -command {DoCmd Save}
$mFile add separator
$mFile add command -label "Exit" -command exit

proc DoCmd {cmd} {
tk_messageBox -icon info -type ok -message $cmd
}
```

The resulting window should resemble Figure 10.11.

FIGURE 10.11

With a minimal amount of Tk code, you can create a functional menu.

If you click the File item on the menu, the figure you see should look like Figure 10.12.

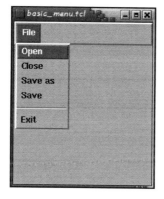

FIGURE 10.12

Clicking the File item opens the associated menu.

The first command, set mainMenu [menu .mainmenu], creates a menu entry. It doesn't have any content, but I'll take care of that in a moment. The next command, . configure -menu $mainMenu, associates the menu I just created with the root window, meaning that the menu entry referenced by $mainMenu is the menu bar for the root window. The next two lines of code add an item to the menu bar. In this case, I'm creating a "File" menu. First, I create a second menu entry named $mainMenu.mFile, which establishes the widget mFile as a child of the main menu—this relationship is necessary so that the mFile menu will display properly when users click the File item on the menu bar. The attribute -tearoff 0, tells Tk that this menu cannot be detached from the menu bar (the default value is -tearoff 1, which permits detaching, or tearing off the menu, to create a new top-level window). The second command, $mainMenu add cascade -label "File" -menu $mFile, adds an item named File to the menu bar (add cascade -label "File"), which, when clicked, opens the menu specified by $mFile (-menu $mFile).

The next block of code adds items to the newly created File menu. Specifically, I add an Open command, a Close command, a Save as command, a Save command, a separator, and an Exit command. The separator is merely a visual aid. Each of the command entries consists of a label and an associated command to carry out the requested operation. In this case, the command is DoCmd *label*, where *label* is the text. DoCmd itself is a simple procedure that uses the tk_messageBox procedure to pop up a window that displays the text passed to DoCmd. The exception is the Exit item, which invokes Tcl's exit command to terminate the script.

To add another menu item, say, Edit, to the menu bar, you would create a second menu item and populate it with commands, for example:

```
set mEdit [menu $mainMenu.mEdit -tearoff 0]
$mainMenu add cascade -label "Edit" -menu $mEdit

$mEdit add command -label "Copy" -command {DoCmd "Copy"}
$mEdit add command -label "Paste" -command {DoCmd "Paste"}
$mEdit add command -label "Cut" -command {DoCmd "Cut"}
$mEdit add command -label "Search" -command {DoCmd "Search"}
$mEdit add command -label "Replace" -command {DoCmd "Replace"}
```

Figure 10.13 shows what the resulting menu would look like.

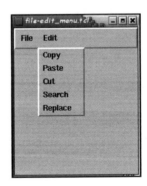

FIGURE 10.13

Use the code in basic_menu.tcl as a template for creating your own menus.

As you can see, creating a Tk menu isn't difficult at all.

BINDING COMMANDS TO EVENTS

In simplest terms, *binding* a command to an event means to arrange for a command or procedure or script to execute when an event occurs. The -command attribute of most Tk widgets does precisely that, it binds or ties the specified command to a particular event, such as selecting a radio button or pressing a command button. Not surprisingly, most events in a Tk application are not tied to pressing keys or mouse clicks. Rather, events occur, quite literally, all the time. Clicking on a window to give it the focus is an event; moving the mouse cursor across a window generates mouse movement events and events when the mouse enters and leaves the window; creating and deleting windows are events; resizing a window is an event; even changing a window's visibility is an event.

Tk, like most GUI frameworks, provides a method for hooking into these (and other) events to bind a command, procedure, or script to them. The command that accomplishes this is the aptly named `bind` command. Its syntax is:

```
bind tag ?event? ?+??cmd?
```

This command binds the command specified by *cmd* to the event specified by *event* that happens to the widget or GUI element specified by *tag*. To put it more directly, when *tag*'s *event* occurs, *cmd* executes. Table 10.5 lists the events that you can *bind*.

TABLE 10.5: BINDABLE EVENTS

Event	Description
Activate	Occurs when a window is activated, usually by receiving focus.
ButtonPress, Button	Generated when a mouse button is pressed; ButtonPress and Button are synonyms.
ButtonRelease	Occurs when a mouse button is released.
Configure	Occurs whenever a window is moved, resized, or its border width changes.
Deactivate	Occurs when a window is deactivated, usually by losing focus.
Destroy	Generated when a window is destroyed, usually by closing or deleting it.
Enter	Delivered to the window that the mouse pointer enters.
Expose	Generated when a window must be redrawn after being uncovered or drawn for the first time.
FocusIn	Sent to a window receiving keyboard input focus.
FocusOut	Sent to a window losing keyboard input focus.
KeyPress, Key	Generated whenever a key is pressed; KeyPress and Key are synonyms.
KeyRelease	Generated whenever a key is released.
Leave	Delivered to the window that the mouse pointer is exiting.
Map	Generated when a window is made viewable by being mapped onto the screen (not minimized or iconified).
Motion	Occurs whenever the mouse pointer is moved.
MouseWheel	Delivered to a window with input focus when a wheel on a mouse is scrolled up or down or clicked.
Unmap	Generated when a window is iconified, minimized, or removed from the active screen.
Visibility	Occurs when a window's visibility changes, such as when another window is moved over it and obscures it or when an obscuring window is moved out of the way.

My discussion of event binding and the `bind` command covers the simplest case, binding a single command or procedure to a single widget. The topic is considerably more sophisticated than I suggest in this section. The goal of this section was to show you that the capability exists, rather than to show you how to use it. I consider it an advanced topic beyond this book's limited scope because it is one of the most complicated parts of Tk programming. I don't want to overwhelm you with minutiae that you might not use for a long time. If you need more information, the `bind` command's man page (`man 3tk bind`) has all of the gory details.

COLORING YOUR WORLD

The Tk widget attributes that set and modify colors, such as `-activebackground` and `foreground`, accept colors in one of two formats: a color name, such as `red`, `blue`, or `green`, or their RGB value specified in hexadecimal (*hex*) format, such as #f00, #0f0, or #0ff (which are red, green, and blue, respectively, specified in 8-bit hex values). The color names that Tk supports are documented in the colors man page (`man 3tk colors`). On UNIX, Linux, and BSD systems, you should be able to view the complete list of colors using the `showrgb` command (part of the X Window System, not Tcl or Tk), shown in the following excerpt, which displays a variety of colors according to their decimal RGB value and their name:

```
$ showrgb
255 250 250             snow
248 248 255             ghost white
248 248 255             GhostWhite
...
139   0   0             DarkRed
144 238 144             light green
144 238 144             LightGreen
```

The complete color list has 752 entries (admittedly, some are duplicates, like ghost *white* and *GhostWhite*), so you'll pardon me for not showing the entire list. These color names are derived from Tk's origins on the X Window System and are supported on all platforms to which Tk has been ported.

If you choose to use the hex format, you can specify each component in 4-, 8-, 12-, or 16-bit format. 4-bit hex values use a single digit for each component; 8-bit hex values use two hex digits; 12-bit hex values use three; and 16-bit hex values use four. Thus, you can specify the color red as #f00, #ff0000, #fff000000, or #ffff00000000.

As a bonus, I've included a simple Tk application, show_colors.tcl in this chapter's code directory, which shows the colors available in the stock Tk distribution. It shows a listbox that contains all of the predefined colors (well, the color *names*) that Tk supports. You select a color from the listbox and click the Set Color button to update a color swatch (actually, a `label` widget) with the currently selected color. Figure 10.14 shows what this script looks like.

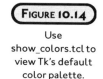

FIGURE 10.14

Use show_colors.tcl to view Tk's default color palette.

I won't describe show_colors.tcl's code because it uses the listbox widget, which you don't learn to use until Chapter 13.

ANALYZING MEMORY TEST

memtest.tcl is the longest script I've created (so far) in this book. Most of it consists of procedure definitions and setup code; the actual execution is pretty simple.

Looking at the Code

```
#!/usr/bin/wish
# memtest.tcl
# Play a Simon-like memory game

# Block 1
# Randomly select a button from a list of buttons
proc SelectButton {buttons} {
    set index [expr {int(rand() * [llength $buttons])}]
    return [lindex $buttons $index]
}
```

```tcl
# Flash randomly selected buttons count times
proc FlashButtons {buttons count} {
    # Create a list of buttons to flash
    for {set i 1} {$i <= $count} {incr i} {
        set btn [SelectButton $buttons]
        lappend flashList $btn
    }

    # Flash the buttons in the list
    foreach btn $flashList {
        $btn flash
        $btn flash
        after 1000
    }

    return $flashList
}

# Compare the flashed buttons to players buttons and display
# the results
proc Score {flashedButtons pressedButtons} {
    global bScore
    global lInfo

    # Disable the score button
    $bScore configure -state disabled

    # Compare the buttons
    if {[llength $flashedButtons] != [llength $pressedButtons]} {
        $lInfo configure -text "Sorry, wrong sequence!"
        return
    }

    if {[lindex $flashedButtons] ne [lindex $pressedButtons]} {
        $lInfo configure -text "Sorry, wrong sequence!"
        return
    }
```

```
    # Only get here if the sequences match
    $lInfo configure -text "You did it!"
    return 0
}


# Block 2
# Play the game
proc PlayGame {buttons} {
    global lInfo
    global bPlay
    global bScore

    # Disable the Play button
    $bPlay configure -state disabled

    # Flash the buttons
    set flashedButtons [FlashButtons $buttons 4]

    # Enable the Score button
    $bScore configure -state normal

    # Tell the player what's next
    $lInfo configure -text "Try to repeat the\nsequence. Then press\nScore to see how
    you\ndid."
    return $flashedButtons
}


# Block 3
# Game buttons
set bRed [button .bred -background red4 -activebackground red \
    -command {lappend pressedButtons $bRed}]
set bBlue [button .bblue -background blue4 -activebackground blue \
    -command {lappend pressedButtons $bBlue}]
set bGreen [button .bgreen -background green4 -activebackground green \
    -command {lappend pressedButtons $bGreen}]
set bYellow [button .byellow -background yellow4 -activebackground yellow \
    -command {lappend pressedButtons $bYellow}]
set bCyan [button .bcyan -background cyan4 -activebackground cyan \
```

```
        -command {lappend pressedButtons $bCyan}]

# List of game buttons
set buttons [list $bRed $bBlue $bGreen $bYellow $bCyan]

# Command buttons
set bPlay [button .bplay -text Play \
    -command {set flashedButtons [PlayGame $buttons]}]
set bScore [button .bscore -text Score -state disabled \
    -command {Score $flashedButtons $pressedButtons}]
set bExit [button .bexit -text Exit -command exit]

# Instruction label
set lInfo [label .linfo  -width 20 -height 4 -justify left \
    -text "Press Play to start"]

# Display
pack $bRed -pady {5 0} -expand true -fill x
pack $bBlue $bGreen $bYellow $bCyan $lInfo -expand true -fill x
pack propagate $lInfo false
pack $bPlay $bScore $bExit -pady {20 0} -side left -expand true -fill x
```

Understanding the Code

As usual, most of the code appears in the procedure definitions that make up Block 1 at the top of the file. The first procedure, SelectButton, selects a button at random from a list of buttons passed to it in the argument buttons and returns the name of that button to the calling procedure.

FlashButtons flashes each button in the list of buttons passed to it as an argument in buttons. The count argument indicates how many buttons to flash. The for loop creates the list of buttons to flash by calling SelectButtons $count times and appending the button name to the $flashList variable. The foreach loop iterates through $flashList, flashing each button twice and then pausing 1000 milliseconds (after 1000), or one second, to create a delay before flashing the next button. After flashing all of the buttons, FlashButton terminates, returning the list of flashed buttons to the calling procedure.

The next procedure, Score, compares the list of buttons the computer generated, passed in flashedButtons, to the list of buttons the player pressed, passed in pressedButtons. First, I disable the Score button to prevent the user from pressing it multiple times and to give the player a visual cue that the game is almost over. I perform two comparisons. If the length of the two lists is different, I know the lists don't match and can terminate the procedure without needing to compare each button. If the lengths match, the second `if` statement compares the lists of buttons in their entirety. If the strings returned by the two `lindex` statements don't match, the procedure terminates. Otherwise, the two lists match, and the player has won. In all cases, I update a label in the game window showing the player whether she won or lost.

Block 2 consists of the `PlayGame` procedure, which handles the bulk of the gameplay. It starts by disabling the Play button, then calls the `FlashButtons` procedure, passing it the list of buttons that was passed to `PlayGame` and the number of buttons to flash. I save the list of buttons returned by `FlashButtons` in the `$flashedButtons` variable so I can return that list to the main game loop. After all of the buttons are flashed, I enable the Score button and then instruct the player to try to replicate the sequence of button presses.

In Block 3, I start creating the game board. First, I create five colored buttons. Their `-command` attributes create entries in the list of buttons pressed by the user (stored in `pressedButtons`). Each button's background color is a darker shade of its active background color. When pressed, this arrangement of colors makes the button noticeably easier to distinguish in its flashing state. I create a list of these game buttons to pass to the various procedures.

The command buttons, naturally, do the work in the program. The Play button, `$bPlay`, invokes the `PlayGame` procedure when pressed. The Score button, `$bScore`, starts out in the disabled state. As described earlier, it will be enabled after the buttons are flashed. This is largely a visual cue to the player to facilitate gameplay, but also serves to prevent unpleasant events if the player presses the Score button while the game buttons are being flashed. `$bScore` calls the `Score` procedure, passing the two lists of buttons to `Score` for evaluation. The Exit button is nothing new and enables the player to exit the game at any time. The instruction label, `$lInfo`, just provides an area where I can display text telling the player how to proceed.

The final lines of code lay out the widgets on the screen. I pack the red button first, to set a more aesthetically pleasing distance between the top of the button and the top edge of the window. Next, I pack the rest of the buttons and the information label in below the red button. The attributes `-expand true -fill x` cause the widgets to expand horizontally to fill their parcels in the window. I pack the Play, Score, and Exit buttons across the window with sizable padding between the instruction label and the tops of the command buttons. While this is partly an aesthetic preference on my part—I don't like windows with widgets jammed together—it is also yet another visual hint to the player that separates the elements of the game to suggest that they have different functions.

With just a few widgets, you can write a reasonably complete Tk application. `buttons`, `radiobuttons`, and `checkbuttons` are common UI elements that enable users to invoke actions and make choices. Knowing how to set and modify colors in a user interface is important because humans use colors as visual cues. Nonetheless, no matter how visually rich and widget-packed you make your user interface, the core of any Tk application is still the Tcl code that ties UI elements to commands and procedures and that provides the logic that makes the application work.

Modifying the Code

Here are some exercises you can try to practice what you learned in this chapter:

10.1 Modify the script to use fewer global variables.

10.2 Modify the Score procedure to perform a single definitive comparison of the flashed and pressed buttons.

WINDOWS, FRAMES, AND MESSAGES

I f you've finished Chapter 10, you've probably decided that the pack geometry manager leaves a lot to be desired. It handles a lot of layout details for you, but it is precisely this lack of control that makes pack hard to use. In this chapter, you learn how to use the grid geometry manager; I think you'll like it better than pack. I'll also introduce you to three more Tk widgets, frames, toplevels (that is, top-level windows), and messages. But first, you get to play my thrilling version of Tic-Tac-Toe.

TIC-TAC-TOE

To play my version of Tic-Tac-Toe, execute the script tic-tac-toe.tcl in this chapter's code directory on the CD. To start the game, click the Play button (see Figure 11.1). Clicking a button changes its text from "?" to "X" or "O," depending on whose turn it is. Notice that you play for both X and O (see Figure 11.2). If you click a button that has already been played, the script gently chides you, as shown in Figure 11.3. When someone has a winner, the winning "line" turns green, and a dialog box pops up to announce the winner (see Figure 11.4). If no one wins, well, nothing happens, so click the Quit button to exit the game.

FIGURE 11.1

Click the Play button to start the game.

FIGURE 11.2

Click the ? buttons to place an X or O on them.

FIGURE 11.3

If you click a marked button, you'll get an error message.

FIGURE 11.4

The first player to mark a line wins.

ON THE GRID: THE GRID GEOMETRY MANAGER

The grid geometry manager lays out widgets in a grid of rows and columns. Each row and column can have a different size (height for rows, widths for columns). You decide the row(s) and column(s) into which each widget is placed and grid adjusts the layout grid to fit the widgets. Much like using HTML tables for Web page layout, grid gives you finer control over the layout of a window. I prefer grid over pack because I find grid to have more predictable results. Or perhaps I'm just a control freak, so I simply prefer the command that gives me more control.

grid offers two placement models, relative and absolute. With *relative placement,* grid determines the row and column sizes based on the contents of each cell. With absolute placement, you specify the row and column positions using grid's -row and -column arguments.

Relative Positioning

When you use grid's relative positioning model, each distinct grid command creates a new row, and the number of columns is determined by the number of widgets given as arguments to the grid commands. The order in which widgets are passed to grid establishes the order in which the widgets appear in the column. grid sets the column width to the width of the widest widget, so, by default, grid centers the rest of the widgets in their respective cells. Row height, similarly, is fixed based on the height of the tallest widget in a cell. The following script uses relative positioning to lay out a 3×3 grid of labels (see rel_grid.tcl in this chapter's code directory):

```
. configure -bg black
wm title . $argv0

for {set i 1} {$i <= 9} {incr i} {
    frame .f$i -bg white -width .30i -height .30i
    label .l$i -bg blue -fg bisque -text $i
    grid propagate .f$i false
    grid .l$i -in .f$i
    if {![expr $i % 3]} {
        grid .f[expr $i - 2] .f[expr $i -1] .f$i -padx 5 -pady 5
    }
}

grid propagate .f5 true
.l5 configure -width 10 -height 10
```

Figure 11.5 shows the window that rel_grid.tcl creates.

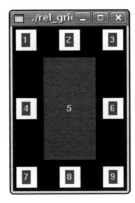

FIGURE 11.5

The grid
geometry
manager using
relative
positioning.

I meanly sneaked in a few additional commands to confuse you. I set the background color of the root window to black to make it easier to see the grid-wise arrangement of the label widgets. The second command, wm title . $argv0, tells the window manager to set the window title to the name of the script (see the sidebar, "Understanding Window Managers," for more information about the wm command).

The for loop creates nine frame widgets named .f1 through .f9 and nine similarly-named label widgets (.l1 through .l9). Each label is numbered for easy identification. I use frames to serve as containers for the label widgets, which means that each frame is both a child widget (referred to as a *slave* in the Tk documentation) of the top-level or root window and a parent (referred to as a *master*) widget of the label widget it contains.

The for loop does most of the work. I created a frame widget that is three-tenths of an inch wide (-width .30i) and tall (-height .30i), locking the frame's size using the grid propagate command. I needed to use grid propagate commands on the frames to prevent them from shrinking or growing to fit the size of their children. The syntax of the grid propagate command is:

```
grid propagate master ?boolean?
```

The *master* parameter specifies the master widget to which the command applies. If *boolean* is true or any value or expression equivalent to true (such as 1), *master* will shrink or grow to fit the size of its largest child widget. If *boolean* is false or any value or expression equivalent to false (such as 0), *master* will not resize.

Next, I draw the frame and its label using grid's -in option to specify the master/slave relationship between the widgets. The argument following -in indicates the widget's master.

Thus, for example, `grid .l4 -in .f4` says that the label widget named `.l4` is a slave widget of the frame widget named `.f4`.

At the end of each row, (when the `$i` loop counter is evenly divisible by 3), I execute the `grid` command for the three frame and label combinations on that row. Each grid command arranges three labels in a three-column wide row. As you can see in Figure 11.5, the resulting figure is a 3x3 grid of `label` widgets numbered consecutively from one to nine, as you move left to right and top to bottom.

The final two commands unlock the middle frame and resize its child label. The purpose of this otherwise gratuitous modification is to demonstrate that the width or height of the largest widget in a cell sets the width or height of the corresponding row or column, respectively.

UNDERSTANDING WINDOW MANAGERS

When you ask Tk to create a widget, it will do so using the windowing system in use on the host OS. Nonetheless, because Tk's roots are in the X Window System, some of its idioms and commands, like the WM command for requesting services from the window manager, might seem out of place on Apple or Windows systems. Readers unfamiliar with UNIX, UNIX-like operating systems such as Linux and the *smörgåsbord* of BSDs, or the X Window System—in other words, Apple and Windows users—are likely to be just as unfamiliar with the notion of a window manager. Apple and Windows systems have the luxury (or handicap, depending on one's perspective) of a windowing system that is tightly integrated into the operating system. With very few exceptions, the UI has one and only one look and feel, and this look and feel is defined and enforced by the OS. You can usually change colors, fonts, and other incidental UI elements, but the primary UI components cannot be altered. To put it succinctly, for Apple and Windows users, the windowing system *is* the window manager.

On UNIX and UNIX-like systems, the windowing system is *not* integrated into the operating system. More important for the purposes of this sidebar is that the windowing system is separate from the window manager. The windowing system used on UNIX and UNIX-like systems is known as the X Window System, or X (not X Windows, X-Window, or X-Windows).

X does not define a user interface. Rather, X (more specifically, the X protocol) defines an architecture and the corresponding low-level drawing operations (known as *primitives*), for building graphical environments. These primitives include drawing and moving windows on a screen and interacting with them using a mouse, keyboard, or other input devices. Two other design features of X are that it is OS-independent and network-transparent. *OS independence* means that X is a user-level application that runs on top of its host OS and that it is not dependent on any particular functionality of the host OS. *Network transparency* means that the system on which an application program executes (the *client* application) does not have to be the same as the system that displays the application's interface (the display *server*).

If X does not define a user interface, who or what does? The window manager. *Window managers* literally manage the placement, behavior, and appearance of windows, buttons, menus, title bars, and the like. This oversimplifies the situation, though. For example, the programming toolkits and libraries used to create a given window manager might enforce a uniform appearance. Alternatively, individual applications, such as point-of-sale systems, might define their own unique interfaces. The point is that there is no "typical" or "standard" X UI. Despite this, Tk almost always does the right thing.

To get a sense of the variety of interfaces created for the X Window System, visit the Window Managers for X Web site at www.xwinman.org.

Absolute Positioning

Absolute positioning using grid's -row and -column arguments enables you to explicitly place widgets. -row and -column both accept a single integer value specifying the (zero-based) row or column, respectively, in which to place the widget. The following script, abs_grid.tcl in this chapter's code directory, creates the same 3×3 grid as rel_grid.tcl using absolute positioning:

```
. configure -bg black
wm title . "abs_grid.tcl"

set row 1
for {set i 1} {$i <= 9} {incr i} {
    frame .f$i -bg white -width .30i -height .30i
    label .l$i -bg blue -fg bisque -text $i
    grid propagate .f$i false
    grid .l$i -in .f$i
    if {![expr $i % 3]} {
        grid .f[expr $i - 2] -row $row -column 0 -padx 5 -pady 5
        grid .f$i -row $row -column 2 -padx 5 -pady 5
        grid .f[expr $i - 1] -row $row -column 1 -padx 5 -pady 5
        incr row
    }
}
```

```
grid propagate .f5 true
.l5 configure -width 10 -height 10
```

Figure 11.6 shows the resulting screen so you can compare it to Figure 11.5.

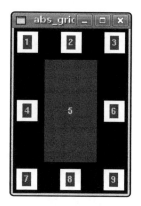

Figure 11.6

The grid
geometry
manager using
absolute
positioning.

In abs_grid.tcl, I used three grid commands rather than one to lay out the frames. At the end of each row, I call grid, but only for a single frame widget. In addition, I used the -row and -column arguments of each widget. When used in this way, grid uses the values specified and does not follow the layout algorithm I described in the previous section. To demonstrate this point, I called grid on the columns out of order (column one, column three, then column two). As you can see from the code for abs_grid.tcl, absolute positioning requires more code (a whopping four lines) than relative positioning, but if you need the additional control, the additional code is the price you have to pay.

Positioning and Padding

To gain more control over where in a cell a widget is placed, you can use grid's -sticky argument to control to which edges of the cell the widget is anchored (yes, this is similar to pack's -anchor option). You may use any combination of the compass points n, s, e, and w (north, south, east, and west, or top, bottom, right, and left, respectively) to indicate where to anchor the widget in its cell. The chief difference between -sticky and -anchor is that -sticky also causes the widget to expand to fill its cell. So, it wouldn't be a stretch, as it were, to suggest that grid's -sticky option combines the functions of pack's -anchor and -fill options. The following script, sticky.tcl in this chapter's code directory on the Web site, shows -sticky's effects:

```
wm title . "sticky.tcl"

set idx 0
foreach i {NW NE SW SE} {
    set col [expr {$idx % 2}]
    set row [expr {$idx / 2}]
    frame .f$i -width 1i -height 1i -bg black -relief groove -borderwidth 2
    grid .f$i -row $row -column $col -sticky nsew
    label .l$i -width 3 -bg blue -fg bisque -text $i
    grid .l$i -row $row -column $col -padx 3 -pady 3 -sticky $i
    incr idx
}
```

FIGURE 11.7

Use -sticky to anchor widgets inside their cells.

Similarly, you can use external (-padx and -pady) and internal (-ipadx and -ipady) padding on the widgets themselves to fine-tune spacing. Padding a widget changes the size of the grid. *External padding* adds space between the edge of a widget and its containing cell, that is, outside the widget's border. *Internal padding*, on the other hand, is added to the space inside the widget's border. The following script, ipad.tcl in this chapter's code directory, illustrates the difference between external and internal padding:

```
set pad [lindex $argv 0]
if {[string length $pad] == 0 || ($pad <=0)} {
    set pad 20
}

wm  title . "ipad.tcl"

frame .container -bg black
```

```
label .lInt -text "Internal Padding" -relief groove
label .lExt -text "External Padding" -relief groove

grid .container -sticky nsew
grid .lInt -ipadx $pad -ipady $pad -in .container
grid .lExt -padx $pad -pady $pad -in .container
```

To execute this script, type the script name followed by a number that specifies the desired padding value to use (the units used are pixels). So, to execute ipad.tcl and request 100 pixels of padding, you would execute the command, ipad.tcl 100. In fact, Figure 11.8 shows one window created by ipad.tcl with precisely that padding. The other window in Figure 11.8 was created with 20 pixels of padding (ipad.tcl 20).

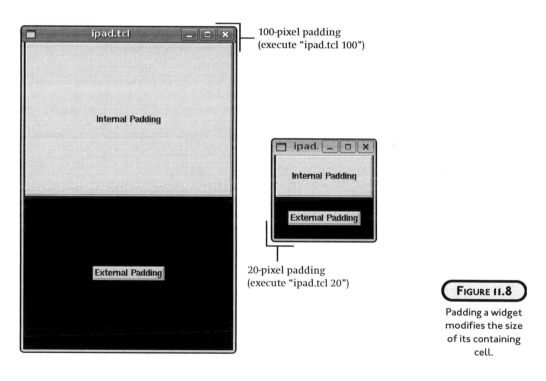

100-pixel padding
(execute "ipad.tcl 100")

20-pixel padding
(execute "ipad.tcl 20")

FIGURE 11.8

Padding a widget modifies the size of its containing cell.

The first line of code in ipad.tcl retrieves the argument passed to the script. Tcl stores command-line arguments passed to the script in a predefined list variable named argv. As a result, you can use standard list options, such as lindex, lsearch, lsort, and so forth, to access command-line arguments. In this case, I use lindex argv 0 to retrieve the single argument and store that value in that integer variable pad. After setting the window title, I created three widgets, a container frame widget (.container), and two label widgets (.lInt and .lExt). As their names suggest, .lInt demonstrates internal padding and .lExt demonstrates external padding.

After drawing the frame with the first grid command, I drew .lInt with the requested amount of internal padding. You can see in Figure 11.8 that internal padding is added inside the border of the .lInt label, enlarging it significantly. Likewise, you can see how the external padding added to the .lExt label is placed outside of the widget's border and inside the border of its containing cell.

Spanning Rows and Columns

Just as a cell can contain multiple widgets, a widget can occupy, or *span*, multiple cells. Spanning behavior is controlled by the aptly named -rowspan and -columnspan attributes. Each attribute accepts a single integer value specifying the number of rows or columns the widget will occupy. The short script that follows, span.tcl in this chapter's code directory, shows a simple example of widgets that span rows and columns:

```
foreach c {red blue violet magenta cyan green} {
    label .l$c -bg $c -width 10 -height 2 -relief groove \
        -text [string totitle $c]
}


grid .lred -row 0 -column 0 -columnspan 2 -sticky nsew
grid .lblue -row 0 -column 2 -rowspan 2 -sticky nsew
grid .lviolet -row 1 -column 0 -columnspan 2 -sticky nsew
grid .lmagenta .lcyan .lgreen -sticky nsew
```

The code is uncomplicated. The foreach loop creates six colored label widgets with a width of ten characters, a height of two lines, and a grooved border. The four grid commands lay out the widgets in various configurations on the master window. The result is the window shown in Figure 11.9.

FIGURE 11.9

Widgets can span multiple rows or columns.

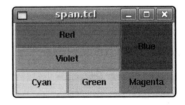

Operating on Rows and Columns

The `grid` options and attributes I've discussed so far have operated at the cell level. There are also options and attributes that apply to entire rows or columns, which can make layout less complicated by applying characteristics, particularly sizing or padding, to a row or a column as a whole rather than applying them to individual cells. This section looks at these more general capabilities.

The all-purpose row- and column-configuration commands are `rowconfigure` and `columnconfigure`:

```
grid rowconfigure master row ?attribute ...?
grid columnconfigure master col ?attribute ...?
```

Each attribute is specified as a -*name value* pair. If you omit *attribute* entirely, `rowconfigure` and `columnconfigure` return the current attributes as a list. If you specify only the attribute -*name*, the return value is its corresponding *value*. Otherwise, `rowconfigure` and `columnconfigure` set the specified attributes, which can be one or more of `-minsize`, `-weight`, `-uniform`, or `-pad`. Table 11.1 describes these attributes.

TABLE 11.1: ROW AND COLUMN ATTRIBUTES

Attribute	Description
`-minsize`	Sets/queries the minimum size of a row or column in screen units (pixels by default).
`-pad`	Sets/queries the amount of padding, in screen units (pixels by default), added to the display area of the largest widget in a row or column.
`-uniform`	Assigns widgets to a group named for the attribute value; used with `-weight` to size and resize widgets as a group.
`-weight`	Sets/queries the rate at which additional space is apportioned to widgets.

I'll start with the simplest example, querying row settings. The code is in attr_query.tcl in this chapter's code directory:

```
wm title . "attr_query.tcl"

set colors [list red blue violet magenta cyan green]
foreach c $colors {
    label .l$c -bg $c -width 10 -height 2 -relief groove \
        -text [string totitle $c]
```

```
}

grid .lred -row 0 -column 0 -columnspan 2 -sticky nsew
grid .lblue -row 0 -column 2 -rowspan 2 -sticky nsew
grid .lviolet -row 1 -column 0 -columnspan 2 -sticky nsew
grid .lcyan .lgreen .lmagenta -sticky nsew

puts [format "%10s%10s%10s" Row Name Value]
puts [string repeat "-" 30]
set row 0
while {$row < 3} {
    set attrs [grid rowconfigure . $row]
    foreach {name value} $attrs {
        puts [format "%10s%10s%10s" $row $name $value]
    }
    incr row
}
```

Readers who have been paying attention will no doubt notice that attr_query.tcl is just span.tcl with code at the end for querying the attributes. After creating a header, I set a loop counter (set row 0) and then loop through each row of widgets, displaying the row number, the attribute name, and the attribute value. I leave querying column attributes as an exercise for the reader.

The output is rather boring, as you can see below, because the row attributes are all at their default settings:

```
$ ./attr_query.tcl
       Row      Name     Value
------------------------------
         0  -minsize         0
         0      -pad         0
         0  -uniform
         0   -weight         0
         1  -minsize         0
         1      -pad         0
         1  -uniform
         1   -weight         0
         2  -minsize         0
         2      -pad         0
```

```
2   -uniform
2   -weight          0
```

Don't Use Console Output in GUI Programs

It is generally considered bad form to use stdout in a GUI program. However, when you are developing an application, common practice is to display debugging information to the console because it is a simple way to obtain information about what is happening inside the script. Users are usually paying attention to the GUI, so console output might not be noticed. More to the point, because GUI scripts are usually started from an icon, they might not even *have* a console attached, so console output will be lost.

Setting a Minimum Size

To assign a minimum size to a row or column, use the -minsize attribute. The default unit is pixels. In the following script, minsize.tcl, I created two rows of two labels. The first row's height is implied by the size of the largest label widget. I set the minimum size of the second row using -minsize, which ensured that the row would be at least, in this case, 50 pixels tall and 50 pixels wide. Here's the code:

```
wm title . "minsize.tcl"
. configure -bg black

label .1Nw -bg #eee -fg black -text NW -relief groove
label .1Ne -bg #ddd -fg black -text NE -relief groove
label .1Sw -bg #ccc -fg black -text SW -relief groove
label .1Se -bg #bbb -fg black -text SE -relief groove

grid .1Nw .1Ne -sticky nsew
grid .1Sw .1Se -sticky nsew

grid rowconfigure . 1 -minsize 50
grid columnconfigure . 1 -minsize 50
```

I defined four labels in various shades of gray, giving each one a grooved border so you could see its edges clearly. The first two grid commands created two rows of labels each containing two labels; that is, I created a 2x2 grid of labels. I used the -sticky nsew widget option to make the labels expand to fill their containing cells. The third grid command used the rowconfigure option to set the minimum size of the second row to 50 pixels. The fourth grid command used columnconfigure to set the minimum size of the second column to 50 pixels. Figure 11.10 shows the resulting window.

Set a row's
minimum size
using the
-minsize
attribute.

As you can see in Figure 11.10, the second row is 50 pixels tall, and the second column is 50 pixels wide. Had I not set the -minsize attribute, all of the labels would have been the same as the NW label.

Padding Rows and Columns

Another way to manipulate the height of a row or the width of a column is to use the -pad attribute. Where padding a widget using the -padx and -pady options creates space between the widget and the edges of its cell, the -pad option grows the overall height of a row or width of a column, allowing more space for displaying a widget. It's easier to show you the difference than describe it, though, so consider the following script, rowpad.tcl, and its resulting windows, shown in Figure 11.11.

```
if {$argc < 1} {
    puts "Please specify a padding option"
    exit 1
} else {
    set opt [lindex $argv 0]
}


. configure -bg black
wm title . "rowpad.tcl"


label .l -width 12 -bg #eee -relief groove


switch $opt \
    "none" {
        .l configure -text "No Padding"
        grid .l -sticky nsew
    } \
    "cell" {
        .l configure -text "Cell Padding"
        grid .l -padx 10 -pady 10 -sticky nsew
```

```
    } \
    "row" {
        .l configure -text "Row Padding"
        grid .l -padx 10 -pady 10 -sticky nsew
        grid rowconfigure . 0 -pad 20
    } \
    default {
        puts "Invalid padding option: $opt"
        exit 1
    };
}
```

I padded the label widget with -padx and -pady for row padding so that you can see that the padding is cumulative, that is, that the amount of padding added to the row with the -pad attribute increases the row's overall height while maintaining the distance between the edge of the cell and the widget itself. Figure 11.11 shows three rowpad.tcl windows to enable you to compare the appearance of each possible padding option. To perform your own comparison, execute the following three commands in a terminal window:

```
$ ./rowpad.tcl none &
$ ./rowpad.tcl cell &
$ ./rowpad.tcl row &
```

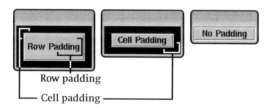

FIGURE 11.11

Padding a row makes it taller.

Resizing Widgets

You might have noticed by now that the widgets in my Tk scripts don't resize themselves if you resize their parent windows. By default, widgets don't grow or shrink when their master grows or shrinks. You can enable resizing by assigning rows and columns a -weight attribute whose value is greater than zero. If the value is zero (the default), resizing is disabled. Otherwise, resizing is enabled. To illustrate, I modified rowpad.tcl to enable resizing both vertically and horizontally. The resulting code follows (see weight.tcl in this chapter's code directory). To make the changes easier to see, I've shown them in bold:

```tcl
set opt [lindex $argv 0]

. configure -bg black
wm title . $argv0

label .l -width 12 -bg #eee -relief groove

switch $opt \
    "none" {
        .l configure -text "No Padding"
        grid .l -sticky nsew
        grid rowconfigure . 0 -weight 1
        grid columnconfigure . 0 -weight 1
    } \
    "cell" {
        .l configure -text "Cell Padding"
        grid .l -padx 10 -pady 10 -sticky nsew
        grid rowconfigure . 0 -weight 1
        grid columnconfigure . 0 -weight 1
    } \
    "row" {
        .l configure -text "Row Padding"
        grid .l -padx 10 -pady 10 -sticky nsew
        grid rowconfigure . 0 -pad 20 -weight 1
        grid columnconfigure . 0 -weight 1
    } \
    default {
        puts "Invalid padding option: $opt"
        exit 1
    };
```

When you execute the script (I used `weight.tcl row`), the initial window looks the same as rowpad.tcl's. However, if you resize the window, you'll see the difference in the behavior of the two scripts (see Figure 11.12).

rowpad.tcl disables row/column resizing

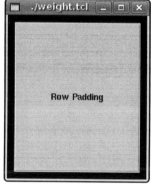

weight.tcl enables row/column resizing

FIGURE 11.12

Set the -weight attribute to enable widgets to resize with their parent windows.

With resizing enabled, the widgets in weight.tcl grow (or shrink) as the master window grows (or shrinks). Not so rowpad.tcl. When its master window grows, the slave windows remain centered in the middle of the master, If you make the master *smaller* than the label, the label will be clipped in the lower right-hand corner. Pretty ugly and probably not what you want your applications to do.

I'VE BEEN FRAMED!

This section and the next deal specifically with widgets that I've already used a good bit: frames and labels. It was necessary to use them without giving you much detail about them because I needed to keep the discussion focused on the particulars of the grid command without getting bogged down in side discussions of the specifics of, say, frames. Hopefully, filling in the gaps now will help you understand more fully some of the preceding sections. This section covers frame widgets and their enhanced counterparts, labelframe widgets. The next section discusses label widgets.

Frames

A frame widget's purpose in life is to be a container for other widgets or to be a spacer between other widgets. It supports a few attributes for setting its width, height, background color, and a 3D border to make the frame appear raised or sunken. I've used the frame widget extensively in this chapter, so I won't repeat that discussion. However, I will describe and demonstrate the -relief attribute, which defines the possible 3D effects that can be applied to most widgets, not just the frame widget. The -relief specifies how the interior of a widget should appear relative to its exterior. It can take one of the values raised, sunken, flat, ridge, solid, or groove. The following script, frame.tcl, shows each possible 3D effect:

```
set row 0
foreach effect {raised sunken flat ridge solid groove} {
    frame .f$effect -width 1i -height .25i -relief $effect -borderwidth 2
    label .l$effect -text $effect

    grid .f$effect
    grid .l$effect -in .f$effect -sticky nsew

    grid propagate .f$effect false
    grid rowconfigure . $row -pad 5

    incr row
}
grid columnconfigure . 0 -pad 5
```

In each iteration of the foreach loop, I define a one-inch-wide and quarter-inch-tall frame with a two-pixel border. Inside each frame, I place a label with one of the possible effects, making it sticky on all sides to fill the frame. Next, I disable propagation to prevent the frames from resizing to fit the size of the labels embedded in them. Finally, before exiting the loop, I place a five-pixel pad around each row. The result is Figure 11.13.

FIGURE 11.13

Frames can have a variety of 3D effects.

Labelframes

As its name suggests, Tk's `labelframe` widget combines the appearance and some of the functionality of both labels and frames. A `labelframe` functions as a frame, serving as a spacer or a container for other widgets. The *label* portion of the name comes from the `labelframe`'s ability to place a label along the border of the widget. Figure 11.14 shows a typical use of a `labelframe`.

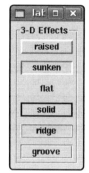

FIGURE 11.14

Labelframes can display a label along their borders.

The code that created Figure 11.14 appears in the following script, which is labelframe.tcl in this chapter's code directory:

```
labelframe .f -text "3D Effects" -width 1i
grid .f -padx 5 -pady 5

foreach effect {raised sunken flat solid ridge groove} {
    label .f.l$effect -text $effect -relief $effect -width 10
    grid .f.l$effect -padx 5 -pady 5
}
```

To establish the master-slave relationship between the labels and the container, I've used the "." notation described in Chapter 9.

The `labelframe` widget has a couple of attributes that behave differently than they do for other widgets or that you have not seen before. In particular, the `-text` attribute is used to create the label that appears along the border. In addition, `labelframes` default to having a `-relief groove` attribute and a `-borderwidth 2` attribute (standard `frame` widgets have no relief and no border by default). The `labelframe`'s different defaults reflect its intended usage, as a container for other widgets and as a design element to create a visual segregation of UI elements.

Two other attributes bear mentioning as well: -labelanchor and -labelwidget. The first, -labelanchor, controls where the default label (the one specified by the -text attribute, if any) will appear. The value can be any of the usual compass points (n, e, sw, ne, and so on) and defaults to nw, meaning that it is placed on the north or top side of the border and on the west or left end of the border. A specification of, for example, -labelanchor es, would place the label on the east or right border at the south or bottom end of the border (see Figure 11.15). The order in which you specify the compass points matters. A specification of es places the label on the east border at the south end; a specification of se places the label on the south border at the east end.

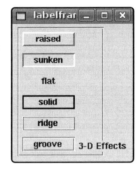

FIGURE 11.15

You can position a labelframe's label in different positions.

The other unique labelframe attribute is -labelwidget. You use this attribute to define your own label for the labelframe and then associate it with the labelframe. If you use -labelwidget, it overrides the value set using the -text attribute. A typical usage of -labelwidget is to use a bitmap or specially styled label instead of the default. For example, the following two commands create a label that has an image rather than text and then associates that label with a labelframe using -labelwidget:

```
label .l -image disc
labelframe .lf -labelwidget .l
```

The corresponding window appears in Figure 11.16.

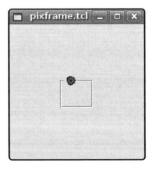

FIGURE 11.16

Using an image for a labelframe's "label."

You haven't learned how to work with images, yet, so I won't go into the code involved here (see Chapter 15, "The Canvas Widget"). If you're curious, though, see pixframe.tcl in this chapter's code directory.

LABELING THE CONTENTS

By now, you and the `label` widget should be on friendly terms, but there are a few character-istics that you haven't seen or used. These attributes include `-textvariable`, `-underline`, and `-wraplength`.

- `-textvariable`—Associates a variable with the label and displays the variable's value, up-dating it automatically as the value changes.
- `-underline`—Specifies the index of a character in the text that should be underlined.
- `-wraplength`—Defines the length *in screen units* at which the text should be wrapped.

The `-wraplength` attribute is defined in an unfortunate manner, screen units (pixels, by default), rather than the number of characters, which is the unit in which the `label` widgets themselves are defined. The `-underline` attribute is equally odd in that it defines the index of the character in the text string that will be underlined and so used as a selection key. This is odd because `label` widgets are read-only and aren't often used interactively. It is useful, though, because if you use a label on a text box, you can cause input focus to shift to the text box when the underlined letter is typed. You'll see how to do this when I discuss text widgets in Chapter 14, "Scrollbar, Scale, and Text Widgets."

The last new `label` attribute, `-textvariable`, enables you to update a `label` widget's text string dynamically to meet the needs of your UI. You might recall that the memtest.tcl script in Chapter 10 updated the instruction label dynamically using the `configure` command; a more elegant way to do it would have been to assign a variable to the label and update the variable. It's a longish script so I won't repeat it here, but you can see the changes in memtest2.tcl in this chapter's code directory.

CREATING NEW WINDOWS

All of the scripts you have seen up to this point show their output in a single window. Often, though, you will want or need to create a separate, stand-alone window in addition to your "main" application window (say, for a modal dialog box). In Tk parlance, such a window is called a *toplevel* and is created with the like-named `toplevel` command. Its syntax is:

```
toplevel name ?options ...?
```

The `toplevel` command returns the pathname of the new window. It is so named because the resulting window is a top-level window; that is, its master is not another widget, but the root window of the screen. A `toplevel` has only two visible features: its background color and an optional 3D border that enables the window to look raised or sunken. Like `frame` and `labelframe` widgets, a `toplevel`'s *raison d'être* is to hold other widgets. This role explains why `toplevels` themselves have few configuration knobs; most of the configuration will be applied to the widgets they contain and most of the decoration of the `toplevel` itself will be handled by the window manager.

The following script, toplevel.tcl in this chapter's code directory, illustrates a simple use of a `toplevel`, creating a window in which to display the source code to the script:

```
proc ShowSource {f} {
    set h 1
    set w 0

    set fileId [open $f r]
    while {[gets $fileId line] != -1} {
        incr h
        append s $line "\n"
        set len [string length $line]
        set w [expr $len > $w ? $len : $w]
    }
    close $fileId

    toplevel .w
    wm title .w "Source Code"
    label .w.l -justify left -height $h -width $w -text $s
    button .w.b -text "Close" -command {wm withdraw .w}
    grid .w.l -sticky w
    grid .w.b -sticky s -pady {30 10}
}


set b [button .b -text "Show Source" -command {ShowSource $argv0}]
set e [button .e -text "Exit" -command exit]
grid $b $e -padx 10 -pady 10
```

The procedure `ShowSource` accepts a single argument, the name of a file to read and display. The first two set commands set the initial height (h) and width (w) of the label in the `toplevel`. The next block of code opens and reads the specified file. Each iteration of the `while` loop reads a line of text, increments the variable h (which is the height, or number of lines read from the file), and appends the line of text read to the variable s, which will be the value assigned to the label's -text attribute. To ensure that the label will be wide enough to display the longest line of text in the file, I use the conditional expression set w [expr $len > $w ? $len : $w]. It compares the current width of the label (stored in $w) to the length of the line just read (stored in $len). If $len is greater than $w, I update $w with $len's value. Otherwise, $w's value remains unchanged. The command button .w.b -text "Close" -command {wm withdraw .w} associates the wm withdraw command with the Close button so that when you click the Close button, the toplevel closes, leaving the "main" or parent window open. The wm withdraw command just withdraws or removes the window on which it is called from the screen without otherwise affecting the rest of the application.

After closing the input file, I lay out the toplevel window, using the variables set in the while loop to configure the label widget that will display the input file. A single grid command displays the file. The "main" part of the script simply defines and displays two buttons, one to create the window (by calling the ShowSource procedure) and one to exit the script. Figure 11.17 shows the main window and the toplevel window created by this script.

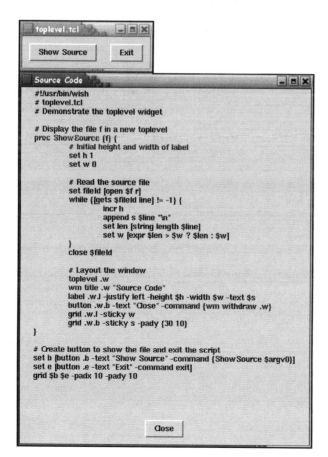

FIGURE 11.17

Top-level windows are separate from the main application window.

You'll notice that if you close the main window using the Exit button, both windows close. However, if you close the `toplevel` using the Close button, the main window remains open. The Exit button, rather the `exit` command, exits the Tcl/tk process, shooting down all the windows it has created.

DID YOU GET THE MESSAGE?

It is certainly useful to be able to create new windows using the `toplevel` command, but for many uses, creating a new top-level window is excessive and more work than you might want or need to do. If you need to show a text string, don't want to have to manually break (wrap) the text, want automatic left-justification, and would like to avoid writing code to handle control characters, then the `message` widget is for you.

The `message` widget's syntax is just like other widgets' syntax:

```
message name ?options ...?
```

In addition to the standard attributes with which you should be familiar by now, the `message` widget has some special attributes that tailor it for displaying text strings using the features I just mentioned. Table 11.2 lists these attributes.

TABLE 11.2: MESSAGE WIDGET ATTRIBUTES	
Attribute	**Description**
`-aspect`	Sets the aspect ratio of the message widget. The ratio is defined as the width of the text to its height, multiplied by 100 (100 * width / height). The aspect ratio defaults to 150.
`-justify`	Defines the justification of the text, defaulting to left-justification.
`-width`	Specifies the length of text lines in the widget.

The default value of `-aspect` is 150, meaning that the text will be one and a half times as wide as it is tall. A value of 200 means that the text would be twice as wide as it is tall. A value of 50, conversely, means that the width of the text would be half of its height. Although the text defaults to left-justification, you can request center- or right-justification with the values `center` or `right`, respectively. The value of the `-width` attribute (in screen units, which are pixels by default) defaults to zero, meaning that the `-aspect` attribute determines the width of the message widget. Accordingly, a *non-zero* for `-width` disables the `-aspect` attribute.

The following script, message.tcl in this chapter's code directory, shows how the message widget looks with its default settings. It displays the README file from the Tk 8.5a6 source distribution:

```
set fileId [open README r]
set msg [read $fileId]
close $fileId

message .m -text $msg
wm title . "README"
grid .m
```

As you can see, it takes a lot less code to display a text file using a message widget than using a toplevel widget. All I had to do was read the input file, store the text in a variable, $msg, and then assign that variable to the message widget's -text attribute. Figure 11.18 shows the resulting window.

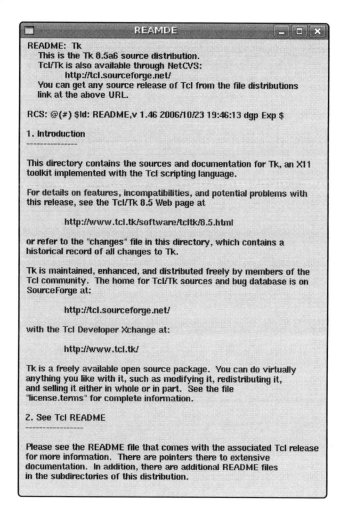

FIGURE 11.18

Message widgets make short work of display text strings.

ANALYZING TIC-TAC-TOE

I think the most difficult part of this game was getting the game-play logic correct, particularly the procedure that identifies whether a particular sequence of buttons represents a winning combination.

Looking at the Code

```
#!/usr/bin/wish
# tic-tac-toe.tcl
# Play a game of Tic-Tac-Toe


# Block 1
# Start the game
proc Start {btns} {
    # Convert the "Play" button to a "Quit" button
    .bExit configure -text "Quit" -command exit

    # Enable the grid buttons
    foreach btn $btns {
        $btn configure -state normal
    }
}

# Disable the grid buttons
proc DisableBtns {} {
    global btns

    foreach btn $btns {
        $btn configure -state disabled
    }
}

# Block 2
# Set "X" or "O" on a button, then check for
# a winning combination
proc SetMark {b} {
    global player X O
```

```
        set mark [$b cget -text]
        # Can only update a button not already pressed
        if {$mark eq "?"} {
            $b configure -text $player
            # Switch players
            if {$player eq "X"} {
                lappend X $b
                CheckWinner $X
                set player "O"
            } else {
                lappend O $b
                CheckWinner $O
                set player "X"
            }
        } else {
            toplevel .w
            message .w.msg -text "Sorry, that square has already been used!"
            grid .w.msg
        }
    }


# Block 3
# Winning button combinations
set winCombos [list {.b1 .b2 .b3} {.b1 .b4 .b7} {.b4 .b5 .b6} \
    {.b1 .b5 .b9} {.b3 .b5 .b7} {.b2 .b5 .b8} {.b3 .b6 .b9} \
    {.b7 .b8 .b9}]

# See if list of buttons passed in "btns" contains a winning
# button combination
proc CheckWinner {btns} {
    global winCombos player

    # Compare known winning button combinations the list of
    # buttons pressed so far
    foreach winCombo $winCombos {
        for {set i 0} {$i < 3} {incr i} {
            set combo [lsort [lrange $btns $i [expr $i + 2]]]
            set ret [string compare $combo $winCombo]
```

```tcl
            if {!$ret} {
                # We have a winner!
                foreach btn $combo {
                    $btn configure -bg green -highlightbackground green
                    $btn flash
                }
                # Announce the winner
                toplevel .w
                message .w.m -aspect 200 -text "Player $player wins!"
                grid .w.m
                # Don't allow further gameplay
                DisableBtns
                return
            }
        }
    }
}


# Block 4
# X always plays first
set player "X"

# Set up the game grid
set row 0
for {set i 1} {$i <= 9} {incr i} {
    button .b$i -text "?" -width 3 -height 3 \
        -state disabled -command "SetMark .b$i"
    if {![expr $i % 3]} {
        grid .b[expr $i - 2] -row $row -column 0
        grid .b[expr $i - 1] -row $row -column 1
        grid .b$i -row $row -column 2
        incr row
    }
    lappend btns .b$i
}


# Start/Quit button
frame .fExit -relief raised -borderwidth 2
```

```
button .bExit -text "Play" -command {Start $btns}
grid .fExit -row 3 -columnspan 3 -sticky nsew
grid .bExit -row 3 -columnspan 3 -in .fExit
grid rowconfigure . 3 -pad 10
```

Understanding the Code

Block 1 defines two utility procedures: Start and DisableBtns. When the script starts, all of the buttons are disabled. The Start procedure, invoked when you click the Play button, enables each button. Start also reconfigures the Play button to be an Exit button, changing both the text on the button and its associated command. The DisableBtns procedure simply loops through each button in the game grid and sets its -state attribute to disabled, effectively preventing further gameplay.

The only procedure in Block 2 is SetMark. It accepts a single argument, the button to mark with an "X" or an "O," depending on who the current player is, which is read from the value of the global variable $player. First, I get the value of the -text attribute for the button passed in. If it is not ?, then the button has already been used or marked, so I create a toplevel window that contains a message widget with text indicating that this square has already been used. Otherwise, I mark the button with an "X" or "O," append the name of the button widget to a list associated with the current player, check to see if the current player has won the game (with the CheckWinner procedure described shortly), and switch players. The variable $X contains a list of all the buttons selected by Player X; $O, likewise, stores a list of the buttons selected by Player O.

The code in Block 3 handles checking to see if a given sequence of buttons contains a winning combination. First, I define a list variable name $winCombos that consists of all the possible combinations of button names that constitute a "win." Each list element, is itself a list of three button combinations. {.b1 .b2 .b3}, for example, are the three buttons across the top of the grid, while {.b3 .b5 .b7} is the diagonal sequence of buttons running from the southwest to the northeast corner of the grid.

CheckWinner does the heavy lifting. It accepts a single argument, a list of marked buttons to check for the known winning combinations stored in $winCombos. The outer loop, the foreach loop, iterates through each possible winning combination until a winner is found or all combinations have been checked.

The inner for loop processes the marked buttons. To do so, I use the lrange command to select three consecutive buttons from the list of marked buttons. I also use the lsort command to sort the list lrange returns in ascending order before I store it in $combo. It is necessary to sort the retrieved values for two reasons. First, the order of buttons in the X and O lists is the order in which they were pressed, which will most likely not be alphabetical. Second, the known winning combinations are sorted in ascending order.

Each iteration of the for loop moves the starting value used with lrange one element into the list of marked buttons. For example, if the marked button list is {.b2 .b3 .b5 .b6}, the three iterations of the for loop will return the following lists. The number to the left of the stylized arrow is the value of the for loop's counter variable, $i:

```
0 → {.b2 .b3 .b5}
1 → {.b3 .b5 .b6}
2 → {.b5 .b6 {}}
```

Yes, the third list has a null or empty element. The inner for loop runs for index values 0, 1, and 2. This is sufficient to cover all possible combinations of button presses because the most buttons either player can press is five; if I haven't found a match by the time I get to the third element in list, I'm not going to find one at all.

Next, I use string compare to compare the marked buttons to the winning combination. Recall that string compare returns zero if the two compared strings are identical, which explains why the if condition is !$ret. If the compared strings are not identical, I proceed to the next combination of marked buttons. Otherwise, when the two button combinations *are* identical, someone has won the game.

To show the winning combination, I change the background of the buttons in the winning combination to green and flash each button. I also use a toplevel window to announce who won, call DisableBtns to prevent further gameplay, and exit the CheckWinner procedure because there is no reason for further comparisons.

Block 4 sets up the game board. I set the default value of the $player variable to "X" because *someone* has to go first. I use a for loop to create the 3x3 grid of buttons. Each button is initially disabled. After creating and laying out each button, I append the button list stored in $btns for use in the Start and DisableBtns procedures in Block 1. Finally, I create the combination Play/Quit button, placing the button in a frame widget to make the layout simpler to manage.

Modifying the Code

Here are some exercises you can try to practice what you learned in this chapter:

11.1 Modify tic-tac-toe.tcl to use both a Play and an Exit button instead of using one button and modifying it dynamically.

11.2 Modify Block 4 of tic-tac-toe.tcl to choose the starting player, either X or O, randomly.

11.3 Modify tic-tac-toe.tcl to show who the current player is.

ENTRY AND SPINBOX WIDGETS

So far, all I've shown you are the read-only widgets such as labels and frames. This is the first of several chapters that discusses Tk's widgets that permit entering text. This chapter introduces the `entry` and `spinbox` widgets. Tk's `entry` widget is a specialized type of text-entry field best-suited to high-speed, head-down data entry but applicable for many types of data entry in which you want to control or validate the data that is input. It displays one line of text that you can edit (or not), subject to restrictions you set using widget-specific attributes and a validation routine that you write. The `spinbox` widget, often referred to as a *spinner* in other GUI toolkits, is based on the entry widget. In addition to enabling text entry in the manner of `entry` widgets, `spinboxes` can also scroll, or *spin*, through a fixed set of values from which you select the desired value (hence their name). The reason I'm covering these two special-purpose text widgets before the all-purpose `text` widget (see Chapter 14) is that the `entry` and `spinbox` widgets support a subset of the features and functionality of the more general text widget. As a result, when you get to Chapter 14, you can build on what you already know.

MAD LIBS REVISTA

Mad Libs Revista rewrites the Mad Libs program from Chapter 4 to use `entry` widgets to create a mad lib silly sentence. To start the game, execute the script g_mad_lib.tcl in this chapter's code directory. Figures 12.1, 12.2, and 12.3 show the game in progress.

FIGURE 12.1

g_mad_lib.tcl's
opening window.

FIGURE 12.2

Type the
requested parts of
speech to play the
game.

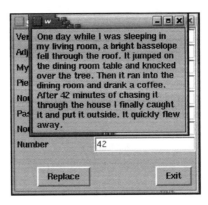

FIGURE 12.3

Click the Replace
button to see the
completed
sentence.

FEATURES OF THE ENTRY AND SPINBOX WIDGETS

The entry and spinbox widgets are very similar. They share many of the same features, attributes, and options. In fact, the spinbox widget is derived from the entry widget. Obviously, they have different behaviors and appearances. In the following discussion, I lump entry and spinbox widgets together to avoid having to repeat myself, but I'll point out where the two widgets differ when necessary.

The entry widget displays a one-line, editable text string. By default, an entry's string is empty. You can select all or part of an entry widget's contents using the mouse, keyboard, or programmatically using widget attributes and commands. If the text in an entry widget is too long to fit entirely within the widget's window, only part of the text will be displayed. This much probably doesn't surprise you. What you might not realize, though, is that you can change the view to display different portions of the text. A spinbox widget has all of the features of an entry widget plus the ability to allow users to spin through a fixed set of values (such as times or dates).

ENTRY AND SPINBOX ATTRIBUTES

In addition to the standard options and attributes entry and spinbox widgets support, they have specific characteristics that I want to highlight (see Table 12.1).

TABLE 12.1: entry AND spinbox ATTRIBUTES

Attribute	Widget	Description
-buttonbackground	S	Background color of the spin buttons themselves.
-buttoncursor	S	Cursor displayed when the mouse pointer hovers over the spin buttons themselves.
-buttondownrelief	S	Relief used for a depressed spin button.
-buttonuprelief	S	Relief used for a raised spin button.
-command	S	Specifies the Tcl command to execute when the spinbutton is invoked.
-exportselecton	B	If true, selected text also becomes the X selection.
-format	B	Defines the format string used when setting the string value (used with -from, -to, and -increment). This must be a format specifier of the form %<pad>.<pad>f, as it will format a floating-point number.
-from	S	Sets the lowest value for a spinbox (in floating point format); used with -to and -increment; -values overrides this setting.
-insertbackground	B	Background color of the insertion area.
-insertborderwidth	B	Width of the border of the insertion area.

Attribute	Widget	Description
-insertofftime	B	If non-zero, the cursor blinks, and this value defines the length of the off portion of the blink cycle in milliseconds.
-insertontime	B	If non-zero, the cursor blinks, and this value defines the length of the on portion of the blink cycle in milliseconds.
-insertwidth	B	Specifies the width in pixels of the insertion cursor.
-invalidcommand, -invcmd	B	Specifies the script to execute if -validatecommand returns 0.
-increment	S	Sets the increment interval between -from and -to.
-readonlybackground	S	Defines the background color when the widget is read-only; defaults to the normal background color.
-selectbackground	B	The background color of selected text.
-selectborderwidth	B	The width of the border around selected text.
-selectforeground	B	The foreground color of selected text.
-show	E	Masks the contents of the entry widget with the specified character, such as *.
-takefocus	B	Controls whether or not the widget accepts focus when using keyboard traversal (using Tab and Shift-Tab). A value of 0 skips the widget, a value of 1 includes the widget, and empty string leaves the decision up to the traversal scripts.
-textvariable	B	The name of a variable whose value is linked to the -text attribute; updates to this variable are reflected immediately in the -text attribute.
-to	B	Sets the highest value for a spinbox; used with -from and -increment; -values overrides this setting.
-validate	B	Determines the mode in which validation should operate; must be one of none (the default), focus, focusin, focusout, key, or all.
-validatecommand, -vcmd	B	Specifies the script to execute for validating input in the widget.
-values	B	Defines list of valid values for the widget's string; overrides -from, -to, and -increment.
-wrap	S	If true, values in a spinbox will roll over (wrap) at the bottom and top of the defined range.
-xscrollcommand	B	Connects the widget to a procedure to use for scrolling the widget's viewable area horizontally.

S: spinbutton only; E: entry only; B: both

Many commands for the entry and spinbox widgets accept index arguments. An *index argument* defines a particular character in the widget's string value. These values are usually used in the context of selecting text or to refer to a portion of a widget's text value that is already selected. You can use one of the following index arguments (out-of-range indices round to the nearest legal value):

- anchor—Sets the anchor point for the selection, which is set with the select from and select adjust widget commands.
- end—Represents the character immediately following the last one in the widget's string.
- insert—Represents the character immediately after the insertion point.
- sel.first—Represents the first selected character.
- sel.last—Represents the last selected character.
- *number*—Specifies the character as a zero-based numeric index.
- @*number*—Specifies *number* as an x-coordinate in the widget's window. The character that spans the specified coordinate will be used. For example, @0 corresponds to the left-most character.

VALIDATING USER INPUT

To use the input validation capabilities of entry and spinbox widgets, set the -validate attribute to one of the values shown in Table 12.2 and set the -validatecommand attribute to a script or procedure that validates the text (by default, validation is disabled). If the validation script returns 1, true, or another valid Tcl Boolean value, the changes to the widget's text will be accepted. Otherwise, the changes will be ignored, and the widget will not accept or show the change.

It is possible to perform percent substitutions on the -validatecommand and -invalidcommand, just as you would in a bind script. Tk recognizes substitutions shown in Table 12.3.

Mixing -textvariable and -validatecommand might cause unpleasant results. If you use -textvariable to set the value of entry and spinbox widgets for read-only purposes, there should be no problems. Problems occur when you try to set -textvariable to a value that your validation command (which is controlled by the -validatecommand). The issue is that setting -textvariable to an invalid value causes the -validate attribute to be reset to none, which means that your -invalidcommand script will not be triggered. Why does validate get set to none? To prevent an infinite loop: setting -textvariable to an invalid value causes -invalidcommand to execute, which might set -textvariable to an invalid value, which causes -invalidcommand to execute. Disabling validation avoids the possibility of the infinite loop.

TABLE 12.2: OPTIONS FOR THE validate **ATTRIBUTE**

Option	Description
all	Executes the validation script for all conditions.
focus	Executes the validation script when the widget receives or loses focus.
focusin	Executes the validation script when the widget receives focus.
focusout	Executes the validation script when the widget loses focus.
key	Executes the validation script when the widget is edited.
none	No validation occurs (default).

TABLE 12.3: PERCENT SUBSTITUTIONS FOR VALIDATION SCRIPTS

Substitution	Description
%d	Validation type (0 for delete, I for insert, -I for focus, forced or textvariable validation).
%i	Index of the character inserted/deleted, if any;, -I otherwise.
%P	The widget's value after the edit.
%s	The widget's value before the edit.
%S	The text string being inserted/deleted, if any;, otherwise an empty string.
%v	The current validation mode (see Table 12.3).
%V	The validation mode that triggered the callback (key, focusin, focusout, forced).
%W	The widget's name.

Likewise, if an error occurs in the -validatecommand or -invalidcommand while evaluating their respective scripts (or if -validatecommand does not return a valid Tcl boolean value), then validation will be disabled. In addition, if you edit the widget's value inside either the -validatecommand or -invalidcommand scripts, validation will be disabled. Again, one reason this occurs is to prevent infinite loops. In addition, editing the widget's value during validation overrides the edit that was being validated.

If You Must Edit During Validation

If you absolutely must edit a widget's value during validation and want to ensure that the -validate option remains set, include the following command in your validation script:

```
%W config -validate %v
```

This command reenables validation. However, your best course of action is to avoid edits during validation and code your scripts to edit widgets *after* validation.

Finally, avoid setting an associated -textVariable during validation, because doing so causes the widget to get out of sync with its associated variable.

BUILDING A BETTER MESSAGE BOX

In Chapter 11, I introduced the toplevel widget and used it to create a crude but effective message box. However, Tk comes with a very nice and easy-to-use message box, created with the tk_messageBox command. Its general syntax is:

```
tk_messageBox ?opt val? ?...?
```

The icons, text, and buttons displayed in the message box depend on the options you specify in *opt* and *val*. Table 12.4 shows the options that tk_messageBox supports.

TABLE 12.4: OPTIONS FOR **tk_messageBox**

Option	Description
-icon *img*	Defines the icon type to display in the message box.
-message *str*	Specifies the message text to display.
-parent *win*	Sets the message box's parent window to *win*; the message box appears over *win*.
-title *str*	Defines the title that appears in the title bar.
-type *type*	Specifies the set of buttons to display in the message box.

When you click one of the buttons in the window, the window closes and returns a text string corresponding to the clicked button. The -type attribute determines the buttons that appear in the window. You can use one of the following values for -type:

- abortretryignore—Displays Abort, Retry, and Ignore buttons, which return abort, retry, or ignore, respectively, when pressed.
- ok—Displays an OK button, which returns ok when pressed.
- okcancel—Displays OK and Cancel buttons, which return ok or cancel, respectively, when pressed.

- retrycancel—Displays Retry and Cancel buttons, which return retry or cancel, respectively, when pressed.
- yesno—Displays Yes and No buttons, which return yes or no, respectively, when pressed.
- yesnocancel—Displays Yes, No, and Cancel buttons, which return yes, no, or cancel, respectively, when pressed.

This chapter's game uses tk_messageBox, so please refer to g_mad_lib.tcl for an example of using this very useful command.

ANALYZING MAD LIBS REVISTA

g_mad_lib.tcl is a classic demonstration that turning a simple, text-based program into a graphical program is rarely a simple "rewrite" at all. Rather, it is a completely new program. In this case, the only element of my original Mad Libs program that survived the rewrite is the source sentence and the code for extracting the text that needed to be replaced.

Looking at the Code

```
#!/usr/bin/wish
# g_mad_lib.tcl
# Demonstrate the entry widget

# Block 1
# Validation command
proc NotEmpty {val} {
    if {$val != {}} {
        return true
    } else {
        tk_messageBox -icon error -type ok -parent . \
            -message "Replacement word or phrase cannot be empty!"
        return false
    }
}

# Block 2
# Find all of the prompts in the text
proc FindPrompts {source} {
    global prompts inputs

    set i 0
```

```
    set j 0
    while {[string first "?" $source $j] != -1} {
        set start [string first "?" $source $j]
        set end [string first "?" $source [expr $start + 1]]
        set j [expr $end + 1];
        set prompt [string range $source [expr $start + 1] \
            [expr $end - 1]]
        lappend prompts [label .l$i -text [string totitle $prompt]]
        lappend inputs [entry .e$i -bg white -validate focusout \
            -vcmd {NotEmpty %P}]
        incr i
    }
}


# Block 3
# Draw the game prompts and entry boxes
proc DisplayPrompts {prompts inputs} {
    set len [llength $prompts]
    for {set i 0} {$i < $len} {incr i} {
        grid [lindex $prompts $i] [lindex $inputs $i] -sticky w
    }
    button .bShow -text "Replace" -command ShowMadLib
    button .bExit -text "Exit" -command exit
    grid .bShow .bExit -padx 5 -pady {20 5} -sticky e
}


# Block 4
# Create a list of replacement phrases from the player's input
proc GetFields {} {
    global inputs

    foreach input $inputs {
        lappend fields [$input get]
    }
    return $fields
}


# Block 5
```

```
# Build and display the completed mad lib
proc ShowMadLib {} {
    global line

    foreach field [GetFields] {
        set start [string first "?" $line]
        set end [string first "?" $line [expr $start + 1]]
        set line [string replace $line $start $end $field]
    }
    toplevel .w
    message .w.m -text $line
    grid .w.m

}


# Block 6
# The source sentence
set line "One day while I was ?verb ending in -ing? in my living room, "
append line "a ?adjective? ?mythical creature? fell through the roof. "
append line "It jumped on the ?piece of furniture? and knocked over the "
append line "?noun?. Then it ran into the dining room and ?past tense verb? "
append line "a ?noun?. After ?number? minutes of chasing it through the "
append line "house I finally caught it and put it outside. It quickly "
append line "flew away."

# List variables to contain the prompts and the player's input
set prompts {}
set inputs {}

# Parse the source sentence
FindPrompts $line

# Display the game window
DisplayPrompts $prompts $inputs
```

Understanding the Code

As usual, g_mad_lib.tcl begins with procedure definitions. Block 1 defines my validation routine, NotEmpty. It accepts a single argument, the text string the player types in an entry widget.

If the text is not empty, NotEmpty returns true. Otherwise, I display a message box complaining that the field cannot be empty and then return false.

Block 2 defines the FindPrompts procedure, which accepts a string argument, $source, that stores the sentence to parse. First, I declare two global variables, $prompts and $inputs. $prompts is a list variable containing labels (actually, variable references to label widgets) that display the prompts for the items the player must provide. $inputs stores variable references to the entry widgets in which the player types.

Next, I create two counter variables, $i and $j. $i increments by one each iteration of the loop; I use it to create sequentially numbered label and entry widgets. $j helps me keep track of my current position in the $source string, as I will explain shortly.

As with the original Mad Lib program, I use a while loop to iterate through the string, using the string first command to locate text situated between pairs of question marks. The algorithm I use in g_mad_lib.tcl is slightly different. Whereas in mad_lib.tcl I replaced text on-the-fly as I parsed the source sentence, in g_mad_lib.tcl all I want to do is extract the prompts; I perform the replacements in a separate statement. As a result, I need to keep track of the position of the second or closing question mark so I can start the search for the next prompt at that position. The method I use is the following:

1. Search for the first or opening ?, starting from the index stored in $j, which is 0 for the first iteration of the loop. Store this value in the variable $start.
2. Search for the second or closing ?, starting at the character index immediately following the index stored in $start. Store this value in the variable $end.
3. Set $j to the character index immediately following the index stored in $end. The next search will start from this index in the string.
4. Extract the text between the two ?s and store it in the variable $prompt.
5. Create a label widget using the value of $prompt and append a variable reference to the newly created label widget to the list variable $prompts. I could have combined Steps 4 and 5, but I didn't want a line of code extending over several lines. Breaking it up into two operations also makes the code easier to read. Otherwise, it would have looked something like the following:

```
lappend prompts [label .l$i -text [string totitle \
    [string range $source [expr $start + 1] [expr $end · 1]]]]
```

6. Create an entry widget corresponding to the label widget created in Step 5 and append a variable reference to the newly created widget to the list variable $inputs. I set the -validate attribute to focusout and -vcmd to NotEmpty %P. This means that when input focus leaves the entry widget, the NotEmpty procedure will be called with the value of the edited text in the widget.

7. Increment the value of $i.

8. Repeat Steps 1–7 until no more ?s are found in $source, at which point the loop and the procedure terminate.

Block 3 consists of the DisplayPrompts procedure. It creates the game window shown in Figures 12.1, 12.2, and 12.3 at the beginning of this chapter. DisplayPrompts accepts two arguments, the $prompts and $inputs variables populated by the FindPrompts procedure. After determining the number of elements in the $prompts list, I use a for loop to iterate through both $prompts and $inputs, laying out rows that contain a label widget and its associated entry widget and sticking them to the west or left side of the parent (root) window. Next, DisplayPrompts creates two buttons, .bShow, which invokes the ShowMadLib procedure, and .bExit, which exits the program. These buttons appear on their own row.

The GetFields procedure in Block 4 iterates through the entry widgets, extracting their text strings and appending the extracted values to the $fields list variable. It returns the completed list of fields to the calling procedure, which is ShowMadLib, defined in Block 5. ShowMadLib, in turn, iterates through the source sentence a second time, this time replacing text between ?s with the player-provided input. After completing the string replacements, I create a new toplevel window, embed a message widget in it containing the modified sentence, and display the completed Mad Lib.

Modifying the Code

Here are some exercises you can try to practice what you learned in this chapter:

1. As it is, you can click the Replace button in g_mad_lib.tcl without providing any input in the entry widgets. Modify g_mad_lib.tcl to require all entry widgets to have valid text.

2. Modify g_lib_mad.tcl to read its source sentence from a file rather than using a hard-coded sentence.

3. The validation scheme in g_mad_lib.tcl has the annoying side effect of not allowing the player to click in one entry widget and then click in a second one without entering text. If you change your mind this way, the validation routine nags you with a message box telling you that the first entry is still empty. Fix the validation routine.

LISTBOX WIDGETS

This chapter shows you how to use Tk's listbox widget. A listbox displays a series of read-only text lines. The list is vertically scrollable and can be scrolled horizontally as necessary. You can select zero, one, or more items in a list, so the listbox widget has methods for determining which items are selected (and for selecting items programmatically). You can add and delete items from a listbox, but items themselves cannot be edited. As usual, you can also control the colors, relief, and other visual attributes of listbox widgets.

MATCHING LISTS

The idea of the this chapter's game is to select related words and phrases from adjacent listboxes. After you create each match, click the Match button to record your selection. After you have matched all of the words in the left-hand listbox with their matching definitions in the right-hand listbox, click the Score button to see how you did. To start the game, execute the matches.tcl script in this chapter's code directory. Figures 13.1–13.5 illustrate the game's screens.

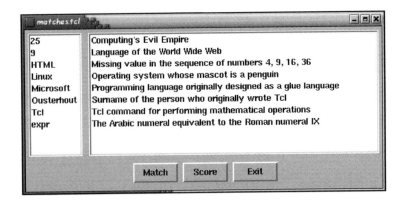

FIGURE 13.1

Match the words on the left to the definitions on the right.

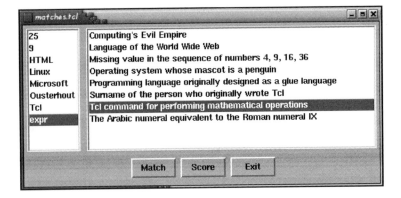

FIGURE 13.2

After selecting a word and a definition, click the Match button.

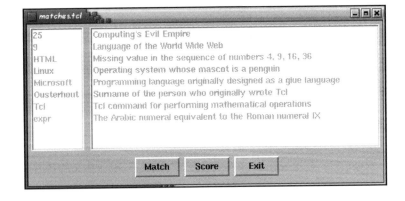

FIGURE 13.3

Click the Score button after creating your matches.

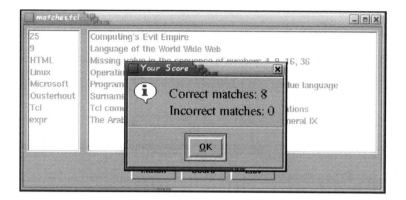

FIGURE 13.4

A perfect score!

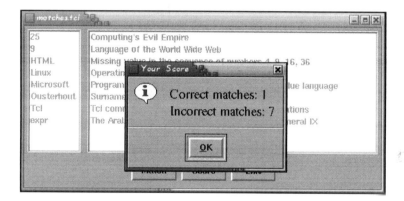

FIGURE 13.5

Maybe I need to try again.

CREATING A LISTBOX

Back in Chapter 10, I provided an extra script, show_colors.tcl, which used a `listbox` widget. I'm going to use various versions of that script to introduce you to the features of Tk's `listbox` widget. I'll start by creating a listbox and populating it with some names of colors, as shown below (see list_create.tcl in this chapter's code directory):

```
proc GetColors {colorFile} {
    set fileId [open $colorFile r]
    while {[gets $fileId line] > 0} {
        lappend colors [string trim [lrange $line 0 end]]
    }
    close $fileId
    return $colors
}

listbox .colorlist -bg white
```

```
set colors [GetColors "colors.txt"]
foreach color $colors {
    .colorlist insert end $color
}

button .bexit -text "Exit" -command exit

grid .colorlist -padx 5 -pady 5 -sticky nsew
grid .eExit -pady {0 5}
```

The GetColors procedure is a helper procedure. It reads the file passed as its sole argument and creates a list of colors ($colors) from the contents of that file. It returns the list of colors to the calling procedure. Figure 13.6 shows the list_create.tcl's window.

FIGURE 13.6

The listbox widget is easy to create and to populate.

At the moment, all you can do is select a color name (as shown in the figure) and scroll the list using a mouse wheel (if your mouse has one) or by left-clicking and dragging down to scroll down the list or dragging up to scroll up the list. You'll notice when scrolling the list that the selected color name, if any, scrolls out of view. You'll probably also notice that you can only select a single item at a time; this is the default behavior but it can be changed. I'll discuss this in the next section, "Selecting Listbox Content."

Creating the listbox is simple: The listbox command creates a listbox widget named .colorlist and gives it a white background. To populate the list, I invoke the GetColors procedure, saving the list of color names it returns in the variable $colors. Next, I use a foreach loop to iterate over each color name and add it to the listbox using the listbox widget's insert command:

```
.colorlist insert end $color
```

The insert command adds an item to a listbox at a specified index. In this case, I used the special keyword end, which means the color name is added to the end of bottom of the list. To specify a particular location, I could have specified a particular index value.

I create an Exit button (.bexit) for the sake of convenience, and then lay out the list and the button using the grid command.

The inverse of inserting an item into a list is removing an item from a list. You accomplish this using the delete command. The following script, item_delete.tcl, adds a Delete button to the list_create.tcl script. I've shown the code additions in boldface so you can see how the script has changed:

```tcl
proc GetColors {colorFile} {
    set fileId [open $colorFile r]
    while {[gets $fileId line] > 0} {
        lappend colors [string trim [lrange $line 0 end]]
    }
    close $fileId
    return $colors
}


proc DelItems {w} {
    $w delete 0 4
}


listbox .colorlist -bg white
set colors [GetColors "colors.txt"]
foreach color $colors {
    .colorlist insert end $color
}


button .bexit -text "Exit" -command exit
button .bdelete -text "Delete" -command {DelItems .colorlist}

grid .colorlist -padx 5 -pady 5 -columnspan 2 -sticky nsew
grid .bdelete .bexit -pady {0 5}
```

With four additional lines of code, I can now delete color names from the list. The key line of code is $w delete 0 4 in the DelItems procedure. The syntax for the listbox's delete procedure is:

listbox delete *first* ?*last*?

Here, *listbox* does not refer to the listbox command itself, but the name of a listbox widget or a variable reference to a listbox widget. *first* and *last* represent the indices, inclusive, of items that should be deleted from the list. If you omit *last*, only a single item will be deleted. Otherwise, all the items between and including *first* and *last* will be deleted. So, in the case of item_delete.tcl, my Delete button is hard-wired to delete the first five colors in this list. This isn't terribly useful, but it shows the basic technique. I'll show you how to delete specific items in the next section.

Figures 13.7 and 13.8 show the item_delete.tcl's window before and after deleting colors from the list.

FIGURE 13.7

Click the Delete button to delete the first five entries in the list.

FIGURE 13.8

After deletion, there are five fewer colors in this list.

SELECTING LISTBOX CONTENT

In the item_delete.tcl script, I deleted color names from the list arbitrarily. This is not terribly useful. The usual sequence of events is for the user to select one or more items and then click a Delete or Remove button to delete the selected items. First, you need to know how to create listbox widgets that support selecting multiple items. Then you need to know how to reference the selected items.

Setting the Selection Mode

You can set the selection mode using the listbox widget's -selectmode attribute, which, for the purposes of this book, must be one of the values in Table 13.1.

TABLE 13.1: VALUES FOR THE -selectmode ATTRIBUTE

Value	Description
single	Only a single item can be selected with mouse button 1.
browse	Only a single item can be selected with mouse button 1, and you can drag the selection with button 1.
multiple	Multiple items can be selected with mouse button 1, and clicking an item toggles its selected state.
extended	Multiple items can be selected with mouse button 1. Clicking an item unselects everything else and sets a new selection anchor.

In browse mode, you can click and drag the selection with mouse button 1. If the selection mode is multiple or extended, you can select multiple items simultaneously, including items that aren't adjacent to each other. In multiple mode, clicking mouse button 1 on a list item toggles its selected state but does not affect other items' selected state.

In extended mode, clicking mouse button 1 on a list item selects it, unselects everything else, and sets the selecting anchor to selected item. If you then drag the mouse (with mouse button 1 pressed), you extend the selection to include all of the items between the anchor and the element under the mouse. You can also click an item to set the anchor and then Shift+Click (press the Shift key while clicking mouse button 1) on another item to select all of the items between the anchor and the Shift+Clicked item. Finally, in extended mode, to add a nonadjacent item to a selection, Ctrl+Click it (press the Control key while clicking mouse button 1).

NOTE — The Selection Mode Can Be Arbitrarily Defined

The default bindings defined for the Tk listbox widget expect the -selectmode attribute to be one of the values shown in Table 13.1. However, if you modify the bindings, you can use an arbitrary value to which your customized binding will respond. I do not address binding in this book, so I've stuck to the default attributes.

In Figure 13.9, I show how the multiple selection mode works while Figure 13.10 shows how extended selection mode works. To create Figure in 13.9, I modified list_create.tcl, adding -selectmode multiple to the listbox command:

```
listbox .colorlist -bg white -selectmode multiple
```

See select_mult.tcl in this chapter's code directory.

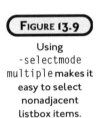

FIGURE 13.9

Using -selectmode multiple makes it easy to select nonadjacent listbox items.

To create Figure 13.10, I specified -selectmode extended when creating the listbox:

```
listbox .colorlist -bg white -selectmode extended
```

See select_ext.tcl in this chapter's code directory.

FIGURE 13.10

Click and drag to select multiple adjacent items in the extended selection mode.

Determining the Selected Items

You're probably thinking something like, "Swell, Kurt. But how do I find out *what* items are selected? " Well, you'll need a goat, a chicken foot, some blood, and... Wait, wrong book. The listbox widget has two commands for retrieving indices of selected items. They are:

- *listbox* index active—Returns the index of the active item.
- *listbox* curselection—Returns a list of indices of selected lines.
- *listbox* get *first* ?*last*?—Returns the lines between and including *first* and, if specified, *last*, where *first* and *last* are index values.

As before, *listbox* does not refer to the listbox command itself, but to the name of a listbox widget or a variable reference to a listbox widget. Each of these commands is best used in different circumstances. The index command, for example, returns the numerical index that corresponds to its argument. In this case, I used the keyword active, which corresponds to the activated item in the list. It is best used when you are interested in the active element, which does not necessarily correspond to all of the selected elements. Table 13.2 lists other possible values for all listbox index and other listbox operations that require index arguments.

TABLE 13.2: LISTBOX INDEX VALUES

Value	Description
0	Index of the first item.
active	Index of the active (activated) item.
anchor	Index of the current selection's anchor point.
end	Index of the last item.
num	Item *num* in the listbox, counting from zero.
@x,y	The item nearest the listbox-relative coordinates given by *x* and *y*.

If there are, or might be, multiple items selected in a listbox, the best command to use is *listbox* curselection, which returns a list of all the indices of selected items. For the Delete button in the color picker script I've been using in this chapter, the curselection command is the one I'll use (more about that very shortly). Finally, if you know the index or indices of the listbox items in which you're interested, you can use *listbox* get, passing it the index or range of consecutive indices. The useful feature of the get operation is that it returns the text of the specified items, rather than their indices.

Using what I've just discussed, the following listing shows yet another variation of the list_create.tcl script that enables you to delete all of the selected colors (see list_delete.tcl in this chapter's code directory):

```
proc GetColors {colorFile} {
    set fileId [open $colorFile r]
```

```
    while {[gets $fileId line] > 0} {
        lappend colors [string trim [lrange $line 0 end]]
    }
    close $fileId
    return $colors
}

proc DelItems {w} {
    set s [$w curselection]
    set colors [lsort -decreasing -integer $s]
    foreach color $colors {
        $w delete $color
    }
}

listbox .colorlist -selectmode multiple -bg white
foreach color [GetColors "colors.txt"] {
    .colorlist insert end $color
}

button .bdel -text "Delete" -command {DelItems .colorlist}
button .bexit -text "Exit" -command exit

grid .colorlist -padx 5 -pady 5 -columnspan 2
grid .bdel .bexit -pady {0 5}
```

The real guts of list_delete.tcl reside in the DelItems procedure. It accepts a single argument, the widget on which to operate. The first set command retrieves the indices of selected items in the widget, storing this list in the variable $s. This is a junk variable, so I didn't bother giving it a meaningful name. The next set operation sorts that list in descending numeric order. The reason I wanted the list in descending order was to preserve the ordering of items in the list as I deleted items. If I delete from the "bottom" of the list, the order of items above the deleted item won't change. If I delete from the "top" of the list, each deletion changes the index value of all of the items below the deleted item. After sorting the list, deleting the items is a simple matter of iterating through the sorted list with a foreach and calling $w delete against each index value.

The other significant change to the script was wiring the Delete button to the new DelItems script. Figures 13.11 and 13.12 show the color list before and after deleting some randomly selected colors.

FIGURE 13.11

Select the colors you want to delete then click the Delete button.

FIGURE 13.12

The selected colors are gone!

Had I not sorted the retrieved indices in descending numeric order, instead of deleting the colors snow, GhostWhite, gainsboro, and OldLace, I would have deleted snow, white smoke, FloralWhite, and AntiqueWhite.

Selecting Items Programmatically

Another task you'll surely want to perform is to select list items programmatically, that is, with code. Table 13.3 shows the operations you have at your disposal for performing selection-related activities in code.

The next script, auto_select.tcl in this chapter's code directory, uses selection set to select the list items between index values 200 and 204 inclusive and the see command to scroll the selected items into view:

TABLE 13.3: SELECTION COMMANDS FOR THE LISTBOX WIDGET

Command	Description
listbox nearest *y*	Returns the index of the value closest to the specified widget-relative *y* coordinate.
listbox scan mark *x y*	Starts a scrolling operation for the specified widget-relative *x* and *y* coordinates (usually used with the scan dragto operation).
listbox scan dragto *x y*	Scrolls from a previously set mark (see the scan mark operation) to the specified widget-relative *x* and *y* coordinates.
listbox see *index*	Scrolls the specified *index* so it is visible in the listbox.
listbox selection anchor *index*	Anchors the selection at the item specified by *index*.
listbox selection clear *first* ?*last*?	Clears selected items between and including the index values specified by *first* and *last* (if *last* is specified).
listbox selection includes *index*	Returns 1 if the current selection includes the item specified by *index*.
listbox selection set *first* ?*last*?	Creates a selection consisting of the items between and including the index values specified by *first* and *last* (if *last* is specified).

```
proc GetColors {colorFile} {
    set fileId [open $colorFile r]
    while {[gets $fileId line] > 0} {
        lappend colors [string trim [lrange $line 0 end]]
    }
    close $fileId
    return $colors
}

listbox .colorlist -bg white
set colors [GetColors "colors.txt"]
set i 0
foreach color $colors {
    set item [format "%3d  %s" $i $color]
    puts $item
    .colorlist insert end $item
```

```
    incr i
}

button .bexit -text "Exit" -command exit
button .bselect -text  "Select" -command {.colorlist selection set 200 204}
button .bscroll -text "Scroll" -command {.colorlist see 200}

grid .colorlist -padx 5 -pady 5 -sticky nsew -columnspan 2
grid .bselect .bscroll -padx 5 -pady {0 5} -sticky nsew
grid .bexit -pady {0 5} -columnspan 2
```

As with the other scripts in this chapter, auto_select.tcl is a modified version of list_create.tcl. In this case, I modified the `foreach` loop to show the index value of each item in the list in addition to its text string. I also added two `button` widgets to implement the selection (`.bselect`) and scrolling (`.bscroll`) functionality. `.bselect`'s -command attribute executes the command `.colorlist selection set 200 204`. The -command attribute for `.bscroll`, similarly, scrolls the list so that the item at index value 200 appears in the center of the `listbox` widget's viewable area. Figures 13.13, 13.14, and 13.15 show the initial window, the results after scrolling the window (clicking the Scroll button), and the window after clicking the Select button, respectively.

FIGURE 13.13

The index values help you see the effects of the Select and Scroll buttons.

In case you were wondering, you can also click the Select button first, followed by the Scroll button. I won't get into the philosophical question of whether or not selected items are really selected if you can't see them, but what I will guarantee is that when you click Scroll, the items I selected are, in fact, selected.

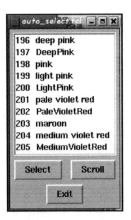

FIGURE 13.14

The Scroll button moves the item at index 200 to the center of the list.

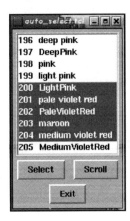

FIGURE 13.15

Clicking the Select button programmatically selects the requested items.

ANALYZING MATCHING LISTS

The Matching Lists games is arguably the most involved script you've seen in this book. It's certainly one of the most complete, using a wide selection of the Tcl and Tk elements I've introduced in this book, including arrays, lists, sorting, frames, buttons, mathematical expressions, and, of course, the `listbox` widget.

Looking at the Code

```
#!/usr/bin/wish
# matches.tcl
# Match words and phrases in two lists

# Block 1
# Variable needed in the procedures
```

```
set matches {}

# Words and their definitions
array set items {
    "HTML" "Language of the World Wide Web"
    "Tcl" "Programming language originally designed as a glue language"
    "Ousterhout" "Surname of the person who originally wrote Tcl"
    "expr" "Tcl command for performing mathematical operations"
    "9" "The Arabic numeral equivalent to the Roman numeral IX"
    "25" "Missing value in the sequence of numbers 4, 9, 16, 36"
    "Microsoft" "Computing's Evil Empire"
    "Linux" "Operating system whose mascot is a penguin"
}

# Block 2
# Match the selected word and the selected definition and mark
# them "disabled"
proc MatchSels {} {
    global lWords lDefs matches

    # Get the current selections
    set w [$lWords curselection]
    set d [$lDefs curselection]

    # Map the indices to their text values
    set word [$lWords get $w]
    set def [$lDefs get $d]

    # Append the matched pair to the list matches
    lappend matches $word $def

    # "Disable" the current selections
    $lWords itemconfigure $w -foreground grey
    $lDefs itemconfigure $d -foreground grey

    # Clear the current selections
    $lWords selection clear $w
    $lDefs selection clear $d
```

```
}


# Block 3
# Compare player's matches to the source array
proc ScoreMatches {} {
    global matches items
    set correct 0
    set incorrect 0

    foreach {word def} $matches {
        if {$def eq $items($word)} {
            incr correct
        } else {
            incr incorrect
        }
    }

    tk_messageBox -title "Your Score" -type ok -icon info \
        -message "Correct matches: $correct\nIncorrect matches: $incorrect"
}


# Block 4
# Define the widgets
set lWords [listbox .lwords -selectmode single -bg white \
    -exportselection false]
set lDefs [listbox .ldefs -selectmode single -bg white \
    -exportselection false]
set fButtons [frame .fbuttons]
set bMatch [button .bmarch -width 5 -text "Match" -command MatchSels]
set bScore [button .bscore -width 5 -text "Score" -command ScoreMatches]
set bExit [button .bexit -width 5 -text "Exit" -command exit]

# Lay 'em out
grid $lWords $lDefs -padx 5 -pady 5
grid $fButtons -columnspan 2 -padx 5 -pady 5
grid $bMatch $bScore $bExit -in .fbuttons -sticky nsew \
    -padx {5 0} -pady {0 5}
```

```
# Block 5
# Parse the items array for words and their definitions
foreach {word def} [array get items] {
    lappend words $word
    lappend defs $def
}


# Block 6
# Populate and resize the words listbox
set wordLen 0
foreach word [lsort -ascii $words] {
    set newLen [string length $word]
    set wordLen [expr $newLen > $wordLen ? $newLen : $wordLen]

    $lWords insert end $word
}
$lWords configure -width $wordLen


# Populate and resize the definitions listbox
set defLen 0
foreach def [lsort -ascii $defs] {
    set newLen [string length $def]
    set defLen [expr $newLen > $defLen ? $newLen : $defLen]
    $lDefs insert end $def
}
$lDefs configure -width $defLen
```

Understanding the Code

Block 1 consists of variable definitions. The $matches list stores a list of matched words and definitions created when the player clicks the Match button. The $items array is the source list of the words and definitions used to populate the two listbox widgets. It also serves as the master list against which the player's matches are scored.

In Block 2, I define the MatchSels procedure, which is invoked each time the player clicks the Match button. I declare the global variables $lWords, $lDefs, and matches because I will be modifying them. $lWords stores the list of words extracted from the $items array, while $lDefs stores the list of definitions, also extracted from the $items array. I define these two variables later in the program, but I declare them here so I can access them inside the procedure.

To create the player's match, I have to find out which items are selected and store the matched word and definition pair. The procedure is straightforward:

1. Get the index of the currently selected word using the curselection operation on the words listbox (set w [$lWords curselection]).
2. Get the index of the currently selected definition using the curselection operation on the definitions listbox (set d [$lDefs curselection]).
3. Fetch the text string corresponding to the index value $w and store it in the $word variable (set word [$lWords get $w]).
4. Fetch the text string corresponding to the index value $d and store it in the $def variable (set def [$lDefs get $d]).
5. Append the matched $word and $def to the $matches list (lappend matches $word $def).

Finally, as a visual aid for the player, I change the font color of items that have been matched. Although the items aren't actually disabled, making them gray emulates a common GUI idiom of "graying out" disabled items. The itemconfigure operation and its related itemcget operation allow you to set and retrieve, respectively, individual list items rather than the listbox itself or the list as a whole. Similarly, after completing the match, I clear the selected items using the selection clear operation to give the player a visual cue that I made the match and as a hint to continue.

The ScoreMatches procedure defined in Block 3 compares the player's matches, stored in the $matches list, to the master list of words and definitions stored in the $items array. Again, these two variables are defined in the global scope, so in order to access them inside the procedure, I declare them as global variables. I also declare two procedure local variables, $correct and $incorrect, whose sole purpose is to keep track of the number of correct and incorrect matches.

The actual comparison is simple enough. Iterating through the player's list of matches, I first break each pair of matched items into a word ($word) and a definition ($def). I compare the string value of the definition to the corresponding definition of $word from the $items array, using $word to index into the $items array. If the value returned by $items($word) is identical to $def, the match is correct, and I increment $correct accordingly. Otherwise, the match is incorrect, and I increment $incorrect. After iterating through each pair of matched items in the $matches list, I use tk_messageBox to display the results.

Block 4 defines and lays out the widgets I'll need, two listbox widgets, a frame to hold the buttons, and the button widgets. I used the single selection mode on the listboxes to prevent the player from trying to match two words to a single definition (or vice versa).

I specified -exportselection false to make it possible to select items from more than one listbox at a time. By default, the listbox widget exports its selection to the X Window System selection buffer (the clipboard under Windows). Because there can only be a single selection buffer at any one time, you can only select items from a single listbox widget. I needed to be able to select items from more than one listbox; setting -exportselection false avoids this limitation. It also prevents selections from being accessed using the selection buffer (clipboard), but matches.tcl doesn't need the selection buffer, so this wasn't a problem.

I used a frame widget as a container for the buttons so the buttons would be nicely centered beneath the two listbox widgets. You'll see why this is necessary when you get to Block 6. Beyond this one wrinkle, gridding out the widgets is routine.

The code in Block 5 parses the $items array, storing the words into the $words list and the definitions into the $defs list.

The code in Block 6 is somewhat more involved. The goal I want to achieve is to make each listbox just wide enough to hold the widest list item (measured in characters) and also to modify the order of items as I insert them into the listbox. If I don't need to modify the order of the list items, the words and their correct definitions end up side-by-side in the two listboxes, which doesn't present much of a challenge to the player.

First, I set the variable $wordLen to 0. At the top of the foreach loop, I sort the contents of the $words list in (ascending) alphabetical order. Then, for each item in the list, I check its length in characters. I use expr's conditional operator (expr $wordLen > $newLen ? $wordLen : $newLen) to update the value of $wordLen if the length of the current word (stored in $newLen) is longer (if it isn't, $wordLen is unchanged). Finally, I insert the current word at the end or bottom of the $lWords listbox. After processing all of the words on the $words list, I use the value of $wordLen to update the width of the $lWords listbox ($lWords configure -width $wordLen). The second foreach loop in Block 6 uses the same technique for the $defs list and the $lDefs listbox, so I'll spare you a repeat of the explanation.

At this point, the setup is complete, and the game is ready to play.

Modifying the Code

Here are some exercises you can try to practice what you learned in this chapter:

13.1. Modify the MatchSels procedure to detect if the player has already selected a word or definition and to prevent reuse of a previously selected word or definition.

13.2. Modify the ScoreMatches procedure to set the foreground color of correctly matched words and definitions to green and incorrectly matched words and definitions to red.

13.3. Modify the script to disable the Score button at the beginning of the game. Similarly, disable the Match button and enable the Score button after all items have been matched.

SCROLLBAR, SCALE, AND TEXT WIDGETS

Scrollbars allow you or your users to scroll the viewable area of a window. A *scale widget* is a slider whose value changes as the slider is moved. Text widgets provide areas for displaying and editing text. Except for very short text documents or small objects of any variety, you will need to use vertical or horizontal scrollbars (or both) to allow users to view different portions of a window's content. In a text document, for example, you'd add a vertical scrollbar to enable users to scroll the document up and down. If you're writing a game that needs a player map, similarly, chances are good that you would need both vertical and horizontal scrollbars so users could look at different parts of the map.

Text widgets are used, well, to display text. In the context of a game, you might not need to display long sections of text, but most other applications usually do involve text display and manipulation. As you will see later in the chapter, Tk's text widget is a full-featured text display and manipulation tool. The price of this feature set is that the text widget is complex.

WORD SEARCH

This chapter's program, gword_search.tcl, presents a simplified version of the classic word search puzzle to illustrate how to program Tk's text widget. The game shows users a randomly ordered collection of letters from which the player must select a word made up of consecutive letters. The player selects a word from the jumble of letters and clicks the Score button. If the correct target word is selected, the word is highlighted in green and disabled. If the selected word is incorrect or isn't the target word, the selection is highlighted in red. To start the game, execute the gword_search.tcl script found in this chapter's code directory. Figures 14.1 through 14.3 show the progress of the game.

Select a word from the letter jumble and click the Score button.

A correctly selected word is highlighted in green.

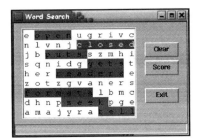

An incorrectly selected word is highlighted in red.

Using the Scrollbars to Move the Viewport

The scrollbar command creates a scrollbar widget, which is used to change the visible area, referred to as the *viewport*, of another widget. Scrollbars work with four of Tk's standard widgets: entry widgets, text widgets, listbox widgets, and canvas widgets. Although they only work with these four standard widgets, the scrollbar protocol is general enough that you can use it to control widgets that you create, but creating a widget from scratch, as opposed to using Tk's stock widgets, is not a subject I'll cover in this book. I do describe how you can interact with the scrollbar protocol directly instead of using its built-in defaults, however, but I think you'll see that this is not an undertaking for the faint of heart.

Scrollbars can move the viewport horizontally, vertically, or both. They consist of a slider, a trough in which the slider moves, and arrows at each end of the trough. The position and size of the slider provide a visual cue about how much of the document is visible in the associated window. For example, if the slider in a vertical scrollbar covers the top third of the area between the two arrows, it means that the associated window displays the top third of its document.

Simple Scrolling

The best way to get started is to look at an example, simple_scroll.tcl, in this chapter's code directory. It uses the text widget that you will learn about later in the chapter, but the principles for connecting a scrollbar to a scrollbar-supporting widget are the same, regardless of the widget to which the scrollbar is connected:

```
proc ReadFile {f} {
    set fileId [open $f r]
    set input [read $fileId]
    close $fileId
    return $input
}

set t [text .t -background #ffffff]
$t insert end [ReadFile "README"]

set sb [scrollbar .y -command [list $t yview]]
$t configure -wrap word -yscrollcommand [list $sb set]

grid $t $sb -sticky nsew
grid columnconfigure . 0 -weight 1
grid rowconfigure . 0 -weight 1
grid columnconfigure . 1 -weight 0
```

The most important two lines of code in simple_scroll.tcl are

```
set sb [scrollbar .y -command [list $t yview]]
$t configure -wrap word -yscrollcommand [list $sb set]
```

because they connect the scrollbar and the text widgets together. The first line invokes the text widget's yview operation when the scrollbar is repositioned. In effect, the first command wires the text widget's display to the scrollbar so that moving the slider up moves the viewport up, and moving the slider down moves the viewport down. If the scrollbar had been oriented horizontally, I would have invoked the text widget's xview operation.

The second command completes the circuit, so to speak, wiring the scrollbar to the text widget by invoking the scrollbar's set operation whenever the view in the text widget changes. Thus, if you use the up or down arrow keys to change the text viewed in the text widget, the slider's position in the scrollbar changes accordingly.

A Confession of Confusion

For some reason, when I was first learning Tk, the connections between the scrollbar widget and the widgets on which they operated confused me. I finally settled on this formulation of the relationship:

- The scrollbar's -command attribute must invoke the connected widget's scrolling operation, which is yview for vertical movement or xview for horizontal movement.
- The connected widget's scrolling attribute (which is either -yscrollcommand for vertical scrolling or -xscrollcommand for horizontal movement) must invoke the scrollbar's set operation.

Perhaps I'm just easy to confuse, but these two rules work for me, so I hope they help you.

The four grid commands are important, too:

```
grid $t $sb -sticky nsew
grid columnconfigure . 0 -weight 1
grid rowconfigure . 0 -weight 1
grid columnconfigure . 1 -weight 0
```

The first command lays out the text widget, followed by the scrollbar. The order in which the widgets are passed to the grid command ensures that the scrollbar appears on the right side of the text widget. The second and third grid commands assign a weight of 1 to column 0 and row 0. Recall from Chapter 11 that the -weight option for the grid command controls whether or not the specified column or row resizes when the master resizes. A non-zero value means that they will resize. Bear in mind that column 0 and row 0 in this case corresponds to the text widget. The last grid command sets the weight of column 1 (the second column) to 0, meaning that this column (which happens to contain the scrollbar) *won't* resize horizontally when the master widget resizes. Putting it all together, then, when you resize the window containing the text and scrollbar widget, the second, third, and fourth grid commands allow the text widget to resize in both the horizontal and vertical directions while constraining the scrollbar widget to resize only vertically while its width remains static.

Figures 14.4 and 14.5 show what simple_scroll.tcl's window looks like.

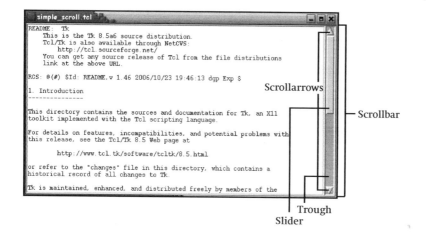

Scrollarrows

Scrollbar

Trough

Slider

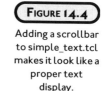

FIGURE 14.4

Adding a scrollbar to simple_text.tcl makes it look like a proper text display.

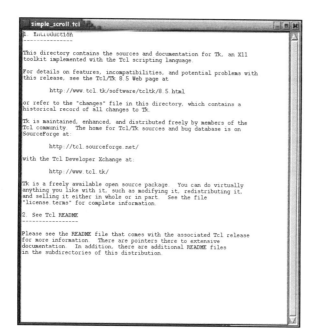

FIGURE 14.5

When the display shows all of the text, the slider doesn't move.

The documentation for the `scrollbar` widget describes the scrollbar in terms of the following five components:

1. **arrow1**—The arrow at the top left end of the scrollbar.
2. **trough1**—The space between the `slider` and `arrow1`.
3. **slider**—The rectangular box in the scrollbar that indicates the amount and location of text visible in the associated widget.
4. **trough2**—The space between the `slider` and `arrow2`.
5. **arrow2**—The arrow at the bottom or right end of the scrollbar.

For the most part, I won't use these terms, but they appear in the documentation and some `scrollbar`-related operations use them, so you should be aware of them and to what they refer. Figure 14.6 shows each of these widget parts as they are described in the `scrollbar` documentation.

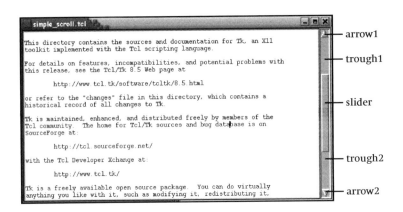

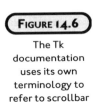

FIGURE 14.6

The Tk documentation uses its own terminology to refer to scrollbar components.

If you play with the window created by simple_scroll.tcl, notice that the size of the slider (its height in the trough) corresponds proportionately to the size of what is available in the viewport, relative to the total size of the item you are viewing through the viewport. For example, in Figure 14.4, the slider is just over half the size of the scrollbar, indicating that approximately half of the document is visible in the associated text widget. In Figure 14.5, on the other hand, the slider extends the full length of the trough, which means you are viewing the entire document.

Similarly, the location of the slider corresponds roughly to where in the item being viewed the viewport resides. In Figure 14.4, the top of the slider is anchored against the top of the scrollbar, so you can surmise that you are looking at the top of the document. In Figure 14.5, however, the resized window shows all the document, so the slider is anchored to the top and the bottom of the scroll trough.

The behavior I've described in this section relies on the default values for the scrollbar protocol and its default bindings. The *scrollbar protocol* defines the messages exchanged between scrollbar widgets and the scrollable widgets (entry, text, listbox, and canvas widgets) to which they are related. Thus, when you use the mouse or keyboard to scroll the text widget in simple_scroll.tcl, it sends messages to the scrollbar indicating the text's current position in the text widget, which the scrollbar uses to adjust its appearance (such as the slider's height and its location in the trough). Likewise, when you use the slider to scroll the text in the text widget, the scrollbar widget sends messages to the text widget telling it how to update the text displayed in the viewport.

The information to take away from this is that scrollbars have a protocol that defines how scrollbars and their associated widgets stay in sync. I have relied on the default values of the protocol. You should be able to do the same for a long time before you need to dig into the innards of the protocol and learn to use other scrollbar commands and attributes to modify the protocol's default behavior.

Similarly, my description of Tk's scrollbar widget assumes that you use its default bindings. You have less need to modify the default bindings for the scrollbar widget than you do to tweak the protocol settings. The capability exists (using the bind command described in Chapter 10), and it isn't difficult or complicated to do so. However, most users have been heavily conditioned to expect scrollbars to behave a certain way. Consequently, changing that behavior in the absence of a compelling reason to do so violates the principle of least surprise and will usually confuse, if not downright annoy, your users.

NOTE

The Principle of Least Surprise

When applied to user interfaces, the Principle of Least Surprise, also known as the Principle of Least Astonishment, the Rule of Least Surprise, or the Rule of Least Astonishment, boils down to, "When creating a user interface, do the least surprising thing." As Eric Raymond writes in *The Art of UNIX Programming* (http://www.faqs.org/docs/artu/ch11s01.html):

> The Rule of Least Surprise is a general principle in the design of all kinds of interfaces, not just software: "Do the least surprising thing." Thus, to design usable interfaces, it's best when possible not to design an entire new interface model (Eric Steven Raymond, *The Art of UNIX Programming*, Chapter 11).

In other words, if it isn't broken, don't fix it.

Probing the scrollbar **Protocol**

As explained in the previous section, when you move a scrollbar, it calls the command specified by its -command attribute, passing some additional parameters that specify the requested operation. The related widget (suppose it is a text widget) responds to this command (using its -xview or -yview attribute, for example) to update the display. To complete the scrolling operation, the scrollbar's position and size have to be updated. This is accomplished by the text widget invoking the command specified in its -xscrollcommand or -yscrollcommand attribute (the set command in simple_scroll.tcl), passing parameters back to the scrollbar that tell the scrollbar how to update its size and position.

The scrollbar's set command takes two arguments, *first* and *last*, real numbers between zero and one (0.0 and 1.0) that indicate the position of the top and bottom (or left and right for horizontal scrollbars) of the widget's display. The *first* argument specifies the (relative) position of the top of the widget; the *last* argument specifies the (relative) position of the bottom of the widget's viewport. In effect, *first* indicates an offset: how far down from the top or in from the left of the item being viewed in the widget the viewport is. Similarly, *last* indicates how much of the item in the widget is currently in the viewport.

In the following script, mod_scroll.tcl, I've modified the simple_scroll.tcl script presented earlier, replacing the scrollbar's set command with a wrapper procedure, Scroll, that displays the values passed to the set command:

```
proc ReadFile {f} {
    set fileId [open $f r]
    set input [read $fileId]
    close $fileId
    return $input
}


proc Scroll {sb args} {
    foreach {first last} $args {
        puts "first=$first, last=$last"
    }
}


set t [text .t -background #ffffff]
$t insert end [ReadFile "README"]
```

```
set sb [scrollbar .y -command [list $t yview]]
$t configure -wrap word -yscrollcommand {Scroll $sb}

grid $t $sb -sticky nsew
Marta Justak, 14tclbook-Fi.doc
grid columnconfigure . 0 -weight 1
grid rowconfigure . 0 -weight 1
grid columnconfigure . 1 -weight 0
```

The key piece of code is the Scroll procedure. It takes the scrollbar widget as a required argument. The keyword args specifies optional arguments. Before executing the scrollbar's set command, it displays the values of the arguments passed to set. Astute readers will notice that the script itself does not pass values to the set command. If you don't explicitly pass values, the scrollbar protocol makes some intelligent assumptions on your behalf—the purpose of this script is to show you what those "intelligent assumptions" are.

To generate the output below, I started the script, which displayed the first two lines of output. When the scrollbar is first mapped, it has no length, thus the offset and size are both 0 (first=0, last=0). The second line of output appears after the text widget is filled with the text read from the input file. The offset is still 0 because the viewport is at the top of the widget. The size value, though, has changed to reflect the fact that just over half of the document (last=0.521739) is visible in the viewport.

Next, I pressed Ctrl+End to scroll to the end of the document, resulting in the third line of output, first=0.478261, last=1. This output indicates that the top of the viewport is just under halfway through the document being displayed. The bottom of the document is visible, as indicated by the output last=1. Finally, I clicked arrow1 (the arrow at the top of the scrollbar) twice, scrolling two units up into the document, resulting in the fourth and fifth lines of output:

```
$ ./mod_scroll.tcl
first=0, last=0
first=0, last=0.521739
first=0.478261, last=1
first=0.456522, last=0.978261
first=0.434783, last=0.956522
```

The point of this is to demonstrate that you can, if you wish, interact directly with the scrollbar protocol, but that doing so is ugly and, in most cases, unnecessary.

USING THE scale WIDGET

Tk's scale widget, referred to as a *slider* in other GUI toolkits, displays a slider that can move back and forth or up and down in a trough. You decide the range of values the widget displays by assigning numeric values with the -from and -to attributes. As the slider moves along the trough, the scale widget's current value changes. You can access the current value of the widget through its -variable attribute.

The following example uses a scale widget to set the maximum amount of time, in seconds, allowed to elapse between turns (see interval.tcl in this chapter's code directory on the Web site):

```
scale .s -from 30 -to 60 -orient horizontal -length 200 \
    -label "Time out duration (secs):" -tickinterval 5 -showvalue true
grid .s -padx 10 -pady 10
```

The scale command creates a scale widget whose value ranges from 30 to 60. It will be laid out horizontally. The attribute -tickinterval 5 creates tick marks below the slider that increment in units of 5. The -showvalue true attributes cause the scale widget to display its current value between the top of the scale itself and the label.

Figure 14.7 shows the resulting window.

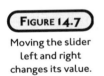

FIGURE 14.7

Moving the slider
left and right
changes its value.

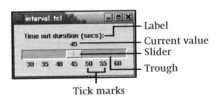

The scale widget supports a reasonably standard set of attributes that control its size, appearance, and behavior. Table 14.1 highlights the scale-specific attributes that you need to know or that you haven't encountered in the discussions of widgets in the previous chapters. As usual, for more information and to view the full list of both standard and scale widget-specific options, please refer to the scale man page (man 3tk scale).

Although the scale widget supports a rich set of attributes, the list of operations you can perform with it is limited, which is perhaps unsurprising when you consider that its function is limited to moving a slider back and forth (or up and down) in a trough. Table 14.2 lists the operations you can perform on a scale widget.

TABLE 14.1: ATTRIBUTES OF THE SCALE WIDGET

Attribute	Description
-bigincrement	Defines the size of "Large" increments by which to adjust the scale.
-cursor	Specifies the mouse cursor to display when the mouse hovers over the scale widget.
-digits	Sets the number of significant digits to retain when converting scale values to string values.
-from	Defines the smallest value the scale widget can take (displayed on the left or at the top of the widget).
-label	Specifies the text label that appears above or to the left of the scale itself.
-length	Sets the length of the widget in screen units (pixels by default).
-orient	Defines the orientation of the widget; must be either horizontal or vertical.
-repeatdelay	Specifies the number of milliseconds a button or key must be pressed before it begins to auto-repeat.
-repeatinterval	Sets the number of milliseconds between auto-repeats.
-resolution	Defines the value to which the scale itself and the tick marks will be rounded; defaults to 1, meaning values will be integral.
-showvalue	If true, the current value of the scale will be displayed.
-sliderlength	Specifies the length of the slider in screen units (pixels by default).
-sliderrelief	Sets the relief style of the slider.
-tickinterval	Defines the interval between tick marks.
-to	Specifies the largest value the scale widget can take (displayed on the right or at the bottom of the widget).
-troughcolor	Sets the color of the trough.
-variable	Defines the variable whose value is the widget's current value.

TABLE 14.2: OPERATIONS FOR THE SCALE WIDGET

Operation	Description
$s coords ?value?	Returns a two-element list consisting of the x and y coordinates of the point along the center of the trough that corresponds to value, or to the scale's current value if value is omitted.
$s get ?x y ?	Returns the scale's current value or, if x or y are specified, the value of the widget at the indicated coordinate(s).
$s identify x y	Returns a string indicating what part of the scale lies under the specified x and y coordinates; the returned value will be slider, trough1 (that part of the trough to the left or above the slider), or trough2 (that part of the trough to the right or below the slider).
$s set value	Sets the value of the widget to value, which moves the slider to that position.

USING THE Text WIDGET

The text widget is perhaps Tk's most sophisticated widget. Naturally, you can use it to display and edit text, but its capabilities extend far beyond mere text display and manipulation. A reasonably complete list of the text widget's features includes, in no particular order, the following elements:

- Controlling line spacing and justification
- Setting the font family, size, weight, and color
- Moving around within the text using marks
- Executing commands and setting text attributes using tags
- Displaying images
- Inserting, modifying, and deleting text
- Cutting, copying, and pasting text
- Adjusting tab stops
- Selecting text
- Searching text
- Embedding other Tk widgets into the text widget
- Undoing and redoing edit operations

GETTING STARTED

I'll start with the following script, simple_text.tcl in this chapter's code directory:

```
proc ReadFile {f} {
    set fileId [open $f r]
    set input [read $fileId]
    close $fileId
    return $input
}


set t [text .t -height 25 -width 80 -background #ffffff]
$t insert end [ReadFile "README"]
grid $t
```

This script creates a window consisting of a single text widget that is 25 lines tall (-height 25) and 80 characters wide (-width 80) with a white background (-background #ffffff). After creating the widget, I insert the contents of the file named README at the "end" of the widget ($t insert end [ReadFile "README"]). Because the text widget is initially empty, the "end" in this case is actually the top. The `ReadFile` procedure opens the specified file, reads its contents into a string variable, and then returns that string to the caller. Figure 14.8 shows the resulting figure.

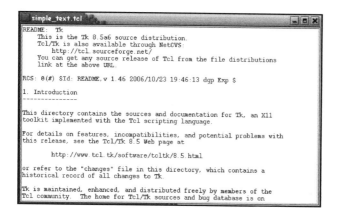

FIGURE 14.8

The `text` widget supports text editing with no additional code.

You can insert, delete, and modify text in the `text` widget immediately, that is, without making any changes in the code. Scrolling is a bit more awkward if you don't have a mouse with a wheel, but you can use the keyboard arrow keys to scroll through the document. Although you can modify the text, you won't be able to save your changes because I haven't provided that functionality. The next few sections add a scrollbar and a menu that allows you to open files, save files, and exit the script.

Before I start showing off the features of the `text` widget, you'll likely want to know the attributes and options you can use. There are a lot of them, as Table 14.3 makes clear, and this is not the complete list (refer to the `text` man page for the comprehensive list).

Adding a Scrollbar

Using what you learned about the `scrollbar` widget in the previous section, adding a `scrollbar` to simple_text.tcl involves just a few lines of code. In the interests of simplicity, I'm only going to add a vertical scrollbar. I'll use the `text` widget's `-wrap` attribute so that text wraps automatically. If you follow the rules I suggested, you need to do three things:

1. Add the `scrollbar` widget to the window.
2. Invoke the `text` widget's `yview` operation in the `scrollbar` widget's `-command` attribute.
3. Invoke the `scrollbar` widget's `set` operation from the `text` widget's `-yscrollcommand` attribute.

TABLE 14.3: ARGUMENTS FOR THE TEXT WIDGET

Argument	Description
-autoseparators	If 1 or true, automatically inserts separators in the undo stack (used with -undo).
-height	Specifies the height of the text widget in lines of text.
-maxundo	Sets the maximum number of undo operations.
-spacing1	Defines the amount of additional space (in screen units) above each line of text.
-spacing2	Defines the amount of additional space above and below wrapped lines of text.
-spacing3	Defines the amount of additional space (in screen units) below each line of text.
-state	Controls whether text can be inserted (normal) or not (disabled) in the widget.
-tabs	Sets the tab stops in the widget.
-undo	If 1 or true, enables the undo mechanism; defaults to 0 (no undo capability).
-width	Specifies the width of the text widget in characters.
-wrap	Defines the wrapping behavior of the widget; must be one of none, char, or word.
-xscrollcommand	Sets the command used to communicate with the horizontal scrollbar widget, if one exists.
-yscrollcommand	Sets the command used to communicate with the vertical scrollbar widget, if one exists.
delete	Deletes a range of characters from the text, as specified by index arguments.
dlineinfo	Returns a five-element list describing the geometry of the area containing the specified index.
dump	Returns the contents of the text widget between specified indices, including information about tags, marks, and embedded windows.
edit	Provides a facility for modifying the contents of the undo stack.
get	Returns a range of characters from the widget.
index	Returns the position that corresponds to the specified index.
insert	Inserts text and optional tags into the widget starting at the specified index.
mark	Provides the ability to create, modify, delete, and interact with text marks.
search	Searches text for a specified pattern, beginning at specific index.
see	Scrolls the text at the specified index into view.
tag	Provides the facility for working with tags.
xview	Changes the horizontal position of the text in the widget.
yview	Changes the vertical position of the text in the widget.

The resulting script, scroll_text.tcl in this chapter's code directory, is shown below:

```
proc ReadFile {f} {
    set fileId [open $f r]
    set input [read $fileId]
    close $fileId
```

```
    return $input
}

set t [text .t -height 25 -width 80 -background #ffffff -wrap word]
set s [scrollbar .s]

$s configure -command [list $t yview]
$t configure -yscrollcommand [list $s set]

$t insert end [ReadFile "README"]

grid $t $s -sticky nsew
grid columnconfigure . 0 -weight 1
grid rowconfigure . 0 -weight 1
grid columnconfigure . 1 -weight 0
```

The ReadFile procedure is unchanged from the previous scripts. I added a new attribute to the command that creates the text widget, -wrap word. This attribute controls how text that is too wide to fit in the text widget is handled. It can be one of three values: none, char, or word. A value of none causes text to be truncated; char allows text to be wrapped at any characters; word breaks text at word boundaries (white space).

The scrollbar command creates a scrollbar widget named .s, a reference to which is stored in the variable $s. I don't specify any attributes when creating the widget, so it assumes default values.

After creating the widgets, the two configure operations connect the scrollbar and text widgets using the rules I gave you in the previous section. I set the scrollbar's -command attribute to the text widget's yview operation. Then I set the text widget's -yscrollcommand attribute to the scrollbar's set operation.

After populating the text widget using my now-familiar ReadFile procedure, I lay out the widgets, using the same procedure described for the simple_scroll.tcl script in the previous section. Figure 14.9 shows the resulting window. Figure 14.10 shows the window when it is scrolled to the bottom of the text widget's contents. Figure 14.11 illustrates selected text. Figure 14.12 proves that you can, in fact, edit the contents of a text widget without writing any code.

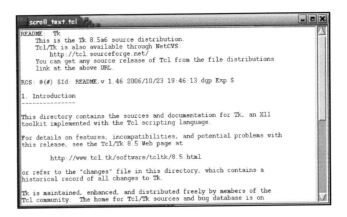

FIGURE 14.9

The text widget now has a linked scrollbar.

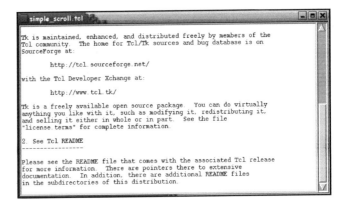

FIGURE 14.10

Use the scrollbar to scroll the viewport to the bottom of the text widget's contents.

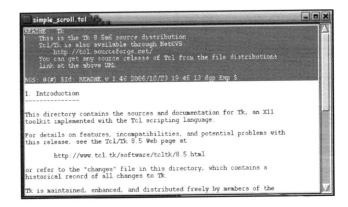

FIGURE 14.11

Selecting text works the way you would expect.

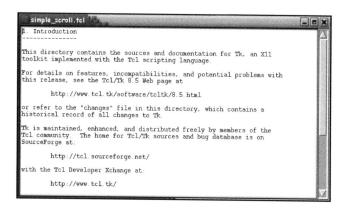

FIGURE 14.12

Yes, Virginia, you can edit text without writing code.

One change from all the scripts I have shown you previously is that I use the `list` command to build the command specified as the attribute for `-command` and `-yscrollcommand`. The reason for this change is that the `list` commands handle quoting and spaces embedded in arguments automatically. Using double quotes for grouping would not deal with the embedded spaces. While using braces around the arguments would handle embedded spaces and accomplish the needed grouping, it would also inhibit substitutions that you might otherwise need performed. Although this is not an issue in these two commands, as your commands become more sophisticated, quoting and embedded spaces become a real consideration, and, as you've seen throughout this book, Tcl (and thus Tk) are more sensitive to white space than other programming languages.

Adding and Populating a Menu

As promised, this section shows you how to add a menu, open an arbitrary file, and save the contents of the `text` widget to an arbitrary file. Although it probably seems like I'm creating a text editor (and, truthfully, I am gradually evolving a simple-minded text editor), what I'm *really* doing is using simple examples to show you how to perform typical operations with and on `text` widgets. I also hope to convey that just a few lines of Tcl and Tk code make it possible to create scripts that are surprisingly capable compared to the amount of code required to implement them.

The following script, menu_text.tcl in this chapter's code directory, shows the latest iteration of the simple_text.tcl script with which I started:

```
proc ReadFile {w} {
    set f [tk_getOpenFile -title "Open file"]
    # Bail if no filename is specified
    if {$f == ""} {
```

```
            return
        } else {
            set fileId [open $f r]
            # Clear the current contents of $w first
            $w delete 1.0 end
            # Read straight from the file into $w
            $w insert end [read $fileId]
            close $fileId
        }
    }

proc SaveText {w} {
    set f [tk_getSaveFile -title "Save file"]
    # Bail if no filename is specified
    if {$f == ""} {
        return
    } else {
        set fileId [open $f w]
        puts -nonewline $fileId [$w get 1.0 "end - 1 chars"]
        close $fileId
    }
}

set t [text .t -height 25 -width 80 -background #ffffff -wrap word]
set s [scrollbar .s]

$s configure -command [list $t yview]
$t configure -yscrollcommand [list $s set]

set main [menu .main]
. config -menu $main
set mFile [menu $main.mFile -tearoff 0]
$main add cascade -label "File" -menu $mFile
$mFile add command -label "Open" -command [list ReadFile $t]
$mFile add command -label "Save" -command [list SaveText $t]
$mFile add separator
$mFile add command -label "Exit" -command exit
```

```
grid $t $s -sticky nsew
grid columnconfigure . 0 -weight 1
grid rowconfigure . 0 -weight 1
grid columnconfigure . 1 -weight 0
```

There's a lot going on in this script. I've modified the ReadFile procedure and added a new one, SaveText. Both accept a single argument, the widget into which to dump the contents of a file (ReadFile) or from which to read the text to save to a file (SaveText). ReadFile uses the tk_getOpenFile command to create a ready-made file open dialog box (see Figure 14.14). tk_getOpenFile returns the name of the file selected in the dialog, so I use that name in the open command. Another change to ReadFile is that I read the contents of the file directly into the text widget, instead of returning the text as a string variable. The condition if {$f == ""} is necessary because the user can close the file open dialog without selecting a file (by clicking the Cancel button). If that happens, I just exit the ReadFile procedure.

The SaveText procedure works similarly. The tk_getSaveFile command creates a ready-made file save dialog box, so if the user selects a file, I open it and use the command puts [-nonewline $fileId [$w get 1.0 "end - 1 chars"] to get the contents of the text widget and save it directly into the file (see Figure 14.17). If the user doesn't select a file in the file save dialog box, I just exit SaveText without taking any action.

The rest of the new code in this script adds the menu and menu entries. First, I create the menu bar itself (set main [menu .main]) and associate it with the root window (. config - menu $main). Next, I create a File menu item and add it to the $main menu. Then I add four entries to the File menu: Open, Save, a separator, and Exit:

1. The Open entry invokes the ReadFile procedure.
2. The Save entry invokes the SaveText procedure.
3. The separator entry creates visual separation between the Open and Save entries and the Exit item.
4. The Exit entry terminates the script (without saving any changes to the contents of the text widget).

The rest of the script consists of the same layout commands that I used in the previous iterations of this script, so I won't rehash them here. Figures 14.13–14.16 show the new Tk features that menu_text.tcl uses.

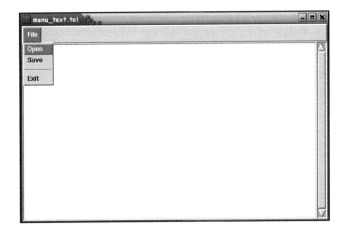

Use the File menu to open and save files and exit the script.

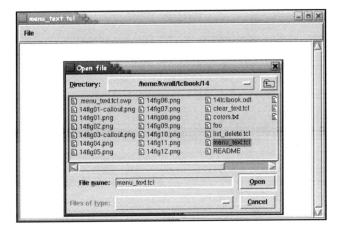

The tk_getOpenFile command creates a fully featured file open dialog.

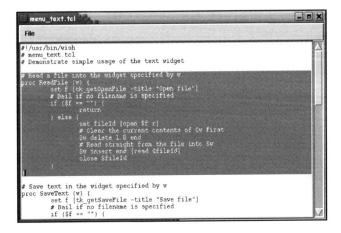

The script is starting to look like a proper, if simple, text editor.

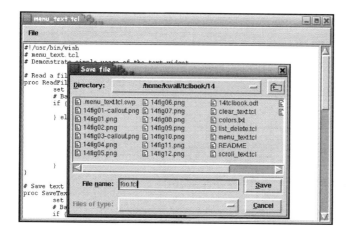

FIGURE 14.16

Save your changes using the dialog created by `tk_getSaveFile`.

USING MARKS AND TAGS

I think you'll derive the most benefit from marks and tags. Marks are beneficial because they enable you to move around within the contents of a `text` widget programmatically, find where the user (or at least the current insertion point) is in the text, and modify the contents of the widget (in terms of adding or deleting text). Tags are most commonly used to apply visual attributes to the text in a `text` widget. Other uses of tags include binding commands to ranges of text and manipulating the text selection. Marks and tags are certainly the two features upon which the word search game at the beginning of the chapter relied. Before I get to marks and tags, though, you'll need to know how to find your way around inside a `text` widget.

Text Indices

A fair portion of the commands, options, and attributes for `text` widgets expect one or more index arguments that specify the text within the widget on which to operate. Given the number of operations that you can perform, there is a correspondingly large number of expressions used to specify index values. These expressions fall into two broad categories: bases and modifiers. *Bases* define the starting point for an operation. *Modifiers* define the direction in which an operation works or the number of characters on which to operate. All text operations require a base or starting point; modifiers are optional. Table 14.4 lists the expressions used to specify text index values and whether the expression represents a base value or a modifier.

The following script, index_text.tcl, illustrates how to use some of the text indexing operations shown in Table 14.4.

TABLE 14.4:   EXPRESSIONS USED FOR TEXT INDICES

Expression	Type	Description
- *N* chars	Modifier	Moves the index backward by *N* characters.
- *N* lines	Modifier	Moves the index backward by *N* lines.
@*x,y*	Base	Refers to the character that covers the pixel at widget-relative coordinates *x* and *y*.
+ *N* chars	Modifier	Moves the index forward by *N* characters.
+ *N* lines	Modifier	Moves the index forward by *N* lines.
end	Base	Refers to character immediately following the last newline.
line.char	Base	Refers to character on line *line* at character position *char*. Line numbers are 1-based; character positions are 0-based.
lineend	Modifier	Moves the index to the last character (the newline) on the line.
linestart	Modifier	Moves the index to the first character on the line.
mark	Base	Refers to the character immediately following the mark named *mark*.
tag.first	Base	Refers to the first character in the tag named *tag*.
tag.last	Base	Refers to the last character in the tag named *tag*.
wordend	Modifier	Moves the index to end of the word containing the current index.
wordstart	Modifier	Moves the index to the beginning of the word containing the current index.

```tcl
proc ReadFile {f} {
    set fileId [open $f r]
    set input [read $fileId]
    close $fileId
    return $input
}

proc DoTag {w c} {
    global status

    $w tag delete t
    $w tag configure t -background [$w cget -foreground]
    $w tag configure t -foreground [$w cget -background]
    $w tag add t [$w index insert] "[$w index insert] $c"

    $status configure -text "Current tag range: [$w tag ranges t]"
}
```

```
set t [text .t -height 25 -width 80 -background #ffffff]
$t insert end [ReadFile "README"]

set f [frame .f]
set b1 [button $f.b1 -text "+ 5 chars" -command [list DoTag $t "+ 5 chars"]]
set b2 [button $f.b2 -text "+ 5 lines" -command [list DoTag $t "+ 5 lines"]]
set b3 [button $f.b3 -text "lineend" -command [list DoTag $t lineend]]
set b4 [button $f.b4 -text "wordend" -command [list DoTag $t wordend]]

set status [label .status -relief sunken -anchor w]

grid $f -sticky nsew
grid $b1 $b2 $b3 $b4 -sticky nsew
grid $t -sticky nsew
grid $status -sticky nsew
```

The script uses tags (and marks), which you haven't learned how to use yet, but they are only a means to an end, providing visual evidence of how text indices work. The gist of the script is just this: Using your mouse, click somewhere in the text with the left mouse button. This sets the insertion point (see Figure 14.17). After setting the insertion point, click one of the buttons at the top of the window. This moves the index from the insert point to the index specified on the button label (five characters forward, five lines forward, the end of the current word, or the end of the current line). In addition to moving the index point, the DoTag highlights the range of text (Figure 14.18) between the insertion point and the specified index, resulting in a visual illustration that the index has, in fact moved.

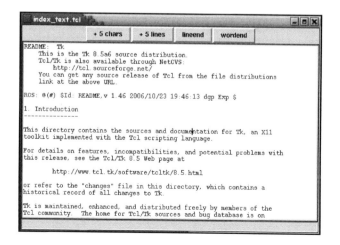

Click somewhere in the text to set the insert point.

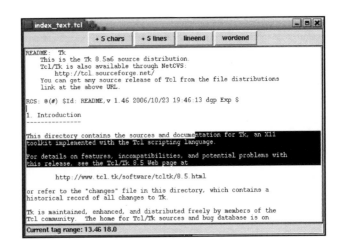

 FIGURE 14.18

The highlighted
text includes the
text between the
insertion point and
the requested
index.

Hitting the Mark

In Tk's terminology, a *text mark* is a name that refers to a space between two particular characters. Marks are ordinarily used as reference points in operations that require indices. You can use any character when naming marks, but I recommend *not* using strictly numeric names, the plus sign (+), the minus sign (-), or spaces, because these elements are used when performing index arithmetic. Names containing these characters potentially complicate index math.

In addition to the marks you create, widgets that support marks include a few predefined marks that cannot be deleted with the mark unset operation listed in Table 14.5. The two most important predefined marks are insert, which refers to the location of the insertion point (where text will be inserted), and current, which refers to the character closest to the mouse cursor. Marks are also *persistent*. If the text surrounding a mark is deleted, the mark remains in place.

Notice that a mark resides *between* two characters. Depending on the value of the mark's gravity (which defaults to right), text will be inserted to the left or the right of the mark. If a mark's gravity is left, text will be inserted to the left of the mark; right gravity means that text will be inserted to the right of the mark. Referring back to index_text.tcl, for example, the expression $t index insert returns the index of the character immediately to the right of the insert mark.

Table 14.5 lists the supported mark operations, which are invoked using the mark command after the name of the widget that supports them (such as text widgets).

The following script, mark_text.tcl in this chapter's code directory, shows all of the currently defined marks in a text widget when you click the Show Marks button.

TABLE 14.5: SUPPORTED MARK OPERATIONS

Operation	Description
$t mark gravity *name* ?*direction*?	If *direction* is not specified, returns the gravity of the mark denoted by *name*; otherwise, sets the gravity of the specified mark to either right or left (defaults to right).
$t mark names	Returns a list of all currently defined marks.
$t mark next *index*	Returns the name of the next mark occurring at or after *index*, if any, or the empty string otherwise.
$t mark previous *index*	Returns the name of the next mark occurring at or before *index*, if any, or the empty string otherwise.
$t mark set *name index*	Defines a mark named *name* immediately before the character specified by *index*.
$t mark unset *name*?...?	Deletes the mark or marks specified by *name*.

```
proc ReadFile {f} {
    set fileId [open $f r]
    set input [read $fileId]
    close $fileId
    return $input
}

proc ShowMarks {t} {
    global status

    foreach m [$t mark names] {
        append s "$m: [$t index $m], "
    }
    $status configure -text "[string trimright $s {, }]"
}

set t [text .t -height 25 -width 80 -background #ffffff]
$t insert end [ReadFile "README"]

set f [frame .f]
set b [button $f.b -text "Show Marks" -command [list ShowMarks $t]]
set e [button $f.e -text "Exit" -command exit]
```

```
set status [label .status -relief sunken -anchor w]

grid $f -sticky nsew
grid $b $e -sticky nsew
grid $t -sticky nsew
grid $status -sticky nsew
```

The workhorse code in this script is the `ShowMarks` procedure, which is invoked by the button `b`. `ShowMarks` iterates through the list of mark names returned by the `mark names` command, appending the name of each mark and the index value to which it corresponds to the string variable `$s`. After exiting the `foreach` loop, I update the text of the label that appears below the `text` widget with the value of this string, after removing the terminating comma and space.

As you can see in the following figures, the list and value of marks defined automatically by the `text` widget changes, depending on the state of the text in the widget. For example, in Figure 14.19, I've just started the script and have neither selected any text nor placed an insertion point using the mouse or keyboard. As a result, the `insert` mark is at index 46.0, that is, on line 46, character 0, which corresponds to the beginning of the line just past the end of the file. The `current` mark is at index 1.0, because that was the character closest to the mouse cursor when I clicked the Show Marks button.

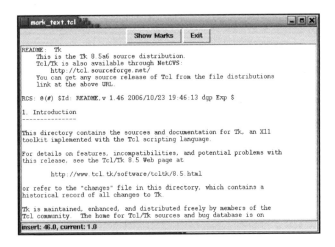

FIGURE 14.19

A newly populated text widget only has two predefined marks.

After placing the insertion point (see Figure 14.20), there's a third mark automatically defined, `anchor`, with a value of 13.31, in addition to `insert` (at 13.31) and `current` (still at 1.0). Recall from Chapter 13 that an anchor point is the base from which a selection begins.

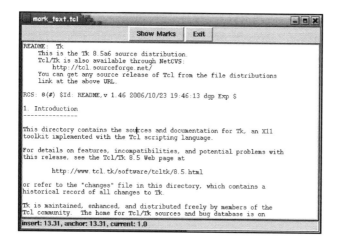

FIGURE 14.20

After placing an insertion point, the text widget defines a third mark.

Notice what happens when I double-click on the word sources on line 13 to select it. Selecting text changes the marks subtly, as you can see in Figure 14.21.

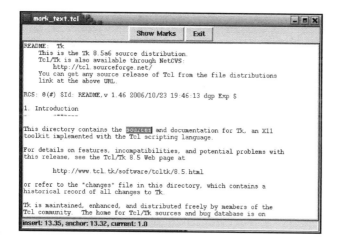

FIGURE 14.21

Selecting text sets the anchor mark where the selection began.

The anchor mark moved to where I double-clicked index 13.32, which corresponds to the space between the letters r and c in the word sources. The insert mark, meanwhile, moved to the end of the word sources, or index value 13.35.

Tag, You're It!

Tags are a special annotation for text, similar to marks but far more capable and versatile. Whereas text marks are used for positioning and movement purposes, tags have a wider variety of uses. They are most commonly used to apply visual attributes to the text in a text widget, including some that are not available as global attributes (such as strikethrough and stippling). Table 14.7 lists all of the text attributes you can apply with tags. Other uses include bind commands to ranges of text, and manipulating the text selection (described in Chapter 13). In addition, unlike marks, one tag can be applied to multiple ranges of text, and multiple tags can be applied to a single range of text.

Table 14.6 lists the operations you can perform with text tags.

TABLE 14.6: TAG OPERATIONS

Operation	Description
`$t tag add` *name start* `?`*stop*`?` `?...?`	Applies the tag *name* to the text from the index *start* up to but not including *stop*, or just *start* if *stop* isn't specified.
`$t tag bind` *name* `?`*seq*`?` `?`*script*`?`	Returns the binding(s) defined for the tag *name* or assigns the script *script* to sequence in *seq* and applies this binding to *name*.
`$t tag delete` *name* `?...?`	Deletes the tag specified by *name*.
`$t tag lower` *name* `?`*below*`?`	Assigns the lowest available priority to the tag *name* or makes its priority less than the priority assigned to the tag *below*.
`$t tag nextrange` *name start* `?`*stop*`?`	Returns a two-element list of indices for the next range to which the tag *name* is applied.
`$t tag prevrange` *name start* `?`*stop*`?`	Returns a two-element list of indices for the previous range to which the tag *name* is applied.
`$t tag raise` *name* `?`*above*`?`	Assigns the highest available priority to the tag *name* or makes its priority higher than the priority assigned to the tag *above*.
`$t tag ranges` *name*	Returns a list of all the index ranges to which the tag *name* has been applied.
`$t tag remove` *name start* `?`*stop*`?`	Removes the tag *name* from index specified by *start* or, if *stop* is specified, from the index range from *start* up to but not including *stop*.

TABLE 14.7: SUPPORTED TAG ATTRIBUTES

Attribute	Description
`-background` *color*	Sets the background color of the tagged text.
`-bgstipple` *bitmap*	Defines the bitmap used for the background stipple.
`-borderwidth` *pixels*	Specifies the width of the border for 3D effects.
`-elide` *boolean*	If `true` (or the equivalent), text tagged with this attribute is hidden.
`-fgstipple` *bitmap*	Defines the bitmap used for the foreground stipple.
`-font` *fontname*	Sets the font used for the tagged text.
`-foreground` *color*	Specifies the foreground color of the tagged text.
`-justify` *type*	Defines the justification of the tagged text (`left`, `center`, or `right`).
`-lmargin1` *pixels*	Sets the spacing for left indentation of tagged text.
`-lmargin2` *pixels*	Sets the spacing for left indentation of tagged text that gets wrapped.
`-offset` *pixels*	Specifies the offset from the baseline for superscripted (positive) or subscripted (negative) text.
`-overstrike` *boolean*	If `true` (or the equivalent), text tagged with this attribute is displayed with a horizontal line through it (also referred to as *strikethrough*).
`-relief` *type*	Defines the type of relief, which must be one of `flat`, `sunken`, `raised`, `groove`, `solid`, or `ridge`.
`-rmargin` *pixels*	Sets the size of the right-hand margin.
`-spacing1` *pixels*	Specifies the amount of space above a line.
`-spacing2` *pixels*	Specifies the amount of space above the wrapped part of a line.
`-spacing3` *pixels*	Specifies the amount of space below a line.
`-tabs` *tablist*	Defines the tab stops for the tagged text.
`-underline` *boolean*	If `true` (or the equivalent), the tagged text is underlined.
`wrap` *mode*	Sets the line wrap style, which must be one of `none` (the default), `char`, or `word`.

ANALYZING WORD SEARCH

Readers can use this program to experiment with text attributes, manipulating the insertion point, modifying line spacing, and keeping track of the text cursor.

Looking at the Code

```
#!/usr/bin/wish
# gword_search.tcl
# Word search game

# Block 1
# Read the puzzle data from the specified file
```

```
proc ReadFile {f} {
    global words lines

    set fileId [open $f r]
    while {[gets $fileId input] > -1} {
        lappend words [lindex $input 0]
        lappend lines [lrange $input 1 end]
    }

    close $fileId
}
# Block 2
# Clears all tags
proc Clear {t} {
    $t tag remove correct 1.0 end
    $t tag remove incorrect 1.0 end
}


# Block 3
# Determine if the text selected in t is the target word
proc Score {t} {
    global lStatus words

    # The starting and ending points of the selection
    if {[$t compare anchor < insert]} {
        set start [$t index anchor]
        set end [$t index insert]
    } else {
        set start [$t index insert]
        set end [$t index anchor]
    }

    # Fetch the selected text
    set word [join [string trim [selection get]] ""]

    # Determine the line number of the selected text     set n [string range $start 0
[expr [string first "." $start] - 1]]
```

```
    # What's the target word?
    set target [lindex $words [expr $n - 1]]

    # Is it a match?
    if {$word == $target } {
        $t tag add correct $start $end
    } else {
        $t tag add incorrect $start $end
    }
}


# Block 4
# Define the widgets
set fPuzzle [frame .fpuzzle]
set fButtons [frame .fbuttons]
set lStatus [label .lstatus -relief sunken -borderwidth 2 -anchor w]
set puzzle [text $fPuzzle.puzzle -width 21 -height 9 -bg #ffffff \
    -font "Courier"]
set bScore [button $fButtons.bscore -text "Score" -anchor n \
    -command [list Score $puzzle]]
set bClear [button $fButtons.bclear -text "Clear" -anchor n \
    -command [list Clear $puzzle]]
set bExit [button $fButtons.bexit -text "Exit" -anchor n -command exit]

# Display the widgets
grid $fPuzzle -column 0 -row 0 -padx {10 5} -pady 10
grid $fButtons -column 1 -row 0 -padx {5 10} -pady 10
grid $puzzle -padx {5 0}
grid $bClear -sticky nsew -padx {5 5} -pady {10 2}
grid $bScore -sticky nsew -padx {5 5} -pady {2 2}
grid $bExit -sticky nsew -padx {5 5} -pady {20 10}
grid $lStatus -columnspan 2 -sticky nsew
wm title . "Word Search"

# Block 5
# Populate the text widget
set words {}
set lines {}
```

```
ReadFile "puzzle.txt"
for {set i 0} {$i < [llength $lines]} {incr i} {
    $puzzle insert end [format "%s\n" [lindex $lines $i]]
}


# Make the puzzle text read-only
$puzzle configure -state disabled


# Define tags
$puzzle tag configure correct -background "dark green"
$puzzle tag configure incorrect -background "dark red"
```

Understanding the Code

The ReadFile procedure in Block 1 opens the file whose name is specified as an argument and then parses the contents of the file into two lists: words and lines. These variables are declared global to enable ReadFile to access and modify them. The $words list contains the target words, and the $lines list contains the jumbled letters that make up the puzzle itself. The format of the puzzle data file is a word followed by a space followed by a series of 11 space-delimited letters:

```
open e o p e n u g r i v c

...

""  z o t z g v a n e r s

...

tell a m a j y r a t e l l
```

Notice that once again, the puzzle contains a line that lacks a valid word.

Block 2 defines the Clear procedure, which removes the two tags from the puzzle text. It is called when the player presses the Clear button to reset the game board and restart the game.

In Block 3, I define the Score procedure that is invoked when the player presses the Score button after selecting a candidate word. The first if-else block determines the starting and ending points of the selection. The conditional evaluation is necessary because the anchor point of a selection isn't necessarily the beginning point of a selection. I'm going to use the starting and ending points of the selection (saved in the $start and $end variables, respectively) to add a tag to the selected text, and the syntax for adding a tag requires that the start value should be less than the end value.

Next, I retrieve the selected word using four levels of Tcl command substitution. Reading from the inside out of the expression `set word [join [string trim [selection get]] ""]`, I do the following:

1. Use `selection get` to fetch the text of the selection from the clipboard.
2. Use the `string trim` command to remove any leading and trailing spaces from the text returned by `selection get`.
3. Use the `join` command to remove embedded space characters from the string returned by `string trim`.
4. Save the string returned by `join` in the variable `$word`.

Once I know the word the player has selected, I need to find from which line of the puzzle the player selected the word so I can use that line number to index into the list of target words (stored in `$words`) to see if I have a match. To determine the line number, I use the `string first` command to parse the line number of the index value stored in `$start`. I store the line number in the variable `$n` and then use the `lindex list` command to extract the corresponding word from the list of target words. Because the `text` widget's lines are numbered from one while lists are numbered from zero, I have to subtract 1 from the value stored in `$n` to extract the correct word from the list of target words. I store the target word in the string variable `$target`.

Finally, I compare the word the player selected (`$word`) to the target word (`$target`). If they match, I add the tag `correct` to the text range that the player selected, which highlights it in green. If the two strings don't match, I add the tag `incorrect` to the text range, which highlights it in red. After tagging the selected text range, the procedure exits.

In Block 4, I define and display the widgets that make up the game. The only remarkable feature in this block involves being careful when defining the `text` widget itself. Specifically, when displaying the puzzle text, I use a monospace font, Courier, to make sure that each letter takes up the same amount of vertical and horizontal space in the `text` widget. This measure ensures that the letters line up evenly both horizontally and vertically. If I use a proportionally spaced font, such as Times, the letters will not align properly.

After I lay out the various widgets, I populate the `text` widget with the puzzle data. First, I read the data file (puzzle.txt) with the `ReadFile` procedure, which stores data in the `$words` and `$lines` lists as I described earlier. Next, I iterate over the `$lines` list and insert each line into the `text` widget. Once the `text` widget is populated, I make it read-only by setting its `-state` attribute to `disabled` (`$puzzle configure -state disabled`). The purpose of this step was to keep the player from accidentally editing the contents of the `text` widget during the game. I have to disable the `text` widget *after* populating it because it is not possible to insert, delete, or modify text in a `text` widget, even programmatically, if it is `disabled`.

The last step is to define the two tags, `correct` and `incorrect`, that I use to tag the text as the user plays the game. The tags are simple: The `correct` tag has a `-background` attribute of "dark green" while the incorrect tag has a "dark red" attribute.

At this point, the game is ready to play.

Modifying the Code

Here are some exercises you can try to practice what you learned in this chapter:

14.1 Modify gword_search.tcl to keep track of the number of correct and incorrect selections and to display the results at the end of the game.

14.2 Modify the `Clear` procedure in gword_search.tcl to clear only incorrect guesses.

THE CANVAS WIDGET

T his chapter shows you how to use one of Tk's most complex widgets, the canvas widget. The canvas is a general purpose widget you can use to display drawing primitives, such as arcs, lines, polygons, and other shapes; images in a variety of formats; text; and even other embedded widgets. The objects in a canvas widget can, like the text in a text box, have tags, and you can assign tagged objects their own event bindings and display attributes. With some work on your part, you can even animate the objects in a canvas. Animation and embedded widgets exceed the scope of this book, but I will show you how to use many of the canvas widget's other features in this chapter. First, however, you get to solve a puzzle.

GOT THE PICTURE?

This chapter's program, Got the Picture, challenges you to solve a puzzle (see puzzle.tcl in this chapter's code directory). It starts with an image of a Byzantine gladiolus. When you click the Start button, the picture is divided into 12 rectangular tiles and mixed up on the game board. Your task is to rearrange the pieces and reconstruct the original picture. To do so, select two pieces to swap their position on the board and then click the Swap button. Figures 15.1–15.4 show the game at various stages.

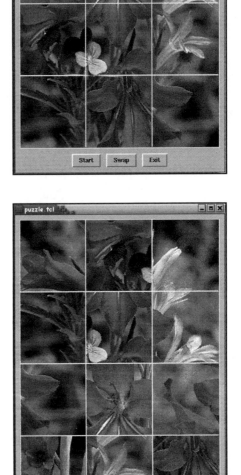

FIGURE 15.1

The gladiolus is pretty to look at when you first start the game.

FIGURE 15.2

Click the start button to jumble the picture.

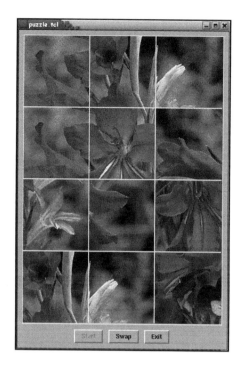

FIGURE 15.3

Select two tiles and pick the Swap button to rearrange the puzzle pieces.

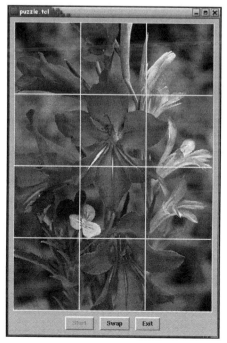

FIGURE 15.4

After rebuilding the original picture, click Exit to close the window.

THE CANVAS WIDGET

As the name itself suggests, the canvas widget creates a blank area on which you draw or paint to your heart's programmatic content (a blank canvas, get it?). As I remarked in the introduction, the canvas widget is one of the most complex widgets in the Tk toolkit, if not *the* most complex. The downside of this complexity is that you have a lot to learn. The upside is that the canvas widget is immensely capable, and there is little you can't do with it. I'll start with a *pro forma* listing of the attributes and operations that are unique to the canvas widget or whose usage in the context of the canvas widget differs from what you have encountered before. Table 15.1 lists the attributes, and Table 15.2 lists the operations.

TABLE 15.1: ATTRIBUTES FOR THE CANVAS WIDGET

Attribute	Description
-closeenough	Specifies a floating point value that controls how close to an object the mouse cursor must be before it is "close enough" to be considered inside the item (defaults to 1.0).
-confine	If true (the default), the canvas' view is restricted to the region defined by -scrollregion.
-height	Specifies the canvas widget's height in any valid coordinate form.
-scrollregion	Specifies a list of coordinates of a rectangular region (left, top, right, and bottom, in that order), considered the viewable area of a canvas widget.
-state	Specifies the canvas widget's default state, which must be one of normal, active, or hidden.
-width	Specifies the canvas widget's width, in any valid coordinate form.
-xscrollcommand	Specifies the command sent to a scrollbar widget's set operation when the canvas widget is scrolled horizontally.
-xscrollincrement	Specifies the increment (in screen units) in which the view moves when the view is scrolled horizontally.
-yscrollcommand	Specifies the command sent to a scrollbar widget's set operation when the canvas widget is scrolled vertically.
-yscrollincrement	Specifies the increment (in screen units) in which the view moves when the view is scrolled vertically.

A dry, soulless recitation of the canvas widget's attributes and operations won't get you anywhere near a state of productivity with it. To get started, you'll need to know the canvas widget's coordinate system.

TABLE 15.2:   OPERATIONS FOR THE CANVAS WIDGET

Operation

```
$c addtag tag search ?arg ...?
$c canvasx screenx ?spacing?
$c canvasy screeny ?spacing?
$c coords id ?x y?
$c create type x y ?...?
$c dchars id first ?last?
$c delete ?id ...?
$c dtag id ?tag?
$c find cmd ?...?
$c gettags id
$c icursor id index
$c index id index
$c insert id before str
$c move id xAmt yAmt
$c postscript ?...?
$c scale id xStart yStart xScale yScale
$c select option ?id arg?
$c type id
$c xview arg ?...?
$c view arg ?...?
```

The Coordinate System

Before I proceed, let me define a convention for referring to points that I'll use throughout the rest of this chapter. Points on canvas widgets are uniquely identified by Cartesian coordinates in the form (x,y), where x refers to a point's X coordinate and y refers to its Y coordinate. To refer to a pair of X and Y coordinates, I'll use the notation (x,y). So, for example, (0,0) describes the point whose X and Y coordinates are both 0; (640,480) refers to a point whose X coordinate is 640 and whose Y coordinate is 480.

With that bit of housekeeping out of way, the canvas widget is laid out in a coordinate system whose origin is the upper left-hand corner of the screen. That corner has the X and Y coordinates (0,0). X, the horizontal position, increases as you move to the right across the canvas, and Y increases as you move down the widget. The width of the canvas is set by the like named -width attribute. The height, similarly, is determined by the -height attribute. Figure 15.5 illustrates the point, so to speak.

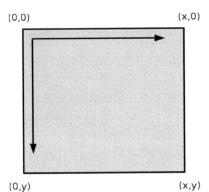

(0,0)   (x,0)

(0,y)   (x,y)

FIGURE 15.5

X increases from left to right; Y increases from top to bottom.

As you can see in Figure 15.5, the upper right-hand corner has the coordinates (x,0), the lower left-hand corner has the coordinates (0,y), and the lower right-hand corner has the coordinates (x,y).

Be default, widgets are dimensioned in pixels. You can change the units by appending one of the following letters to use the corresponding unit:

- c—Centimeters
- i—Inches
- m—Millimeters
- p—Points

A "point" in this context refers to traditional printer's points, which are $\frac{1}{72}$". The examples I use in this chapter will be defined in terms of pixels.

The following script shows a simple `canvas` widget with some embedded text.

```
set c [canvas .c -width 320 -height 240 -bg white -relief sunken]
$c create text 100 100 -text "Hello, Tcl/Tk World!"
grid $c
```

The first command creates a `canvas` widget that is 320 pixels wide and 240 pixels tall with a white background. The entire widget has a sunken relief. The second command draws the text `Hello, Tcl/Tk World!` on the canvas at the coordinates (100,100). Figure 15.6 shows the resulting figure.

Using Canvas Objects

The canvas widget has a number of built-in drawing primitives that you can use to compose more sophisticated content. *Drawing primitives* describe the basic drawing operations that the widget supports. Tk's documentation refers to drawing primitives as *canvas objects,* so that's the terminology I'll use. The list of supported canvas objects includes the following, arranged in alphabetical order:

- arc—Arcs, or curved line segments
- bitmaps—Bitmaps, or two-color graphic images
- image—Images, either bitmaps or one of several full-color graphic formats
- line—Straight lines
- oval—Ovals, or any closed, circular shape
- polygon—Polygons, made up of a number of connected line segments
- rectangle—Rectangles, or any close, rectilinear shape
- window—Embedded windows, or other widgets embedded in a canvas widget

The following sections discuss drawing each of these objects, with the exception of the window object. I omit discussion of window objects because I consider embedded windows to be an advanced topic that you probably won't need until you progress further in your Tk scripting.

Each class of canvas objects has a number of attributes that you can use to define its behavior and appearance. Not surprisingly, some object attributes are unique to the object in question; other attributes are common to all canvas objects. To avoid considerable tedium and repetition, Table 15.3 lists these common or shared attributes.

TABLE 15.3   SHARED CANVAS OBJECT ATTRIBUTES

Attribute	Description
-activedash *pattern*	Defines the dash pattern of a line or outline enclosing an object in its active state.
-activefill *color*	Defines an object's fill color in its active state.
-activeoutline *color*	Defines an object's outline color in its active state.
-activeoutlinestipple *bitmap*	Defines the stipple pattern used to draw the outline of an object in its active state.
-activestipple *bitmap*	Defines the stipple pattern used to fill an object in its active state.
-activewidth *width*	Defines the width of the outline drawn around an object's region in its active state; *width* can be any valid coordinate form.
-dash *pattern*	Defines the dash pattern of a line or outline of an object in its normal state.
-dashoffset *offset*	Defines the offset into an object where the dashes appear; used with -dash.
-disableddash *pattern*	Defines the dash pattern of a line or outline of an object in its disabled state.
-disabledfill *color*	Defines the fill color of an object in its disabled state.
-disabledoutline *color*	Defines the color of the outline when an outlined object is in its disabled state.
-disabledoutlinestipple *bitmap*	Defines the stipple pattern used to draw the outline of an object in its disabled state.
-disabledstipple *bitmap*	Defines the stipple pattern used to fill an object in its disabled state.
-disabledwidth *width*	Defines the width of the outline drawn around an object's region in its disabled state; *width* can be any valid coordinate form.
-fill *color*	Defines the fill color of an object in its normal state.
-offset *offset*	Defines the offset of stipples in either x, y coordinates or *side*, where *side* is center or one of the standard compass points (n, ne, e, se, s, sw, w, or nw).
-outline *color*	Defines the color of the outline when an outlined object is in its normal state.
-outlinestipple *bitmap*	Defines the stipple pattern used to draw the outline of an object in its normal state.
-state *state*	Defines an object's state (one of normal, active, or hidden), overriding the global state of the canvas object itself.
-stipple *bitmap*	Defines the stipple pattern used to fill an object in its normal state.
-tags *taglist*	Defines a list of one or more tags to apply to an object.
-width *width*	Defines the width of the outline drawn around an object's region in its normal state; *width* can be any valid coordinate form.

The dash-related attributes bear on the canvas widget's (relatively new) ability to draw lines and outlines using dashed lines. Each dash-related attribute accepts a single argument, *pattern*, which defines the appearance of the dashed line. To demonstrate my earlier comment about the canvas widget's complexity, the *pattern* argument can take one of two forms: a list of integers whose values define the length of the line segments used to draw the dashed line, or a string that defines the proportions of the line segments used to draw the dashed line.

Drawing Arcs

An *arc* is a section of an oval defined by two angles: a *start* and an *extent*.

Use the following command to create arc objects:

```
$c create arc coords ?attr ...?
```

$c refers to the canvas widget on which the arc object is being drawn. The *coords* argument defines opposite corners of a rectangular region that would serve as the bounding box of an oval. Instead of an oval, though, an arc object consists of a curved line segment along an oval. The line segment begins at the angle specified by the -start attribute and extends through the angle specified by the -extent attribute. The *attr* argument specifies the attributes, if any, to apply to the resulting object. The return value of the create arc command is an identifier or handle that can be used in calls to the itemcget and itemconfigure commands and other commands that require an item identifier that refers to a canvas object.

The arc object supports the object-specific attributes listed in Table 15.4.

TABLE 15.4: ARC OBJECT ATTRIBUTES	
Attribute	**Description**
-extent *degrees*	Specifies the length in *degrees* of the arc's angular range.
-start *degrees*	Specifies the beginning of the arc's angular range in degrees.
-style *type*	Specifies the arc style, which must be one of pieslice, chord, or arc.

An arc is drawn in the *counter-clockwise* direction from -start through -extent, starting at the 3 o'clock position. The -extent attribute defines the length of the arc, not its endpoint. Thus, if -start is 30 and -extent is 60, you wind up with a 90-degree arc. The *degrees* argument can be specified with negative values. If the -extent attribute is greater than 360 or less than -360, then the value applied will be *degrees* modulo 360.

The following script, arc.tcl in this chapter's code directory, illustrates each of the possible arc styles:

```
set c [canvas .c -width 300 -height 300 -bg "white"]

$c create oval 10 10 290 290 -fill "#dddddd" -outline "#dddddd"

$c create arc 10 10 290 290 -start 90 -extent 60 -style arc \
    -outline "red" -activeoutline "dark red" -activewidth 5

$c create arc 10 10 290 290 -start 0 -extent 45 -style pieslice \
    -fill "light blue" -outline "light blue" \
    -activeoutline "dark blue" -activewidth 5

$c create arc 10 10 290 290 -start 180 -extent 90 -style chord \
    -fill "yellow" -outline "yellow" \
    -activeoutline "orange" -activewidth 5

grid $c
```

The canvas object is 300×300 pixels square with a white background. I created four canvas objects to place on the canvas: an oval and three arcs. Its purpose in this program is to show that the three arc objects are part of the same oval. I filled each arc with a different color so that you can tell them apart and recognize the difference between each of the three arc styles.

The first arc is 60 degrees long, starting from the 90-degree point on the circle and extending 60 degrees (-start 90 -extent 60). It is drawn in the (somewhat confusingly named) arc style, so it lacks an area to fill. The default color (shown when the object is in its normal state) is red (-outline red). Moving the mouse cursor over it changes its state to active, so the -activeoutline color (dark red) and the -activewidth (5 pixels) cause it to stand out.

The second arc is only 30 degrees long. Drawn in the pieslice style, it has a -fill color of sky blue. The -activeoutline and -activewidth attributes are dark blue and 5, respectively. Again, the purpose of using these attributes is to make the object stand out when the cursor hovers over it and to illustrate the behavior of the object in its active state. Notice also that the pieslice style creates an area defined by the arc itself plus two line segments between the center of the oval and the ends of the arc.

The third arc uses the chord style. Its notable feature is that the chord's area is defined by a linear line segment between the arc's endpoints, which are at 180 degrees and 270 degrees.

Figure 15.7 shows arc.tcl's window in a normal state, that is, with none of the embedded objects activated. Figure 15.8 shows the third arc, the yellow chord, activated.

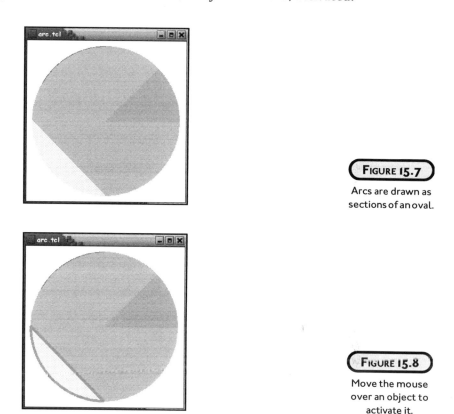

FIGURE 15.7

Arcs are drawn as sections of an oval.

FIGURE 15.8

Move the mouse over an object to activate it.

Drawing Bitmaps

The canvas widget's bitmap object enables you to position and display bitmaps in the canvas. However, these bitmaps are not the colored bitmaps you are accustomed to using as icons, clip art, and the like. Rather, they are a much simpler graphic. In the context of Tk, a *bitmap*, more properly referred to as a *bitmap image*, refers to an image whose pixels can display one of two colors or be transparent. Speaking strictly technically, a bitmap image consists of a foreground color, a background color, a source bitmap, and a mask bitmap. The source and mask bitmaps are a rectangular grid of zeros and ones, and both grids are the same size. In the source bitmap, pixel values of 1 map to a foreground color and pixel values of 0 map to a background color. The mask bitmap controls which portions of the source bitmap you actually see. In the mask bitmap, a value of 0 hides (masks) the corresponding pixel in the source bitmap, causing nothing to be displayed. A value of 1 allows the corresponding pixel from the source bitmap to be displayed.

This background information might be more than you wanted to know about old-fashioned bitmaps, but it is necessary to understanding why `bitmap` objects behave the way they do. Use the following command to create `bitmap` objects:

```
$c create bitmap x y ?attr ...?
```

`$c` refers to the `canvas` widget on which the `bitmap` object is being drawn. The *x* and *y* arguments define a point around which the `bitmap` will be drawn. By default, the bitmap is centered on that point, but you can use the `-anchor` attribute to modify where the `bitmap` will be positioned relative to the specified coordinates. The *attr* argument specifies the attributes, if any, you want applied to the `bitmap` object. The `bitmap` object supports the object-specific attributes listed in Table 15.5.

TABLE 15.5: BITMAP OBJECT ATTRIBUTES

Attribute	Description
-activebackground *bitmap*	Specifies the color of the bitmap's 0-valued pixels in its `active` states. If omitted or if *color* empty string, nothing is displayed, resulting in a transparent effect.
-activebitmap *bitmap*	Specifies the bitmap to display in its active state.
-activeforeground *color*	Specifies the color to use for the bitmap's 1-valued pixels in active, defaulting to black.
-anchor *pos*	Positions the bitmap relative its positioning point, defaulting to center.
-background *color*	Specifies the color of the bitmap's 0-valued pixels in its `normal` state. If omitted or if *color* empty string, nothing is displayed, resulting in a transparent effect.
-bitmap *bitmap*	Specifies the bitmap to display in its normal state.
-disabledbackground *bitmap*	Specifies the color of the bitmap's 0-valued pixels in its `disabled` state. If omitted or if *color* empty string, nothing is displayed, resulting in a transparent effect.
-disabledbitmap *bitmap*	Specifies the bitmap to display in its disabled state.
-disabledforeground *color*	Specifies the color to use for the bitmap's 1-valued pixels in its disabled state, defaulting to black.
-foreground *color*	Specifies the color to use for the bitmap's 1-valued pixels in its normal state, defaulting to black.

Tk's bitmaps are primitive in comparison to other image formats and, insofar as Tk supports more modern image formats, I'm going to skip further discussion of the canvas widget's bitmap object and direct you instead to the more capable and visually appealing image object discussed next. However, the script bitmap.tcl in this chapter's code directory illustrates how to use the bitmap object.

Still Curious about Bitmaps?

 If you want more information about Tk's notion of bitmaps, a notion that is firmly rooted in Tk's X Window System origins, refer to the manual page for the bitmap command (man 3tk bitmap).

Drawing Images

The image object is Tk's general purpose object for non-bitmap images. Before you use an image object on a canvas widget, you must first create the image using the image create command. Before diving into the specifics of the canvas widget's image object, I need to take a detour through the image command because you need to know how Tk deals with images that aren't bitmaps.

Using the image Command

The image command is used to create and manipulate images. It can create the two-color bitmaps described earlier and non-bitmap images. By *non-bitmap images*, I mean image types other than the simple, two-color graphic objects I've already described.

Why Two Commands for Working with Bitmaps?

 The Tk core has two commands for dealing with the bitmap format due to historical reasons. The original command was bitmap. When Tk was first created, the bitmap command was added specifically to give developers native commands for working with X bitmaps, the simple two-color bitmap format you've already seen. As display technology evolved, Tk lagged behind. Eventually, support for full-color images was added via the image command. However, to preserve backward compatibility with older Tk code, support for the two-color bitmap format was included in the image command, and the original bitmap command was preserved. Tk continues to schlep around the old bitmap support, but most people will want to use the image command because it supports a wider variety of images.

Table 15.6 summarizes the image command's operations.

Operation	Description
image create *type* ?*name*? ?*opts*?	Creates an image of the specified *type*, returning an identifier used in other image operations. If specified, *name* is used as the identifier; otherwise, the identifier is created. Values for *opts* depend of the value of *type*.
image delete *name*	Deletes the image referred to by the identifier specified in *name*.
image height *name*	Returns the height in pixels of the image specified by *name*.
image inuse *name*	Returns a Boolean true if the image specified by *name* is being used by any widget.
image names	Returns a list of all currently defined images.
image type *name*	Returns the type of the image specified by *name*.
image types	Returns a list of all the possible image types.
image width *name*	Returns the width in pixels of the image specified by *name*.

The Tk core only supports two values for the *type* argument, bitmap (the two-color format described previously), and photo which, despite its name, supports several full-color image formats (PPM, PGM, and GIF), image dithering, and gamma correction. Support for many other image formats, such as JPEG, TIFF, and PNG, is available through Tk extensions. To keep things simple, I'll use the photo image type and the GIF format.

The following script creates an image, populates it with a picture of a dahlia from my garden, and displays some information about the image (see image.tcl in this chapter's code directory):

```
set img [image create photo]
$img read dahlia.gif

set f [frame .f -bg "white"]
set top [label $f.top -image $img -bg "white"]
set nfo [label $f.nfo -bg "white"]

lappend data \
    "Handle: $img\n" \
    "Height: [image height $img]\n" \
    "Width : [image width $img]\n" \
```

```
    "In use: [image inuse $img]\n" \
    "Type   : [image type $img]"
foreach datum $data {
        append t $datum
}
$nfo configure -text $t -justify left

grid $f -sticky nsew
grid $top -sticky nsew
grid $nfo -sticky w
```

For the purposes of the present discussion, the first two lines of code are the most important because they show how to create an image and how to populate it with image data:

```
set img [image create photo]
$img read dahlia.gif
```

The first line creates an image of type photo, storing the returned identifier in the variable $img. Notice that I did not assign an identifier to the created image using the -name attribute. As a result, the image command synthesizes a name by appending an integer to the text image. As you can see in Figure 15.9, the identifier is image1. The second line populates the image by reading the contents of the file dahlia.gif ($img read dahlia.gif).

To display the image, I use a label widget ($top) and set its -image attribute to $img. I used the second label, $nfo, to display some of the information about the image. Figure 15.9 shows the resulting window.

FIGURE 15.9

The image command can display full-color GIFs and two-color bitmaps.

To create and populate the `image` in a single command, I could have written `set img [image create photo -file dahlia.gif]`. The attribute `-file dahlia.gif` tells the `image create` command to read the data for the `image` from the file dahlia.gif.

Using the `image` Canvas Object

The previous section just slapped an `image` onto a `label` widget for demonstration purposes. In this section, I'm going to describe how to take an `image` created with image create and paint it on a `canvas`. Use the following command to create `image` objects:

```
$c create image x y ?attr ...?
```

`$c` refers to the `canvas` widget on which the `image` object is being drawn. The *x* and *y* arguments define a point around which the `image` object will be drawn. By default, the image is centered on that point, but you can use the `-anchor` attribute to modify where the `bitmap` will be positioned relative to the specified coordinates. The *attr* arguments, if any, list the object attributes you want to apply to the resulting `image` object. Of the common options listed in Table 15.7, the `image` object supports only the `-state` and `-tags` attributes, but it also supports the object-specific attributes listed in Table 15.7.

TABLE 15.7: IMAGE OBJECT ATTRIBUTES

Attribute	Description
`-activeimage` *name*	Specifies the image to display in the object's `active` state, where *name* is the return value of an `image create` operation.
`-anchor` *pos*	Positions the bitmap relative to its positioning point, defaulting to `center`.
`-disabledimage` *name*	Specifies the image to display in the object's `disabled`, where *name* is the return value of an `image create` operation.
`-image` *name*	Specifies the image to display in the object's `normal` state, where *name* is the return value of an `image create` operation.

The following script, c_image.tcl in this chapter's code directory, demonstrates how to use the image object:

```
set img [image create photo dahlia -file "dahlia.gif"]

set w [image width $img]
set h [image height $img]
set x [expr $w / 2]
```

```
set y [expr $h / 2]

set c [canvas .c -background "white" -height $h -width $w]
$c create image $x $y -image $img

grid $c -sticky nsew
```

The first command uses the `image` command discussed in the previous section to create an image. Unlike the earlier example, I use the `-file` attribute to specify the contents of the image object and also define the identifier I want assigned to the resulting image. The next two commands get the width and height of the image, storing them in the variables $w and $h, respectively. I'll use these values to dimension the `canvas` widget when I define it. I also will use the width and height values to calculate the center of the image, storing these values in the variable $x and $y, respectively. I use the values to specify the anchor point of the `image` object when I create it.

Next, I define the canvas widget, using the width and height values just described (`set c [canvas .c -background "white" -height $h -width $w]`). Similarly, the following command, `$c create image $x $y -image $img`, creates the `image` object to draw on the `canvas` widget. Unlike the bitmap example you saw earlier, I used an image identifier rather than a filename to create the image. Both methods are acceptable; the reason I used the identifier rather than a filename is to demonstrate the proper syntax.

Figure 15.10 shows c_image.tcl's window.

FIGURE 15.10

Full-color images have greater visual appeal than two-color bitmaps.

Drawing Lines

The line object is used to draw both straight and curved lines. In the simplest case, a straight line, you specify a starting and ending point. To draw curved lines, you can use either a series of joined line segments, or you can draw a spline and instruct the canvas to smooth the spline. In addition, you (or your users) can draw lines using the mouse. The example script you'll see shortly uses the mouse to draw the lines. Other features of the canvas widget's line object include varying the width of the line itself, the ability to place arrows at one or both ends of a line segment, and being able to specify the appearance of the points (vertexes) at which two lines meet.

Use the following command to create line objects:

```
$c create line coords ?attr ...?
```

$c refers to the canvas widget on which the line object is being drawn. The coords variable is a list of two or more pairs of (x,y) coordinates defining points along the line at which line segments are joined. The attr arguments specify the attributes you want to apply to a line segment.

The line object supports the object-specific attributes listed in Table 15.8.

TABLE 15.8: LINE OBJECT ATTRIBUTES

Attribute	Description
-arrow *where*	Specifies if and how many arrowheads to draw at the ends of the line; *where* must be one of none, first, last, or both (defaults to none).
-arrowshape {*N L W*}	Specifies the arrowhead shape where (*N L W*) is a three-element list defining the size of the arrowhead.
-capstyle *style*	Specifies how to draw line caps, where style is one of butt, projecting, or round and defaults to butt; not used with -arrow or -arrowshape.
-joinstyle *style*	Specifies how to draw line joints, where *style* is one of bevel, miter, or round and defaults to miter; not used if the line only has two points.
-smooth *boolean*	Specifies if the line should be smoothed; used with -splinesteps.
-splinesteps *number*	Specifies the number of line segments used to smooth a curve; used with -smooth.

If you specify the -arrow attribute, you can use the -arrowshape {*N L W*} attribute to specify a three-element list that defines the arrow's characteristics. The list elements define the lengths of arrow components, as described on the next page:

- N—The first list element defines length of the neck, of the arrow, which is the part of the arrowhead that touches the line.
- L—The second list element defines overall length of the arrow from its base or neck to its tip.
- W—The third list element defines the distance from the outside edge of the line to each of the trailing points.

Figure 15.11 shows the parts of an arrow.

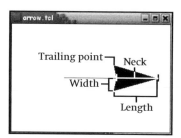

FIGURE 15.11

Who knew that drawing arrowheads on a line could be so complicated?

Tk attempts to use an internally defined heuristic to set the arrowhead size if you omit -arrowshape. In particular, if you request arrows but don't specify -arrowshape, the neck of the arrow will be eight pixels long, the length of the arrow will be ten pixels long, and the width of the arrow will be three pixels. Thus, the equivalent -arrowshape attribute would be arrowshape {8 10 3}.

If you want to experiment with the -arrowshape attribute, you can use the script arrow.tcl in this chapter's code directory. It's the script I used to create Figure 15.11.

The following script, arrows.tcl in this chapter's code directory, shows you how to use the -arrow and -arrowshape attributes:

```
set c [canvas .c -width 300 -height 300 -bg "white"]

set l1 [$c create line 60 10 60 290 -arrow none]
set l2 [$c create line 120 10 120 290 -arrow first -arrowshape {8 10 3}]
set l3 [$c create line 180 10 180 290 -arrow last -arrowshape {16 20 6}]
set l4 [$c create line 240 10 240 290 -arrow both -arrowshape {40 45 13}]

grid $c -sticky nsew
```

After creating a canvas, I create four line objects named l1 through l4. Each line is perfectly vertical because the endpoints of each line have the same X coordinate. Similarly, they are all the same length, 280 pixels, because they share common starting and ending Y coordinates (10 and 290, respectively). The only difference between them is the shape and location of the arrows: l1 has no arrows; l2 has an arrow at its first endpoint, which is the point (120,10); l3 has an arrow at its last (or second) endpoint, which is the point (280,290); l4 has somewhat oversized arrows at both ends of the line.

Each arrowhead is bigger than the one on the line preceding it. As I mentioned earlier, the default shape corresponds to the attribute `-arrowshape {8 10 3}`, so I could have written the command for creating the line l2 as `set l2 [$c create line 120 10 120 290 -arrow first]`.

Figure 15.12 shows what the lines and arrows in arrows.tcl look like.

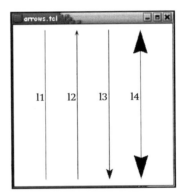

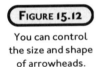

FIGURE 15.12

You can control the size and shape of arrowheads.

Table 15.8 shows that the `-smooth` attribute accepts a Boolean argument. If you specify `-smooth false` (or `-smooth 0`), the line will not be smoothed; `-smooth true` or `-smooth 1` causes the line to be smoothed using a Bezier curve.

A Slight Oversimplification

Only Bezier curve smoothing is supported in the Tk core, so the `-smooth` attribute behaves as I described: Setting it to `true` results in a line that has been smoothed using a Bezier curve. However, Tk supports loading smoothing algorithms from external libraries at runtime. If this is done (a topic that is well beyond this book's scope), then the argument to `-smooth` can also be the name of a smoothing algorithm to apply.

The next script, lines.tcl, creates a series of line segments and joins them using the `-joinstyle` attribute:

```
proc RandomInt {min max} {
    return [expr int($min + (rand() * ($max - $min + 1)))]
```

```
}

proc MakePoint {} {
    set x [RandomInt 0 300]
    set y [RandomInt 0 300]
    return [list $x $y]
}

for {set i 0} {$i < 6} {incr i} {
    lappend coords [MakePoint]
}
set c [canvas .c -width 300 -height 300 -bg "white"]
$c create line [join $coords] -width 5 -joinstyle round
grid $c -sticky nsew
```

The RandomInt procedure should be familiar to you by this point, so I'm going to skip yet another description of it. The MakePoint procedure calls RandomInt twice to create a pair of coordinates that define a single point on the canvas, returning that point as a two-element list. The for loop calls MakePoint six times to create a list of coordinates that I pass to the create line command (after exiting the for loop). The resulting "line" is actually five line segments joined, in this case, using -joinstyle round. This style of line joints, shown in Figure 15.13, gives the joints between each line segment a rounded or smooth look. Figure 15.14 uses beveled joints, which look rougher and in most cases appear to be squared off rather than forming a cleanly drawn joint. Figure 15.15 uses the default join type, -joinstyle miter, which creates sharp, fitted joints that look as if they were created by a miter saw (hence the name).

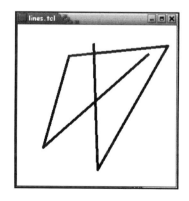

FIGURE 15.13

Rounded joints are smooth and soft.

FIGURE 15.14

Beveled joints
look rough and
jagged.

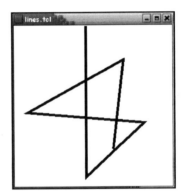

FIGURE 15.15

Mitered joints
appear sharp and
fitted.

How do you draw a curve? Draw a segmented line, as shown in the previous example, and then apply smoothing. Specify `-smooth true` if you want to create lines that are smoothed instead of having pronounced angles at each joint between line segments. Increasing the number of points on the curve results in a smoother curve. To do so, specify `-splinesteps` *num*, which causes each curve to be approximated using *num* line segments. The next script illustrates using the `-smooth` and `-splinesteps` attributes:

```
proc RandomInt {min max} {
    return [expr int($min + (rand() * ($max - $min + 1)))]
}


proc MakePoint {} {
    set x [RandomInt 0 639]
    set y [RandomInt 0 479]
    return [list $x $y]
}
```

```
proc Smooth {c line num} {
    if {$num == 0} {
        $c itemconfigure $line -smooth false
    } else {
        $c itemconfigure $line -smooth true -splinesteps $num
    }
}


for {set i 0} {$i < 20} {incr i} {
    lappend coords [MakePoint]
}

set c [canvas .c -width 640 -height 480 -bg "white"]
set f [frame .f -width 640 -bg "white"]
set ln [$c create line [join $coords] -width 3]

set b0 [button $f.b0 -width 10 -text "0 Splines" \
    -command "Smooth $c $ln 0"]
set b2 [button $f.b2 -width 10 -text "2 Splines" \
    -command "Smooth $c $ln 2"]
set b3 [button $f.b3 -width 10 -text "3 Splines" \
    -command "Smooth $c $ln 3"]
set b10 [button $f.b10 -width 10 -text "10 Splines" \
    -command "Smooth $c $ln 10"]
set b50 [button $f.b50 -width 10 -text "50 Splines" \
    -command "Smooth $c $ln 50"]
set b100 [button $f.b100 -width 10 -text "100 Splines" \
    -command "Smooth $c $ln 100"]

grid $c -sticky nsew -columnspan 4
grid $f -sticky nsew -columnspan 4
grid $b2 $b3 $b10 $b50 $b100 -pady 10 -padx 10
```

When you initially start this script, you will see a randomly generated collection of joined line segments. There are five buttons at the bottom of the window that apply smoothing to the generated line, using two, three, ten, 50, and 100 splines. A sixth button removes all smoothing, reverting the line to its original, unsmoothed state.

The RandomInt and MakePoint procedures are the same as they were in the previous section. The Smooth procedure smoothes the line displayed in the window. It accepts three arguments: the canvas widget and line object ($c and $line, respectively) on which to operate, and an integer value, $num, that specifies how many splines to use for smoothing the line. If $num is 0, I disable smoothing completely by setting $line's -smooth attribute to false. This causes the line to revert to its original, unsmoothed configuration. Otherwise, I set -smooth true and pass $num to the -splinesteps attribute.

As in lines.tcl earlier, I use a for loop to generate a number of X and Y coordinate values to use when creating the line. In this script, I wanted a complex line, so I generated 20 points. Next, I define a canvas widget, a frame widget to contain the smoothing buttons, and the line itself, passing the $coords list I populated in the for loop. After I create the six buttons to invoke the Smooth procedure, I display the widgets using the grid and the script is ready to go.

Figures 15.16–15.21 show each smoothing option applied to the same figure.

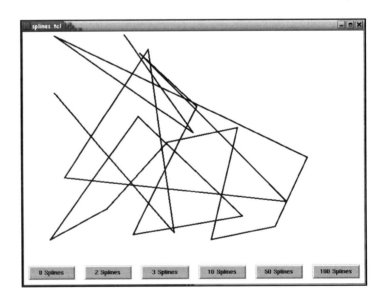

FIGURE 15.16

The unsmoothed line is hideous to behold.

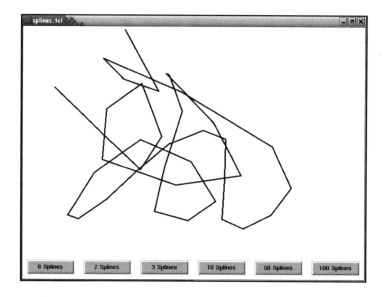

FIGURE 15.17

Two splines don't make much of a difference.

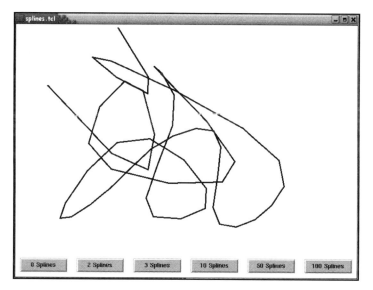

FIGURE 15.18

Three splines begin to soften the line.

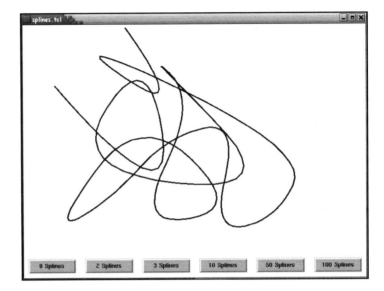

FIGURE 15.19

Ten splines result in a nice smooth figure.

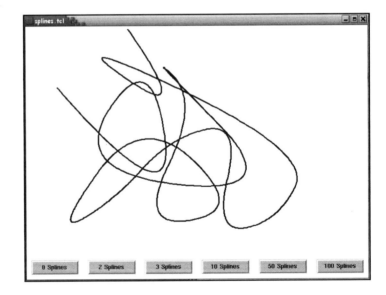

FIGURE 15.20

Fifty splines doesn't make an appreciable difference.

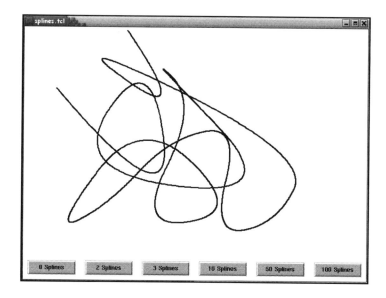

FIGURE 15.21

One hundred
splines is overkill.

As you can see from these six figures, the sweet spot for smoothing a line, or at least the line in *this* program, is somewhere between three and ten points.

OF SPLINES AND BÉZIERS

In computer graphics, a *spline* refers to a smooth curve that passes through two or more points. Splines are generated using mathematical formulas, the details of which are either fascinating (to a graphics hound) or dreadfully boring (to mere mortals). There are many different ways in which to calculate splines, but one of the most common is to use Bézier (pronounced bez-ee-ay) curves. Bézier curves are (somewhat incorrectly) named for the French engineer and mathematician Pierre Bézier, who popularized this method for smoothing a series of line segments. As I explained earlier, Tk's support for splines is limited to Bézier curves in the standard release.

The Bézier method requires at least three points to define a curve, the two endpoints of the line segment and a third point, referred to as a *handle*, situated somewhere along the curve. The endpoints are called *anchors* or *anchor points*. Handles, alternatively known as *tangent points* or *nodes*, define the shape of the curve. By moving the handles, you can modify the shape of the curve. As far as Tk is concerned, the more handles you provide (using the -splinesteps attribute), the smoother the resulting curve. For more information than you might want about calculating Bezier curves, I recommend the Wikipedia article on the subject (see http://en.wikipedia.org/wiki/Bezier_curve).

Drawing Ovals

The oval canvas object is defined just like the `arc` object, by specifying two sets of coordinates that create a bounding box. If the bounding box is square, the resulting oval will be circular; otherwise, you wind up with a non-circular ovoid shape.

Use the following command to create `oval` objects:

```
$c create oval coords ?attr ...?
```

`$c` refers to the `canvas` widget on which the `oval` object is being drawn. The `coords` arguments consist of two (x,y) coordinates that define the `oval`'s bounding box. As usual, `attr` specifies any attributes you want applied to the object. Note that if `coords` defines a square bounding box, the resulting oval will be circular.

The `oval` object lacks object-specific attributes, but does support the common object attributes listed in Table 15.3 earlier in the chapter. Most of the time, you will want to set either the color of the oval's interior, its outline, or both. The following script, oval.tcl in this chapter's code directory, illustrates several ovals:

```
set c [canvas .c -width 240 -height 100 -bg "white"]

$c create oval 10 10 90 90 -width 5 -fill "sky blue" -outline "dark blue"
$c create oval 110 10 140 90 -width 5 -fill "chartreuse" -outline "dark green"
$c create oval 150 30 230 70 -width 5 -fill "yellow" -outline "orange"

grid $c -sticky nsew
```

This is a pretty simple script, drawing three ovals. The first is a sky blue circle with a dark blue outline. The second is a vertically elongated chartreuse oval with a dark outline. The third is a horizontally stretched oval with a yellow background and an orange foreground. Figure15.22 shows the resulting window.

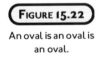

FIGURE 15.22

An oval is an oval is an oval.

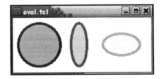

Drawing Polygons

The `canvas` widget's `polygon` object is just what the name implies, a polygon made up of an arbitrary number of line segments. Like the `line` object, the resulting shape can be smoothed. Use the following command to create `polygon` objects:

```
$c create polygon coords ?attr ...?
```

$c refers to the canvas widget on which the polygon object is being drawn. The *coords* argument is a list of at least three (x,y) coordinates that define line segments, joined at their endpoints to form the vertexes of the closed shape. Also like the line object, you can specify a particular join style for the vertexes, and, if you want a curved polygon rather than a linear one, you can use the -smooth and -splinesteps attributes to apply a smoothing algorithm. In addition to the common canvas object attributes listed in Table 15.3, the polygon object supports the object-specific attributes shown in Table 15.9.

TABLE 15.9:   POLYGON OBJECT ATTRIBUTES

Attribute	Description
-joinstyle *style*	Specifies how to draw line joints, where *style* is one of bevel, miter, or round and defaults to miter; not used if the line only has two points.
-smooth *method*	Specifies the algorithm used to smooth the line; used with -splinesteps.
-splinesteps *number*	Specifies the number of line segments used to smooth a curve; used with -smooth.

The following script, polygon.tcl in this chapter's code directory, shows you how to program the polygon object.

```
proc Smooth {c line num} {
    if {$num == 0} {
        $c itemconfigure $line -smooth false
    } else {
        $c itemconfigure $line -smooth true -splinesteps $num
    }
}


set c [canvas .c -width 400 -height 400 -bg "white"]
set f [frame .f -width 400 -bg "white"]

set x 80
set y 80
set coords {160 80 240 80 240 160 320 160 320 240 240 240 \
    240 320 160 320 160 240 80 240 80 160 160 160}
set poly [$c create polygon $coords -width 5 \
```

```
     -fill "blue violet" -outline violet]

set b0 [button $f.b0 -width 8 -text "0 Splines" \
    -command "Smooth $c $poly 0"]
set b2 [button $f.b2 -width 8 -text "2 Splines" \
    -command "Smooth $c $poly 2"]
set b10 [button $f.b10 -width 8 -text "10 Splines" \
    -command "Smooth $c $poly 10"]
set b50 [button $f.b50 -width 8 -text "50 Splines" \
    -command "Smooth $c $poly 50"]

grid $c -sticky nsew -columnspan 4
grid $f -sticky nsew -columnspan 4
grid $b0 $b2 $b10 $b50 -pady 10 -padx 5
```

This script is very similar to the splines.tcl script presented earlier in the chapter. The most significant difference is that instead of generating the points randomly, I specify them manually:

```
set coords {160 80 240 80 240 160 320 160 320 240 240 240 \
    240 320 160 320 160 240 80 240 80 160 160 160}
```

Starting from the upper left-hand corner of the polygon I want to draw (see Figure 15.23), I define each vertex in order, moving clockwise around the figure until I get to the last point. Defining them in order ensures that the line segments are connected properly. The smoothing buttons include a different mix of smoothing options, but, other than the different canvas object and the smaller set of smoothing buttons, not much is new here. Figures 15.23–15.26 show the original polygon and the results after applying 2, 10, and 50 splines for smoothing.

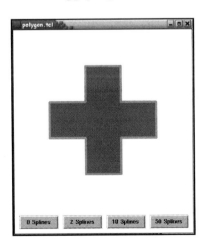

FIGURE 15.23

The original polygon is crisp and sharp.

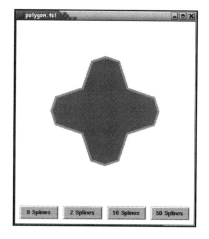

FIGURE 15.24

Adding two
splines makes it
angular, but not
smooth.

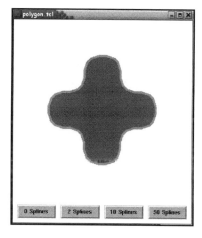

FIGURE 15.25

Even after adding
10 splines, the
polygon still
displays a hint of
linearity.

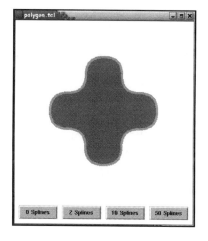

FIGURE 15.26

The addition of 50
splines removes
all visible straight
lines.

Drawing Text

The `canvas` widget's `text` object displays a string of characters, arranged in one or more lines, on the canvas. Like the other `canvas` objects you have seen in this chapter, the text object supports a variety of formatting operations. In addition, unlike the other `canvas` objects, the `text` object also allows you to use text insertion and manipulation commands such as `insert`, `index`, `select`, `icursor`, and so forth.

To create a `text` object, use the following command:

```
$c create text x y ?attr ...?
```

`$c` refers to the `canvas` widget on which the `text` object is being drawn. The arguments *x* and *y* define an *anchor point* on which the text is centered (using the `-anchor` attribute described in Table 15.10). As usual, you can specify one or more attributes to further define the text object being created. The `text` object supports the object-specific attributes listed in Table 15.10.

TABLE 15.10: TEXT OBJECT ATTRIBUTES

Attribute	Description
`-anchor` *pos*	Positions the bitmap relative to its positioning point, defaulting to `center`.
`-font` *name*	Specifies the font to use for the text item; defaults to a system-dependent font.
`-justify` *how*	Specifies text justification, which must be one of `left`, `right`, or `center`; defaults to `left`.
`-text` *string*	Specifies the text to display.
`-width` *length*	Specifies the maximum line length; defaults to zero.

The anchor point defines a point on the canvas relative to which the text object is positioned. The default setting is `-attribute center`, meaning that the text object will be centered on the anchor point. Other values include any one of the compass points n, ne, e, se, s, sw, w, and nw (for north, northeast, east, southeast, south, southwest, west, and northwest, respectively).

The font used the platform-specific font. If you want to specify a particular font, use the `-font` *name* attribute, where *name* is a valid font name for the host platform. The `-justify` option specifies how to justify the text and is meaningful only if the text spans multiple lines.

The `-text string` attribute defines the initial text contents of the `text` object. Newline characters embedded in string create line breaks in the text. At runtime, of course, you can modify the contents of the text object using the `insert` and `delete` commands.

To define the width of the text, use the -width attribute (no surprise there). If -width is zero (the default setting), text is broken into lines at newline characters. Otherwise, the text will be broken at *length*. In this case, lines that exceed *length* are broken immediately before the space character closest to *length*.

The following script, plain_text.tcl, shows a simple example of the canvas widget's text object:

```
proc ReadFile {f} {
    set fileId [open $f r]
    set s [read $fileId]
    close $fileId
    return $s
}


set c [canvas .c -bg "white"]
set t [$c create text 0 0 -anchor nw]
$c insert $t end [ReadFile "README"]


grid $c -sticky nsew
grid rowconfigure . 0 -weight 1
grid columnconfigure . 0 -weight 1
```

You've seen almost all of this code before. The only new elements are the two lines that create and populate the text widget:

```
set t [$c create text 0 0 -anchor nw]
$c insert $t end [ReadFile "README"]
```

The first line creates a text object, $t, with an anchor point of (0,0) and anchor position of nw. The result is a text object nailed to the upper left-hand corner of the canvas. The second line invokes the ReadFile procedure on the now-familiar README file and inserts the returned string at the "end" of the text object. Insofar as the text object is initially empty, the "end" is also the beginning or top. To display the window, I pin the canvas widget to all four sides of its parent window (grid $c -sticky nsew) and then use the rowconfigure and columnconfigure commands to set the -weight attribute to 1. The rationale is to allow the canvas widget (and its contents) to resize as the parent window resizes. Figure 15.27 shows the resulting window.

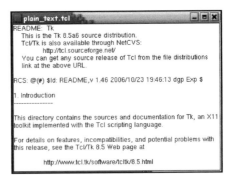

FIGURE 15.27

Resize the window
to view the entire
README file.

ANALYZING GOT THE PICTURE?

In my opinion, puzzle.tcl is the most complicated script I've presented in this book. It uses language features discussed throughout the book. Obviously, I needed to use the canvas widget and other GUI elements such as buttons, frames, and images. It also contains a number of procedures, simple mathematics, list manipulation, looping, conditionals, and event bindings. In short, puzzle.tcl is a complete Tcl and Tk program.

Looking at the Code

```
#!/usr/bin/wish
# puzzle.tcl
# Create a puzzle out of an image

# Block 1
# Initialize the game board
proc InitGame {c img} {
    # Disable the Start button
    uplevel {$f.bstart configure -state disabled}
    # Create puzzle pieces
    set tiles [SplitImage $c $img]
    # Mix up the puzzle pieces
    JumbleImage $c $img $tiles
}

# Block 2
# Draw a 3x4 grid on the image
proc DrawGrid {c img} {
    set incrx 140
    set incry 150
    # Draw horiz lines
    for {set y 0} {$y < 600} {incr y $incry} {
```

```
$c create line 0 $y 419 $y -width 2 -fill yellow
    }
    # Draw vert lines
    for {set x 0} {$x < 420} {incr x $incrx} {
        $c create line $x 0 $x 599 -width 2 -fill yellow
    }
}

# Block 3
# Split the image into 12 tiles
proc SplitImage {c img} {
    # Create 12 tiles
    for {set i 0} {$i < 12} {incr i} {
        lappend tiles [image create photo t$i]
    }

    # Populate the tiles
    set sx 0
    set sy 0
    set ex 140
    set ey 150
    set incrx 140
    set incry 150
    for {set t 1} {$t <= 12} {incr t} {
        [lindex $tiles [expr $t - 1]] copy $img  from $sx $sy $ex $ey
        if {$t % 3 != 0} {
            set sx $ex
            set ex [expr $sx + $incrx]
        } else {
            set sx 0
            set ex $incrx
            set sy $ey
            set ey [expr $sy + $incry]
        }
    }
    return $tiles
}

# Block 4
# Generate a list of random numbers between 0 and 11
proc Randomize {} {
    set nums [list]
    while {[llength $nums] < 12} {
```

```
        set n [expr int((rand() * 12))]
        if {[lsearch -integer $nums $n] == -1} {
            lappend nums $n
        }
    }
    return $nums
}

# Block 5
# Redraw the image in its "puzzle" form
proc JumbleImage {c img parts} {
    # Clear the board
    $img blank

    # Draw the jumbled image
    set sx 0
    set sy 0
    set ex 140
    set ey 150
    set incrx 140
    set incry 150
    set nums [Randomize]
    for {set t 1} {$t <= 12} {incr t} {
        set i [lindex $nums [expr $t - 1]]
        set tile [lindex $parts $i]
        $img copy $tile -to $sx $sy $ex $ey
        if {$t % 3 != 0} {
            set sx $ex
            set ex [expr $sx + $incrx]
        } else {
            set sx 0
            set ex $incrx
            set sy $ey
            set ey [expr $sy + $incry]
        }
    }
    # Pass the (x,y) coordinates under the cursor to SelectTile
    bind $c <Button-1> [list SelectTile %x %y]
}

# Block 6
# When a tile is selected, add it to the list of selected tiles
proc SelectTile {x y} {
```

```
    global selected

    # Map a the (x,y) coordinates to a tile
    if {$x >= 0 && $x < 140 && $y >= 0 && $y < 150} {
        lappend selected 0 0 140 150
    }
    if { $x >= 140 && $x < 280 && $y >= 0 && $y < 150} {
        lappend selected 140 0 280 150
    }
    if {$x >= 280 && $x < 420 && $y >= 0 && $y < 150} {
        lappend selected 280 0 420 150
    }
    if {$x >= 0 && $x < 140 && $y >= 150 && $y < 300} {
        lappend selected 0 150 140 300
    }
    if {$x >= 140 && $x < 280 && $y >= 150 && $y < 300} {
        lappend selected 140 150 280 300
    }
    if {$x >= 280 && $x < 420 && $y >= 150 && $y < 300} {
        lappend selected 280 150 420 300
    }
    if {$x >= 0 && $x < 140 && $y >= 300 && $y < 450} {
        lappend selected 0 300 140 450
    }
    if {$x >= 140 && $x < 280 && $y >= 300 && $y < 450} {
        lappend selected 140 300 280 450
    }
    if {$x >= 280 && $x < 420 && $y >= 300 && $y < 450} {
        lappend selected 280 300 420 450
    }
    if {$x >= 0 && $x < 140 && $y >= 450 && $y < 600} {
        lappend selected 0 450 140 600
    }
    if {$x >= 140 && $x < 280 && $y >= 450 && $y < 600} {
        lappend selected 140 450 280 600
    }
    if {$x >= 280 && $x < 420 && $y >= 450 && $y < 600} {
        lappend selected 280 450 420 600
    }
}

# Swap the tiles
proc SwapTiles {c img} {
```

```
    global selected

    image create photo src
    image create photo temp
    set x1 [lindex $selected 0]
    set y1 [lindex $selected 1]
    set x2 [lindex $selected 2]
    set y2 [lindex $selected 3]
    set x3 [lindex $selected 4]
    set y3 [lindex $selected 5]
    set x4 [lindex $selected 6]
    set y4 [lindex $selected 7]

    # Get the image from the first tile
    src copy $img -from $x1 $y1 $x2 $y2

    # Get the image from the second tile
    temp copy $img -from $x3 $y3 $x4 $y4

    # Put the first image in the second one's grid
    $img copy src -to $x3 $y3 $x4 $y4

    # Put the second image in the first one's grid
    $img copy temp -to $x1 $y1 $x2 $y2

    # Clear the list variable
    unset selected
}

# Block 7
# Layout the UI
# Create the image
set img [image create photo -file "gladiola.gif"]
set w [image width $img]
set h [image height $img]

# Canvas to display the puzzle
set c [canvas .c -width $w -height $h]

# Image object to contain the puzzle
set puzzle [$c create image 0 0 -image $img -anchor nw]
DrawGrid $c $img
```

```
# Buttons to control the game
set f [frame .fbuttons -width $w -height 100]
set bStart [button $f.bstart -text "Start" \
    -command [list InitGame $c $img]]
set selected {}
set bSwap [button $f.bswap -text "Swap" -command [list SwapTiles $c $img]]
set bExit [button $f.bexit -text "Exit" -command exit]

# Display the widgets
grid $c -sticky nsew -pady {10 0} -padx 10
grid $f -sticky nsew
grid $bStart $bSwap $bExit -pady 10 -padx 5
```

Understanding the Code

The InitGame procedure in Block 1 is invoked when the player clicks the Start button. It initializes the game board after it has been created. InitGame takes two arguments: the canvas widget on which to draw ($c) and the image object to use. I disable the Start button to prevent accidentally redrawing the board in mid-game. Next, I call the SplitImage procedure, using the $c and $img arguments passed in to InitGame. This procedure splits the displayed image into 12 equally-sized tiles that serve as the puzzle pieces. Next, I call the JumbleImage procedure to clear the starting board and redraw the image in its mixed up form. The DrawGrid block 2 procedure just draws a series of yellow horizontal and vertical lines on the canvas. I do this mostly as a visual aid to the player.

Block 3 defines the SplitImage procedure, which takes the same canvas and image arguments described earlier. First, I create 12 empty image items and append them to the list variable $tiles. Next, I iterate over the image, moving from the upper left-hand corner to the lower right-hand corner. In each iteration of the for loop, I copy a 140-pixel by 150-pixel region of the "parent" or main image into one of the tiles. The variable declarations and the if-else statement exist for what I refer to as *bookkeeping* purposes. They help me keep track of the part of the image that I need to copy. After creating the tiles, I return the completed list to the calling procedure.

The Randomize procedure (Block 4) is a helper function. Its purpose is to generate a randomly ordered list of numbers between 0 and 11, inclusive. I use this random ordering to redraw the image in its puzzle, or mixed up form.

In Block 5, I define the JumbleImage procedure. In addition to the standard canvas and image arguments ($c and $img, respectively), JumbleImage accepts a third argument, parts, which is the list of tiles created by the SplitImage procedure I defined earlier. JumbleImage uses the same bookkeeping logic as SplitImage to maintain the X- and Y-coordinate values. There are some key differences, though. The code in question is reproduced below:

```
set nums [Randomize]
for {set t 1} {$t <= 12} {incr t} {
    set i [lindex $nums [expr $t - 1]]
    set tile [lindex $parts $i]
    $img copy $tile -to $sx $sy $ex $ey
```

First, I call Randomize to generate a randomly ordered list of numbers between zero and 11, inclusive. After I initialize the for loop, I extract one of the random numbers from the list. Then I use the number to index into the list of tiles and retrieve the corresponding image from the $tiles array. Then I copy that image to the specified region of the canvas object. In this way, I rearrange the picture to create the puzzle the player has to solve. Finally, I bind a single click of mouse button 1 (the left mouse button) to the procedure SelectTile, passing the object ID of the tile that was clicked.

The two procedures in Block 6 handle the mouse event and arrange for the selected images to be swapped. SelectTile takes the name of a tile as its sole argument and appends that name, which is actually the tile's object ID, and appends it to the global list variable $selected. The SwapTiles procedure, in turn, swaps the images displayed in the two tiles.

The balance of the code (Block 7) defines and displays the game board. I create the source image (rather, the source image *object*) first and then use its width and height to define the canvas widget's width and height. Next, I anchor the canvas widget to the parent window's upper left-hand corner and then call DrawGrid to superimpose the grid lines over the image.

I use a frame widget as a container for the various button widgets that control the game. The Start button invokes the InitGame procedure described earlier. Similarly, I wire the SwapTiles procedure to the Swap button. No application is complete without an Exit button, either, so I provide that as a convenience for the player. Finally, I display the widgets, and the game is ready to play.

Modifying the Code

Here are some exercises you can try to practice what you learned in this chapter:

15.1 Modify the binding for mouse button 1 to give the player visual feedback that the selected tile is, in fact, selected.

15.2 Modify the code in Block 6 to prevent the user from selecting more than two tiles.

Tcl Command Summary

This appendix summarizes all the Tcl commands available in Tcl version 8.4.14. It lists each command and a short description of the command's use or purpose.

Command	Description
after	Execute a command after a specified delay.
append	Append data to a variable.
array	Access and manipulate array variables.
binary	Insert and extract data from binary strings.
break	Abort the current loop command.
case	Evaluate one of several scripts, depending on the value of a variable or an expression.
catch	Evaluate a script or command, trapping and optionally handling errors or other exception conditions.
cd	Change the working directory.
clock	Fetch and manipulate time.
close	Close an open I/O channel.
concat	Join lists together.

Command	Description
continue	Skip to the next iteration of a loop.
dde	Execute a Dynamic Data Exchange command (Windows only).
encoding	Manipulate character encodings.
eof	Check for end-of-file condition on an open I/O channel.
error	Raise an error.
eval	Evaluate a Tcl script.
exec	Invoke a subprocess.
exit	Terminate the current Tcl script.
expr	Evaluate an expression.
fblocked	Test to see if the most recent input operation emptied the input buffer.
fconfigure	Get and set options on an I/O channel.
fcopy	Copy data between I/O channels.
fileevent	Execute a script or command when an I/O channel becomes readable or writable.
file	Interrogate and modify file names and file attributes.
flush	Flush any currently buffered output for a channel.
foreach	Iterate over the elements of one or more lists.
format	Format a string in the style of the C language sprintf() function.
for	Execute one or more Tcl scripts or commands a fixed number of iterations.
gets	Read an input line from an open I/O channel.
global	Access global variables.
glob	Return the name(s) of files that match shell-style glob patterns.
history	Manipulate the list of recently executed Tcl commands.
if	Execute a script or command if a certain condition is true.
incr	Increment the value of a variable.
info	Interrogate the internal state of the Tcl interpreter.
interp	Create and manipulate Tcl interpreters.
join	Create a string by joining together list elements.
lappend	Append list elements onto a variable.
lindex	Retrieve an element from a list.
linsert	Insert elements into a list.
list	Create a list.
llength	Determine the number of elements in a list.
load	Load external application code and initialize new commands.
lrange	Return one or more elements from a list.

Command	Description
lreplace	Replace elements in a list with new elements.
lsearch	See if a list contains a particular element.
lset	Modify the value of a list element.
lsort	Sort the elements of a list.
memory	Interface with Tcl's memory debugger.
namespace	Create and manipulate the contexts in which commands and variables are visible.
open	Open a file-based or command pipeline I/O channel.
package	Interrogate and manipulate the list of available Tcl pages.
pid	Retrieve process identifiers.
proc	Create a Tcl procedure.
puts	Send output to an open I/O channel.
pwd	Return the absolute path of the current working directory.
read	Read input from an open I/O channel.
regexp	Match a regular expression against a string.
registry	Manipulate the Windows registry.
regsub	Perform regular expression-based substitutions.
rename	Rename or delete an existing command or procedure.
resource	Manipulate Macintosh resources.
return	Return from a procedure, optionally specifying a return value.
scan	Parse a string using conversion specifiers in the style of the C language sscanf() function.
seek	Change the location of the file pointer in an open I/O channel.
set	Set and retrieve variable values.
socket	Open an I/O channel to a TCP network connection.
source	Evaluate a file or resource as a Tcl script.
split	Split a string into a syntactically correct Tcl list, automatically handling quoting.
string	Manipulate strings.
subst	Perform backslash, command, and variable substitution on a string.
switch	Evaluate one of multiple scripts or commands, depending on the value of a control variable.
tell	Interrogate the current location of the "file" pointer in an open I/O channel.
time	Determine the execution time of a script.
trace	Monitor and report variable access, command usage, and command execution.

Command	Description
unknown	Handle attempts to use commands that don't exist.
unset	Delete variables from the current namespace.
update	Process pending events and idle callbacks.
uplevel	Execute a script in a different stack frame.
upvar	Create link to a variable in a different stack frame.
variable	Create and initialize a namespace variable.
vwait	Process events until a specified variable is updated.
while	Execute a script or command as long as a given condition is met.

B

TK COMMAND SUMMARY

This appendix summarizes all the Tk commands available in Tk version 8.4.14. It lists each command and a short description of the command's use or purpose.

Command	Description
bell	Ring the system bell.
bind	Arrange for window manager events to invoke Tcl scripts.
bindtags	Determine which bindings apply to a window, and order of evaluation.
bitmap	Create and manipulate two-color images.
button	Create and manipulate button widgets.
canvas	Create and manipulate canvas widgets.
checkbutton	Create and manipulate check box-style widgets.
clipboard	Interrogate and modify the system clipboard.
console	Control the console on systems without a real console.
destroy	Delete one or more windows.
entry	Create and manipulate text entry widgets.
event	Define virtual events and generate events.
focus	Manage the input focus.

Command	Description
font	Create and inspect fonts.
frame	Create and manipulate frame widgets.
grab	Restrict the mouse pointer and keyboard events to a window.
grid	Geometry manager that arranges widgets in a grid.
image	Create and manipulate images.
labelframe	Create and manipulate labelframe widgets.
label	Create and manipulate label widgets.
listbox	Create and manipulate listbox widgets.
loadTk	Load Tk into a safe interpreter.
lower	Move a window down in the stacking order.
menubutton	Create and manipulate menubutton widgets.
menu	Create and manipulate menu widgets.
message	Create and manipulate message widgets.
option	Add/retrieve window options to/from the option database.
options	Standard options supported by widgets.
pack	Geometry manager that packs around edges of cavity.
panedwindow	Create and manipulate panedwindow widgets.
photo	Create and manipulate full-color images.
place	Geometry manager for fixed or rubber-sheet placement.
radiobutton	Create and manipulate radiobutton widgets.
raise	Move a window up in the stacking order.
scale	Create and manipulate scale widgets.
scrollbar	Create and manipulate scrollbar widgets.
selection	Interrogate and modify the X selection.
send	Execute a command in a different application.
spinbox	Create and manipulate spinbox widgets.
text	Create and manipulate text widgets.
tk	Interrogate and modify Tk's internal state.
tkwait	Wait for variable's value to change or for window to be destroyed.
toplevel	Create and manipulate toplevel widgets.
winfo	Interrogate window-related information.
wm	Communicate with the system window manager.

Index

Made in the USA
Middletown, DE
13 June 2016